The Cardinals and
the Yankees, 1926

The Cardinals and the Yankees, 1926

A Classic Season and St. Louis in Seven

PAUL E. DOUTRICH

McFarland & Company, Inc., Publishers
Jefferson, North Carolina, and London

Library of Congress Cataloguing-in-Publication Data

Doutrich, Paul E.
The Cardinals and the Yankees, 1926 : a classic season and
St. Louis in seven / Paul E. Doutrich.
p.   cm.
Includes bibliographical references and index.

ISBN 978-0-7864-4657-5
softcover : 50# alkaline paper ∞

1. World Series (Baseball) (1926)   2. St. Louis Cardinals
(Baseball team)— History — 20th century.   3. New York
Yankees (Baseball team)— History — 20th century.
4. Baseball — United States— History — 20th century.   I. Title.
GV878.4.D68   2011
796.357'640977866 — dc22   2010048301

British Library cataloguing data are available

On the cover: Grover Cleveland Alexander (top) and Tony Lazzeri
(National Baseball Hall of Fame Library, Cooperstown, New York)

Manufactured in the United States of America

McFarland & Company, Inc., Publishers
Box 611, Jefferson, North Carolina 28640
www.mcfarlandpub.com

To my father,
who taught me the game,
and to Les Bell,
who told me the story.

Table of Contents

Acknowledgments

As with any project there have been many people who have made significant contributions to this book. My son Adam Doutrich played a major role throughout every phase. Most important he was an excellent and thorough research assistant as well as a contemplative sounding board whose consultation often helped to guide my writing. My stepson Mark Medina, a young sports writer for the *Los Angeles Times*, contributed his editorial expertise to improve significantly the early chapters. At York College, Peter Levy and Phil Avillo, as they always do, provided friendship and encouragement along the way. Peter, as my department chair, was able to give me a partial release from my teaching duties and academic responsibilities for one semester. Another colleague, Josh Landau, read a couple of early chapters. His enthusiasm further encouraged my writing.

On a less personal level there were numerous institutions that facilitated my work. Most important among them is the National Baseball Hall of Fame and specifically Freddy Berowski and John Horne, Jr. Freddy was an excellent guide to various research material and John made getting photographs a pleasant experience. Various archives and libraries provided material crucial to the completion of this book. Among them are the Pennsylvania State Library, the Boston Public Library, the New York Public Library, the Cincinnati Historical Society, the Library of Congress, the Chicago Historical Society, and the Missouri Historical Society. Every person I dealt with at these facilities was eager to help and pleasant to work with. The many great resources created by members of the Society for American Baseball Research (SABR) helped me throughout. Retrosheet.org was another incredibly useful tool that saved me hours and hours of research time.

Unquestionably the most important contributor to this work is my wife,

Dr. Cindy Brooks Doutrich. Her patience, encouragement, pride, smiles and laughter enabled me to focus on this project. Writing a book is a solitary activity and often cuts into "family time." Cindy always ran interference for me, accompanied me on research trips and protected my writing time from extraneous demands (ranging from dinner dishes to various meetings). She is the reason I was able to complete this book. Finally, my cat Sparks graciously agreed to sleep either on my lap or the back of my chair rather than across my keyboard or wrapped in research notes where she preferred to be.

Preface

In 1962 I was a 12-year-old Little League shortstop with dreams of future glory. My father was a Harrisburg, Pennsylvania, councilman in charge of the city's recreation activities. That year he organized a new summer program, Baseball School, for city boys between the ages of 12 and 18. On Monday and Wednesday mornings four former major leaguers gave instruction to boys in the Hill section of the city. On Tuesdays and Thursdays they instructed boys in the Uptown section of the city.

The grand Baseball School event that summer was a morning of hitting instruction given by Ted Williams. Two years earlier Williams had retired from the Red Sox and since then had been serving as a spokesman for Sears and Roebuck sporting goods while awaiting his ticket to Cooperstown. My father had contacts with the Sears national headquarters and was able to hire Williams to give the exhibition.

The 90-minute instruction session was amazing, and afterward Williams, my father, two of the baseball school instructors, and a Sears representative had lunch in Williams' hotel suite. To my great joy I was invited to go along.

Throughout the meal Williams asked Les Bell, who was the head Baseball School instructor, questions about ballplayers, batting styles, and the pitchers that Bell had played with and against. Bell had been in the major leagues for eight full seasons beginning in 1925. In his second season, 1926, he hit .325 and, along with Rogers Hornsby and Jim Bottomley, helped carry the Cardinals to the National League pennant and then to a World Series championship over a Yankees team that included Babe Ruth and Lou Gehrig. Just hearing those names was magical to me, but to learn that Mr. Bell, who now coached me twice a week, had actually played with and against such baseball icons cast him in a whole new light.

All through lunch Williams claimed that he was pestering Bell for my benefit. Usually he started his questions by bellowing, "Ah come on Les tell the kid about..." but after awhile the requests focused on one story in particular. "Come on, Les, tell the kid about that goddamned Alexander and how he struck the hell out of Lazzeri... Come on, Les, it's a helluva great story! Tell us the real story about that damned game — the kid needs to know what really happened."

The game he was talking about was the seventh game of the 1926 World Series. Though I didn't know it at the time, it was baseball legend. The newspapers had reported that with the Cardinals up by a run in the seventh inning an inebriated Grover Cleveland Alexander staggered out of the St. Louis bullpen and somehow struck out Tony Lazzeri with bases loaded to win the Series. That's the way the story was usually told, but Bell had a very different version. Williams, who had heard Bell's account numerous times demanded that he tell it to me.

Shortly after Williams' death in 2002 I was asked to describe my encounter with him to a gathering of baseball fans. In preparing contextual material for my story I came to realize that while the seventh-game encounter between Alexander and Lazzeri was a thrilling baseball moment, in fact it was the capstone to an exceptionally exciting season, certainly one of the most exciting in baseball history. I was also surprised to discover that a full account of the 1926 baseball season had not been written.

At the core of the story are the two pennant winners. Like competing protagonists in a good novel, the 1926 Yankees and the Cardinals provide in many ways a study of contrasts. The Yankees were at the epicenter of the baseball world while the Cardinals toiled away at the western fringe of the major leagues. The Yankees franchise was among the most profitable and publicized in baseball. The Cardinals received limited press coverage and the team's ownership had a long history of struggling to generate adequate revenues. In 1926 the two teams took very different paths to their league championships. The Yankees began with a flourish that included a 16-game winning streak and then hung on through the last month of the season as their lead steadily shrank. Meanwhile the Cardinals floundered during the early months of the season but after a couple of key acquisitions the team caught fire and edged out two rival clubs.

The individual players who comprised the two teams also offer interesting contrasts. The Yankees roster featured numerous first- and second-generation Americans including Babe Ruth (German), "Jumping" Joe Dugan (Irish), Tony Lazzeri (Italian) and Lou Gehrig (German). Most of the Cardinals players were home-grown farm boys from the heartland. In 1926 the famous "Murderer's Row" was assembled and began the first Yankees dynasty. Of course the most notable "murderer" was Babe Ruth, who in 1926 had one of the best seasons in his fabled career. Colorful, gregarious and undisciplined, Ruth became the popular image of his team. On the other hand, St. Louis, with a couple of exceptions, was a collection of subdued, low-profile players who conformed to the expectations of their leader, Rogers Hornsby. Unquestionably the best player in the National League and perhaps all of baseball, Hornsby was in many ways the antithesis of Ruth. He was completely focused on his profession, uncompromising, often nasty and an egoist of major proportions. Like Ruth, however, he was acknowledged to be the embodiment of his team.

The story of the 1926 season is also a story that transcends baseball. It is a story that reflects the popular culture of America during the most roaring year in the Roaring Twenties. It includes the adventures of a young daredevil who began to concoct a scheme that a year later would transform him into the world's most acclaimed hero. Meanwhile during this age of the flapper, an American woman won international fame by accomplishing an athletic feat that many thought was impossible. In a decade that included a fundamentalist religious fervor, the disappearance of a nationally known evangelist produced one of the era's most bizarre episodes. At the same time the sudden death of a popular young movie star mesmerized Americans. Gambling, prohibition, and attitudes about immigrants, among other issues, were also wrapped into the summer of 1926. Clearly it was a season flavored by colorful episodes, personalities and events that provide insights not just about baseball but about life in America during the decade.

What follows is an attempt to tell that story. It is the end product of a day many years ago when I sat on the foot of a bed beside Ted Williams and listened to Les Bell's gravelly voice describe a fabled moment at the end of an especially exciting baseball season during a rambunctious time in America.

1

A Radical Shift

Sports championships sometimes come unexpectedly. In baseball a few well timed hits in key situations, a string of opportune pitching performances, or a career year by an otherwise average player can transform a mediocre team into a winner. More often, though, a successful team is nurtured over time. A roster is analyzed and carefully assembled. When failures and injuries occur, effective adjustments are made. Such was the case for the two teams that met in the 1926 World Series.

In 1925, 18 months before their autumn meeting, both the St Louis Cardinals and the New York Yankees were expected to contend for their league's pennant. However, amid high hopes the two teams began the 1925 season losing far more games than they won. Front line players failed to perform while injuries limited other key players, making midseason changes necessary. In addressing their failures both teams lay the foundations for success a year later. For New York the corrections launched the career of a legendary baseball hero. For St Louis the adjustments added new sparkle to an already brilliant star.

The most important Yankees loss in 1925 came even before the first pitch of the season was thrown. It came not as a result of play on the field but rather as a result of the insatiable lifestyle of their bigger than life champion: Babe Ruth. Labeled "the stomach ache heard round the world," the episode occurred amidst an otherwise highly successful spring for a team that appeared ready to dominate the American League.

Yankees manager Miller Huggins had great expectations for the 1925 season. The acquisition of spitball pitcher Urban Shocker fortified a pitching staff that was already among the strongest in the league. The return of Earle Combs from a broken ankle which had sidelined him midway through the previous season added both offensive punch and defensive perfection to the New York lineup. The play of Babe Ruth, who hit at almost a .500 clip through spring training, further bolstered Huggins's confidence. So sure was the Yankees manager that he uncharacteristically boasted to reporters that his club would bring the league pennant back to New York ... no question about it.[1] However, no sooner had the prediction been made than clouds of doubt began to gather over his club.

Babe Ruth had been relatively well behaved throughout the spring, probably because his wife Helen had spent much of the time with him in Florida. That all changed when the Yankees left St. Petersburg for their traditional two-week barnstorming trip back north. Helen returned to New York alone and immediately the Babe went on an escapade that included massive quantities of food, alcohol and women. Carousing around the clock, he only took time out to savage opposing pitchers along the way.

By the end of the first week, the constant indulgences began to catch up with the Babe. During a game in Birmingham he complained of an upset stomach. The next day in Atlanta stomach cramps and a fever forced him out of a game after only one inning. Three days later in Knoxville he was back in the lineup but still visibly ill.

The two-hour train ride from Knoxville to Asheville, North Carolina further aggravated the Babe's condition. Stomach cramps became unbearable and a fever again flared. While disembarking in Asheville Ruth collapsed and had to be carried by two team-

For Babe Ruth 1926 offered a chance to redeem himself after a dismal season the previous year. In true Ruthian fashion the Babe did all that was expected of him and more while adding several chapters to his legend.

mates to a waiting taxi. Upon the advice of a local doctor, team officials decided that Ruth should forego the rest of the trip and immediately return to New York. Loaded onto a northbound train, he and Yankees scout Paul Krichell spent a long, restless night riding toward Grand Central Station.

The next morning, feeling much better, Ruth decided to have breakfast before arriving in New York. Eating what was for him a light meal, the Babe gobbled down several slices of toast, a couple of eggs, some fried potatoes, orange juice and coffee. The results were predictable: a major gastrointestinal explosion. While in the train's men's room attending to his misery the Yankees slugger fainted and gashed his head on the wash basin. By the time he reached New York City, he was covered with blood and again reeling with stomach pains.

At Grand Central Station an ambulance awaited the ailing home run king. With photographers' flashbulbs popping and a swarm of reporters scribbling away, Ruth was strapped onto a stretcher, carried off the train, and rushed to a nearby hospital. On the way he was again seized by another stomach attack and had to be sedated.

For several days rumors swirled throughout the city that Ruth was dying (a few reports even claimed that he had already died). Finally, after almost a week, the Yankees star underwent surgery to treat an internal abscess. Though a complete success, the operation put the Babe out of action for six weeks, and even after rejoining his teammates it would be another six weeks before he could work himself into playing condition.

The loss of Ruth set the tone for the Yankees season. The team fumbled through the spring awaiting its leader's return. With Ruth went much of the Yankees offensive punch. Injuries to several key players further scrambled the batting order and compromised the defense. Meanwhile, the pitching staff, with the exception of Herb Pennock, barely managed mediocrity. As losses mounted, dissension and doubt colored relations between players and management.

Ruth's return in late May did little to immediately solve the Yankees' problems. Thirty pounds lighter and obviously weakened by his ordeal, the Babe was able to play only on a part-time basis through the end of June. Even after regaining the strength needed to finish the games he started, Ruth's production fell far short of expectations. Through late July he had hit only ten home runs and his batting average bobbed around the .250 mark. A late-season surge pushed his final totals closer to respectability but still well beneath Ruthian standards.[2]

On June 2, amid what was becoming a bleak season, fate played an important card on behalf of the Yankees. During pre-game batting practice the team's regular first baseman, Wally Pipp, was inadvertently beaned by

Charlie Caldwell, the batting practice pitcher. Hit squarely on the temple, Pipp went down and was unable to man his usual station at first base.[3] At the time the accident appeared to be just another setback in an already disappointing season. Pipp was a ten-year Yankee veteran who had established himself as a sure-handed fielder, a consistent hitter with three .300 seasons to his credit, and one of the team's best clutch hitters. He also had a reputation as a fierce competitor, a quality apparently lacking on the 1925 club. Filling his shoes even for a game or two would be a difficult task. However, manager Huggins confidently gave the assignment to a young left-handed slugger who had been used only sparingly during the early weeks of the year. The move that day began one of the fabled Yankee careers. Lou Gehrig would remain the Yankees first baseman for the next 14 seasons.

Becoming part of the Yankees starting lineup was the beginning of one long journey and the end of another for Gehrig. The son of German immigrants, he had spent his youth in the Washington Heights section of New York City. His childhood had been a combination of school, sports, and part-time jobs. Though his mother, with whom he had an unusually close relationship, demanded that her son work hard in school, Lou preferred playing fields. In high school he starred as a halfback on the football team as well as on his school's baseball team, both at the plate and on the pitcher's mound. As a student his only noteworthy achievement foreshadowed the future. He had perfect attendance during his high school years.

It was his mother and his athletic prowess that won him admission to Columbia University. Pestered by Mrs. Gehrig, the school's football coach, in an effort to rejuvenate his team's sagging fortunes, helped get Lou enrolled. While he performed well on the gridiron it was on the baseball diamond where he truly excelled. Even before he joined the squad, stories about Gehrig's powerful bat spiced up campus discussions. Students whose dorm rooms faced Columbia's South Field told tales of one wallop that hit a sundial 500 feet from home plate. Others remembered reading about a pitch that Lou, while still in high school, had hit out of Wrigley Field during an all-star game. Once the season started the Columbia baseball coach used him both in the field and on the mound. Lou excelled wherever he was positioned but it was his power at the plate that separated him from fellow players. He batted at a .444 clip with an astounding .937 slugging average, one out of every four of his hits a home run, often of mammoth dimensions.

Much to his mother's chagrin, Gehrig signed a contract with the Yankees in 1923 after his sophomore season. Billed as another Babe Ruth he spent much of his first professional season with Hartford in the Eastern League. After two lonely and unproductive weeks away from home Gehrig did some soul searching and began to show his talent. While he ended the season with a respectable .304 batting average it was his 24 home runs that impressed Yankees management.

The following year Gehrig was again assigned to Hartford. With the parent club contending for a pennant and Wally Pipp having an outstanding season at the plate, manager Miller Huggins felt no urgent need to bring Gehrig to New York. Instead he was given another year to develop. Gehrig responded with a .369 batting average and 37 home runs. It was a performance that earned him a few end-of-the-season starts for the Yankees.[4]

All through the winter of 1924–25 Huggins contemplated how best to use Gehrig's talents during the coming season. A batting order that included both Ruth and Gehrig might produce the most powerful hitting tandem that the game had ever known. The problem was finding a place for the young slugger in the existing lineup. With Wally Pipp solidly entrenched at first base there seemed little opportunity for a poor-fielding rookie in the starting lineup. By December trade rumors had begun to swirl. Perhaps the Yankees might best use Gehrig by trading him to the St. Louis Browns for their discontented 20-game winner, Urban Shocker. The Yankees needed another reliable starter and Shocker was among the best available. Huggins agreed that another pitcher would bolster the New York staff but scoffed at the idea of swapping his future star, even for a 20-game winner. When the deal for Shocker was finally made it was pitcher Joe Bush and two other Yankees, not Lou Gehrig, who were given tickets to St. Louis.

During the first two months of the 1925 season Huggins used Gehrig primarily as a pinch hitter. However, Lou's pinch hitting career came to an end on June 1 when he was sent in to hit for the Yankees shortstop. The following day, with the Yankees mired in seventh place, Huggins gave his young slugger the chance he had been waiting for. In what the *New York Times* labeled "a radical shift" Huggins replaced three of his regular starters. Two substitutions were of little note. Howard Shanks, a light hitting defensive specialist, filled in for Aaron Ward at second base and Benny Bengough was penciled in behind the plate. It was the third part of Huggins' "radical shift" that paid rich dividends. Lou Gehrig was given the ailing Wally Pipp's spot at first base.[5] Lou would remain the Yankees first baseman for the next 2129 games and later become a member of baseball's Hall of Fame.

As the first chapter of the Lou Gehrig saga was being written in New York, 1,000 miles west the Cardinals were beginning a new chapter of their own.

Like the Yankees, the Cardinals expected to contend for a league championship in 1925. Manager Branch Rickey was particularly optimistic as he began to harvest the early products of his elaborate farm system. Of course at the heart of the roster was the league's premier player, Rogers Hornsby.

At the peak of his career, he had batted .424 the previous season, the highest batting average in the twentieth century and Hornsby's second .400 season in three years. If there was a Babe Ruth in the National League it was Rogers Hornsby, and he wore a Cardinals uniform. The team also had a solid nucleus that included future Hall of Famers Jim Bottomley and Jesse Haines. Among the newcomers was Les Bell, the American Association batting champion the previous year. Slick fielding Tommy Thevenow was brought to St Louis to plug the Redbird hole at shortstop. Pitcher Flint Rhem was another gifted young player who was being counted on to shore up the mound crew. With a solid season from the veterans and a bit of help from the young recruits, Rickey anticipated spending the summer in the thick of the National League pennant race. With a little luck he believed the Cardinals might even win their first pennant.

In baseball high hopes in March are often dashed by May. Such was the case for the 1925 Cardinals. By the end of April, despite solid hitting, Rickey's club was entrenched in the National League cellar. May turned out to be even worse as the team lost three out of every four games they played. Of special concern was a beleaguered pitching staff that had almost as many sore arms as it did complete games. Meanwhile, with the exception of Hornsby and Bottomley, Cardinals hitters slumped through the month.

According to the St. Louis press the source of the Cardinals problems was not on the field but in the dugout. Branch Rickey, the team's somewhat eccentric manager, was accused of overmanaging, browbeating, and running players in and out of games for no apparent reasons. Starting players were removed from the

In his first full season as the Yankees first baseman, Lou Gehrig quietly established himself as one of the most powerful hitters in baseball.

lineup at the slightest sign of a slump. Hunches rather than performances seemed to guide decisions. Rickey's constant theorizing and philosophizing also upset fans almost as much as it did players. As the losses mounted, the Cardinals manager was accused of resorting more and more to his own unique understanding of the game rather than well established baseball axioms. Such conjectures turned an essentially simple game into a confusing distraction.[6]

Cardinals star Rogers Hornsby was particularly angry at his manager's quixotic maneuvering. On several occasions Hornsby became so frustrated that he physically confronted Rickey. In one altercation the Cardinals manager threw a punch at his star and had to be restrained because Hornsby had disagreed with a signal to take a pitch.[7] Hornsby moaned to anyone who would listen that Rickey was condescending to his players, often using scholarly words and phrases that few of them understood.[8]

Hornsby was not the only exasperated Cardinal. A devoutly religious man of unbending convictions, Rickey's principles created divisions on the team. Among his most irritating stand was his refusal to appear on the field on Sundays. Instead he hired a substitute manager for Sunday games. Rickey's attitude about alcohol further alienated some players who considered it to be yet another example of his sanctimonious character. While a student at Ohio Wesleyan he had been an active advocate of the temperance crusade. As the Cardinals manager his continuing support for Prohibition chilled relations with several of his players. Hornsby, who rarely imbibed himself, defended his teammates, arguing that a drink after a ball game was simply a way for some players to relax and begin preparing for the next game.

Another who questioned Rickey's field decisions was Sam Breadon, the team's primary owner and president. Breadon was a true Horatio Alger rags-to-riches story. The son of Irish immigrants, he grew up on the tough streets of lower Manhattan during the late nineteenth century. Sammy dropped out of school after the fourth grade because his father had died and he needed to help his mother support his seven siblings. Combining hard work and opportunism he was able to climb into a comfortable but mundane job as a clerk in a Wall Street office. In 1902, at the age of 26, Breadon decided the time had come for him to seek his fortune. Long on ambition but short on cash, he migrated to St. Louis and found a job as an auto mechanic even though he knew nothing about the automobiles. Over the next 15 years he worked his way out of the garage, into the showroom and finally into the executive office of his own Ford and Pierce Arrow dealerships. By 1917 Breadon, who was known to some as "Singin' Sam" and others as "Lucky Sam," had established himself as a successful and respected St. Louis businessman.[9]

An avid Cardinals fan, Breadon, when given an opportunity, added baseball to his list of businesses. Perhaps the poorest and least successful franchise in the major leagues, the Cardinals were owned by heiress Helene Hathaway Robison Britton, or "Lady Bee" as she was affectionately known. With her team attracting fewer and fewer fans, Mrs. Britton became disenchanted with the club and decided in 1916 to sell it. Rather than watch the Cardinals relocate, concerned civic leaders devised a plan they labeled the "Cardinal Idea" which offered various incentives in an effort to attract a local syndicate of investors. By that time a multi-millionaire, "Lucky Sam" was one of the initial purchasers.

One of the tasks confronting the new Cardinals organization was finding a club president. When the team's board of directors polled seven of the city's leading sports writers/editors all seven agreed that the best choice to fill the position was Branch Rickey, who at the time was working as the business manager for the city's other major league team, the Browns. Rickey had already established a reputation as a keen judge of young talent and a baseball innovator. Armed with a law degree as well, he was considered one of the more intelligent men in baseball. Happy to part company with Phil Ball, the Browns' cantankerous owner, Rickey enthusiastically accepted the offer and began a 25-year association with the Cardinals.

By 1919 the "Cardinal Idea" was floundering. To reinvigorate the effort Breadon agreed to increase his investment in the team and join the board of directors. Later in the year, as the club began a reorganization effort, he was asked to become the team president. He accepted the offer with the condition that Rickey be retained as the Cardinals manager and be appointed club vice president. The previous spring Rickey had reluctantly agreed to be the field manager in addition to continuing his duties as club president. Board members were pleased with his on-the-field leadership even though it had limited the time he could devote to off-the-field duties. When told of Breadon's plan, Rickey initially balked at what he considered a demotion but soon recognized the strength of the idea. The new arrangement would enable Rickey to focus on player development and winning games. Meanwhile Breadon would handle the club's marketing and financial matters.[10]

By the time he became the Cardinals president Breadon had come to consider Rickey one of the outstanding young men in baseball. Though very different in their personal behavior the two men shared several important qualities as well as a similar vision for their team. Like Breadon, Rickey had risen from humble beginnings through hard work, personal sacrifice and instinct. The two men also shared an understanding of what it took to succeed, and both were prepared to try the unconventional if doing so might help them achieve their goals. Likewise, both were strong-willed and single-minded in pursuit of their goals. Joining forces in directing the Cardinals, Breadon and Rickey began a relationship that profoundly changed professional baseball. Most importantly they devised a system of farm clubs that revolutionized the way baseball organizations developed talent. They also transformed the Cardinals from a team that regularly finished at the bottom of the league standings into a perennial pennant contender.

Breadon's first notable success was to cut a deal with Browns owner Phil Ball which enabled the Cardinals to move out of their tiny, ramshackle ballpark and into Sportsman's Park just a few blocks away. He then generated some operating capital by selling Cardinal Field. With money in hand, he and Rickey began to purchase minor league franchises where they could get eager young prospects under contract and groom the best of them for the Cardinals. During the next three years the organization quietly purchased teams in Syracuse, Houston, Fort Smith (Arkansas) and Sioux City (Iowa). With its new farm system, which some would later deride as "Rickey's plantation," up and running the Cardinals no longer had to outbid more prosperous franchises for talent. At the same time, Breadon launched a successful public relations campaign in St. Louis that brought new fans to his team.

Unfortunately, while the team was paying debts, building a fan base, and developing players, it was still losing more games than it was winning. By the end of the 1924 season, Breadon among others had concluded that the problem was the team's manager, Branch Rickey. After the season ended the two men met, ostensibly to make plans for the team's immediate future. The general conclusion was that the meeting was instead really a way for Rickey gracefully to step down as manager and devote all his time to player development and running the ever-growing farm system. However, when the 1925 season began he was still at the Cardinals' helm.

Finally on May 30, three days before Lou Gehrig replaced Wally Pipp in New York, a very frustrated Sam Breadon made his own radical shift. With his team stuck in the National League's cellar, he dismissed Rickey as manager. In his place Breadon named a hesitant Rogers Hornsby to be the team's new manager. The move strained the friendship that had grown between Breadon and Rickey though their working relationship remained productive for another 15 years. It also heightened the animosity between Rickey and his replacement and created a web of intrigue within the organization. The final chapter of that feud would not be played out until shortly after the triumphant 1926 season.

Almost immediately after Hornsby took over the Cardinals began winning. Players who had been slumping at the plate began hitting. The ailing pitching staff reversed its fortunes and began putting together complete game victories. And of course the new Cardinals player-manager, who was on his way to his second Triple Crown, kept rattling the ball at better than a .400 clip despite his new duties. By late June Hornsby's crew had won 16 of the 20 games played under their new manager and had lifted themselves three spots in the standings to fifth place.

Throughout the rest of the season the Cardinals continued to play solid baseball. Sheltered within the familiar surroundings of Sportsman's Park and encouraged by increasingly enthusiastic fans, Hornsby's team played especially well at home, winning almost two out of every three games. Away from St. Louis it was a different story. On the road the Cardinals played less than .400 baseball. Still, under the new leadership the team was eventually able to pull itself above the .500 mark, ending the season in fourth place, a respectable finish considering the disappointing start.

Most credited Hornsby for the Cardinals turnaround. His knowledge of the game, both on and off the field, and his relationship with teammates seemed to enable him to mold his players into a unit. Discipline, something that had wavered under Rickey, was more uniformly and fairly administered by Hornsby. Likewise, the new manager spoke in terms that his players understood. He had also given some of the players seldom used by Rickey a chance to prove themselves. In several cases the results were exceptional. By the end of the season the only person in the Cardinal organization still not convinced of Hornsby's managerial skills was Branch Rickey. The disgruntled former manager complained that Hornsby's success was largely a product of scheduling and Rickey's work in preparing the team.

For both the Yankees and the Cardinals, the 1925 season had been a year of disappointment, experimentation and change. By the end of the season both teams had laid the foundations for a successful 1926 season. The Yankees found a new power hitter capable of filling Babe Ruth's shoes if necessary. Meanwhile the Babe had discovered his mortality. His monumental stomach ache, his slow recovery and lackluster performance instilled in Ruth a resolve to dedicate himself to baseball as he had never done before. Soon after the season's last pitch he pledged that in 1926 he would once again produce the way Yankees fans expected.[11] His fellow Yankees quietly seconded their leader's determination and several agreed to join Ruth in his off-season preparations. They were a team accustomed to contending for pennants. The 1925 season had been very frustrating. Next year would be much different.

By the close of the 1925 season the Cardinals were also eager to embark on the following season's chase for their league's pennant. Under Hornsby the Cardinals had become a team and gained confidence. With a year under their belts and a wise field manager at their helm, Cardinals players were ready to challenge for the first pennant in team history.

2

Preparing for the Season

As the 1926 season approached, both the Yankees and the Cardinals were eager to get started. The Cardinals were anxious to continue what they had begun during the last half of the 1925 season. The Yankees were just as anxious to atone for the team's woeful performance the previous year.

Most in the baseball world agreed that the fate of the 1926 Cardinals rested upon the shoulders of their player/manager Rogers Hornsby. No one doubted Hornsby's abilities as a player. In 1925 he had won his fifth consecutive batting championship with a .403 average, the third time in five years that he had finished atop the magical .400 plateau. He had also driven in more runs (143) and hit more home runs (39) than anyone else in the National League, thus earning his second Triple Crown. The performance easily earned him recognition as the league's Most Valuable Player. There was plenty of evidence that the 29-year-old Cardinals star was at the peak of his playing career and would continue to shine for years to come.

Baseball experts were not as confident about Hornsby the manager. He had done an admirable job leading his young club through the last half of the previous campaign. On the other hand, some, including Branch Rickey, contended that Hornsby had simply been the beneficiary of opportune timing. Certainly the Cardinals under Hornsby had won more games than they had under Rickey. However, when the two managers' winning percentages at home and on the road were compared, there was little difference. According to Rickey, Hornsby's success was a product of scheduling. He had managed the club through the bulk of its home schedule while Rickey paid a price for leading the team during much of the away schedule. Additionally, Rickey was not shy about reminding listeners that it was he who had assembled the 1925 team.

Aside from inexperience, the chief worry about Hornsby was his growing gambling habit. When not on the ball field he could often be found at
horse races, which he called "the best sport next to baseball," or dog tracks.[1]
As his baseball success had grown, so too did the size of his bets. By 1922
his gambling cost him hundreds of dollars a week. Occasionally during the
baseball season, when his gambling debts drained his immediate resources,
he tapped players and sportswriters for loans. Once, after his playing career
was over, he admitted to having bet more than $500,000 during his playing
days and claimed that he had won almost as much as he had lost. The last
part of his statement was clearly more boast than fact. While he enjoyed
gambling he never learned to read a racing form properly. Instead he relied
largely on friendly advice, tips, and his own intuition.

In early 1926 Hornsby's gambling became a problem for baseball. Frank
Moore, a well-known bookie from Kentucky, accompanied the Cardinals
star to spring training. Later that year Moore sued Hornsby for unpaid gambling debts and personal loans. The bookie claimed that between December
1925 and March 1926 he had placed bets totaling more than $327,995 for the
Cardinals manager and that Hornsby still owed him $70,000. Hornsby
admitted that the bets had been made but denied that he owed Moore any
money. When the case came to trial late the following year, Hornsby's lawyer
argued that because gambling was illegal in Missouri the courts could not
require Hornsby to pay. A St. Louis jury found in favor of the baseball star.
Upset by the decision, Moore appealed to baseball's czar, Commissioner
Kenesaw Landis. With the shadow of the infamous "Black Sox" scandal still
looming over the game as well as several other more recent high-profile
gambling episodes, Landis, who personally disdained gambling, was especially concerned. Though he sharply rebuked Hornsby, he nevertheless refused
Moore's request.[2]

Of course Hornsby had his defenders. His most important supporter
was the Cardinals president, Sam Breadon. Prior to the 1926 season Breadon
announced that Hornsby "is the greatest manager since John McGraw."[3]
Breadon argued that no one knew more about baseball than Hornsby nor
was anyone more qualified to manage the Cardinals. The Cardinals players
were also ardent Hornsby supporters. Many of the young Cardinals looked
to their manager as a teacher, a big brother, and a hero all rolled into one.
Les Bell, the third baseman, was one of Hornsby's biggest fans. The previous
season the young slugger found himself languishing through a spring slump.
Bell claimed that Hornsby had solved his troubles at the plate by patiently
working with him. The Cardinals manager had suggested adjustments in
Bell's stance and swing and then helped Bell become comfortable with the
changes.[4] There were other players who were equally appreciative of the

opportunities that Hornsby afforded them. None was more grateful than Willie Sherdel, who was given a chance to become a starting pitcher. Then there were players like Tommy Thevenow who idolized Hornsby.

Hornsby's approach to the game served as further inspiration for his players. To the Cardinals manager there was nothing more important than winning, and he dedicated himself completely to that goal. For him the diamond was a battlefield. He proposed in 1926 that: "When you love a game you want to win. That's me. If I don't win a pennant in a year or two I'm through."[5] In an age of particularly fierce competitors who would do whatever it took to win, none fought harder or needed to win more than Rogers Hornsby.

When not on the ballfield or at a race track, Hornsby was preparing himself for the next day's confrontations. The Cardinals manager did not drink or smoke because he felt both activities would diminish his ability to perform on the ballfield. Likewise, he avoided movie theaters and reading because he feared to do so would hurt his ability to see a pitched ball. Adequate sleep and an appropriate diet were also important parts of the Hornsby daily regimen. In an era before night baseball, Hornsby during the season went to bed at 11:00 P.M. and rose at 11:00 A.M. He ate two meals a day, contending that too many meals made ballplayers sluggish and unable to play to their potential.

While he was strict about his own routine, he was far more flexible with his players. His philosophy as a manager was simple: "(Players) do or don't for me. If they do, all right. If they don't, we'll get somebody who does." He admitted that there were some players he liked better than others but vowed that friendships would have nothing to do with decisions made on the field. Hornsby averred: "If some egg that I think is dumber than four humpty dumpties can get out and sock in a run or go in and steal second and score a winning run on a short single, wouldn't I be a square head to let my belief that he's dumb stand in the way of the team's success." His team would have no curfews or "team detectives" to tell him who was behaving and who was not. Hornsby pledged that "we won't interfere with anybody's liberty or pursuit of happiness, but if they won't play good baseball they can do their pursuing in the bush leagues."[6] The bottom line for the Cardinals manager was winning. If each player committed himself to winning as Hornsby did, the team would win. If any player did not dedicate himself, the entire team would suffer and adjustments would have to be made. This simple philosophy was happily embraced by most of Hornsby's teammates.

In his element on the diamond, Hornsby was not a particularly pleasant person off the field. His confrontations with various baseball owners and front office administrators became legendary. At least four times during his managerial career he was replaced because of ugly confrontations with team officials.[7] Newspaper reporters were also frequent recipients of the ferocious Hornsby wrath. The slugging star was unforgiving when dealing with his critics. While he generally liked children, he had little patience for fans in general. He viewed anyone who did not play baseball with suspicion. With few exceptions he considered ethnic and racial minorities, even if they did play baseball, as inherently degenerate.[8] Most civic organizations from national trade unions and political parties to local Kiwanis and Rotary clubs were also on his hit list. Hornsby was content only at the ball park surrounded by his teammates, and then only if his club was winning and he was performing well.

Though Hornsby had supreme confidence in his own abilities, he well understood that if the Cardinals were to contend for the National League pennant there were several key players who would have to make significant contributions throughout the season. One of those players was shortstop Tommy Thevenow. The young Cardinals infielder had spent the early part of the 1925 season with the team but did not play well. In the field he was unquestionably major league caliber. Some, including Hornsby, even thought that Thevenow might become one of the game's great infielders. However, the youngster's abilities at the plate were a different matter. Offensive improvements would have to be made if Tommy was going to remain in the major leagues. His problems stemmed from an unconventional batting stance and awkward swing. Setting his slender frame into a gawky crouch and clumsily chopping down at pitches, he was simply unable to cope with major league pitching. Even when he did somehow connect with a pitch he generated no power.[9]

During the spring of 1925 the St. Louis coaching staff, assisted by Hornsby, redesigned Thevenow's hitting style with hopes that the slick-fielding rookie might plug a hole in the Cardinals infield. The youngster was instructed to straighten up a bit and lean away from the plate. He was also told to move his hands back from the center of his body and cock them behind his right shoulder. These changes produced a more fluid and powerful swing. To give him some time to perfect his new hitting style, Branch Rickey shipped Thevenow back to the Cardinals AAA farm team in Syracuse. In 140 games with Syracuse Thevenow hit a respectable .270. The performance was good enough to earn him a few end-of-the-season games with the Cardinals and a full-time place on the team the following year.

Thevenow's promotion to the major leagues in 1926 ended a journey that had begun five years earlier in Madison, Indiana. The Cardinals shortstop started his career in organized baseball much the same way many other players of the era had. Upon graduation from high school he joined his town's semi-pro team. Though he hoped to pitch, his exceptional defensive abilities established him as the club's regular shortstop. From Madison he moved on the following year to a town team in Centralia, Illinois. Thevenow had been born in Centralia and claimed "the town (Centralia) sure was baseball crazy."[10] While not in an organized league, the Centralia club played almost every day and was recognized as one of the stronger independent teams in the region. As he had in Madison, Thevenow dazzled local fans with his defensive skills.

Town teams like those in Madison and Centralia were an integral part of baseball in the 1920s. By providing a bit of entertainment and recreation, town teams helped to knit local populations into communities. From Amherst, Massachusetts, to

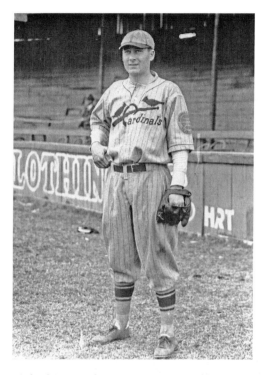

Light-hitting shortstop Tommy Thevenow plugged an obvious hole in the Cardinals infield. During the World Series his glove saved a couple of games and surprisingly his bat won another.

Sisson, California, and from Meeker, Oklahoma, and Eagle Lake, Texas, to Janesville, Wisconsin, and Helena, Montana, town teams had been playing each other since the 1860s. It was in the isolated villages and hamlets throughout America that these teams flourished. An unofficial census in 1925 counted almost 2,000 of town teams in the United States. It was town teams that provided a foundation upon which professional baseball was established during the late nineteenth century.[11]

Local men and boys usually comprised the town team roster. A few played with hopes of becoming a professional but most played simply because they enjoyed the game. Typically player ages ranged from the late teens to the mid-thirties though there were many exceptions. Christy Mathewson, for instance, pitched for the Factoryville (PA) squad when he was only 13. Town teams were usually egalitarian enterprises which reflected the socio-economic mix of the community. Local businessmen or company supervisors and their hired hands played together as equals while their families and friends joined in supporting the club. Rarely were players on these teams paid, though by the turn of the twentieth century "ringers," especially pitchers, could be found on many teams.

Town teams commonly became the focus of impassioned community interest. In countless American villages the fate of the local nine dominated summertime discussions. Oral accounts of games frequently became local lore passed from one generation to the next. For those who played, the town team provided status. A star pitcher or hitter became a local celebrity. For those who simply supported their hometown club, the team was a source of endemic pride. Of course, when teams from neighboring communities met on the playing field, ardent supporters often generated intense and sometimes bitter rivalries.

Game days could be festive occasions. Most clubs played several days each week. On the other hand, some teams limited play to weekends which, in the nation's various Bible belts, meant Saturdays. Rarely was an admission fee charged. Instead ball games became unofficial town meetings. Picnic baskets were packed and toted off for an afternoon or evening at the local diamond. Part of any summertime celebration typically included town folk congregating at the local ball field to watch the home team play. To accommodate the faithful a few towns built bleachers. However, at most fields spectators were expected to provide their own seating. Onlookers often lined fields with chairs, barrels, boxes, packing crates and even horse-drawn carriages. By the twenties some watched from automobiles parked just off the foul lines.

The one universal characteristic of all town baseball fields was that no two fields were the same. Some communities pooled their resources to create a local showcase. Other communities simply gouged out a diamond wherever adequate space could be found. Some fields were carefully tended while others were little more than dust and patches of scrub grass. There were fenced fields with dimensions that responded to the strengths of the home team, as well as open meadows in which players occasionally shared space with grazing livestock. Some fields were flat and level, while others included obstacles ranging from hills to railroad tracks to baselines bordered by streams. Aside from maintaining standard distances between bases and from the pitcher's mound to home plate, each field was truly an entity unto itself.[12]

This was the baseball arena in which Tommy Thevenow and many of his major league peers honed their baseball skills. Two years with town teams brought Thevenow in 1923 to the Joplin (MO) Miners and professional baseball. The stop at Joplin proved to be another success for him. In the field he combined outstanding speed and an excellent arm to almost magically transform certain base hits into sensational outs. As a hitter, despite his awkward stance, he also showed promise, hitting .286 and leading the Western Association in triples. By the end of the season many Miners fans recognized that their team's star shortstop was bound for greater baseball challenges.

There were others who shared the Miners fans' sentiment. One of them was Branch Rickey. The Cardinals manager discovered Thevenow accidentally during the 1923 season. Rickey had been coaxed by Blake Harper, president of the Cardinals' farm team in Fort Smith (Kansas) to watch a prospect that Harper was considering for his squad. Rickey was very busy with his duties as Cardinals manager and the organization's vice president but reluctantly agreed to accompany Harper on a brief scouting trip. The prospect, Ernie Smith, played for Enid in the Western Association. During a midseason contest between Enid and Joplin, Rickey and Harper met to evaluate Smith. Harper was quite impressed but Rickey saw little in Smith. Instead the Cardinals manager became entranced by the Joplin shortstop, Tommy Thevenow. Though he knew absolutely nothing about Thevenow, Rickey immediately decided to add him to the Cardinals' ever-growing collection of minor leaguers. A few weeks later Thevenow's contract was sold to the St. Louis club and Tommy was on his way to the Syracuse Stars, a Cardinals affiliate in the International League.[13]

At Syracuse in 1924 Thevenow continued to reel off spectacular plays on a regular basis. His .271 batting average was certainly not outstanding though it was acceptable in light of his defensive prowess. The performance with the Stars earned him a temporary promotion to the parent club in 1925 and a permanent move to St. Louis in 1926.[14]

In many ways Thevenow's consistent play and steady sojourn through baseball's hinterland reflected the shortstop's personality. In a day when brash, free-spirited players grabbed fan attention, Tommy was an exception. An unassuming player, he was once described by a sports writer as "a tight lipped, silent warrior with the heart of a lion and a baby smile."[15] On the field he confidently went about his business with minimal commotion. Off the field he was equally quiet and mild mannered. He neither drank excessively nor caroused through the night as did several of his fellow Cardinals. Instead he approached baseball as a challenge that required discipline and effort. These qualities earned him much appreciation and respect throughout his career. His work ethic also brought Tommy a bit of glory during the 1926 baseball season.

Thevenow and his Cardinals mates prepared for the season in San Antonio. The previous year, under Branch Rickey, the team had spent spring training in Stockton, California. However, new manager Rogers Hornsby preferred the Texas city for several reasons. Aside from the fact that it was not far from his boyhood home and his ailing mother, he wanted his pitchers to spend a week or so at the nearby sulphur springs in Hot Wells before the preseason officially began. He hoped that the early conditioning would help eliminate the arm problems that had plagued Cardinals hurlers the previous season. With a healthy pitching staff, he was confident that his team would be as good as any club in the National League.

Hornsby's spring training methods departed from those of his predecessor in other ways as well. Rickey had treated the pre-season tune-up as a time of strenuous conditioning both physically and mentally. His camps were marked by relatively rigid discipline and regular classroom strategy sessions. The new Cardinals manager frowned upon an arduous training regimen. He contended that "too much practice is worse than not enough practice, for if the men are driven too hard they become stale before the season opens or they balk and may bring discipline into contempt."[16] Instead he wanted to build his players slowly into playing condition. Rather than the standard two-hour workouts twice each day, Hornsby's crew had one session that began at 11:00 A.M. and concluded by about 2:00 P.M. The rest of the day team members could use as they saw fit.

Hornsby formally opened spring training with his first edict. He informed his players, "If there's anyone in this room who doesn't think we're going to win the pennant go upstairs now and get your money and go home because we don't want you around here."[17] In the days that followed, the team focused on the basics. The Cardinals manager regarded practice games against other major league clubs as unimportant. His team would not be shuffled around the country playing exhibition games when they could be taking batting or fielding practice in their own ball park. Instead of competing against other major league clubs, the Cardinals scheduled warm-ups against nearby minor league teams from Waco, Houston, and San Antonio as well as the University of Texas team. Only once did they play another major league team, the Chicago White Sox, a game that ended in a tie.

The Cardinals' spring performance gave St. Louis fans reason to expect good things. The team had won 25 games in Texas without a loss. The only blemishes on their pre-season record came after returning to St. Louis. Two losses to the city's American League rival, the Browns, only slightly dimmed the Cardinals' spring success. Despite the losses, manager Hornsby promised his team was in great shape and ready to challenge for its first National League pennant. Cardinals hitters were smacking the ball around exceptionally well, and with Thevenow entrenched at shortstop the infield looked solid. There were still a few questions in the outfield but nothing to worry about. Only the pitching staff remained a trouble area, but Hornsby was sure that his mound crew would come around once the season got under

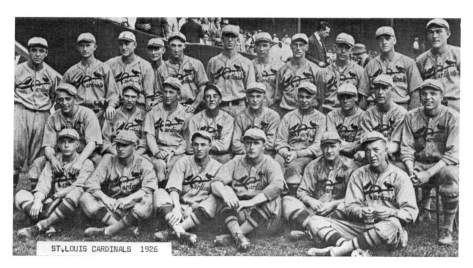

The 1926 St. Louis Cardinals included some of the first players developed through Branch Rickey's controversial farm system. *Back row (left to right):* Allan Sothoron, Wattie Holm, Chick Hafey Art Reinhart, Bill Warwich, George Toporcer, Bill Hallahan, Edgar Clough Flint Rhem; *middle row (left to right):* Jim Bottomley, Lester Bell, Jess Haines, Otto Williams, Rogers Hornsby, Bill Kellifer, Ray Blades, Bill Sherdel, Taylor Douthitt; *front row (left to right):* Billy Southworth, Tommy Thevenow, Vic Keen, Ernie Vick, Bob O'Farrell, Grover Cleveland Alexander.

way. Such assurances were more than enough to convince Redbird support-ers.[18]

The Yankees' spring was more conventional than was the Cardinals pre-season. On March 1 the New Yorkers assembled in St. Petersburg, where they traditionally conducted spring training. Led by a reconditioned Babe Ruth, the team prepared to answer some of the questions that had perplexed their fans for almost a year. Among the most frequently asked question was who would fill the critical second base and shortstop holes in the New York infield. No one argued that the keystone combination from the previous year had been inept, but finding quality replacements seemed difficult. To help shore up the middle of the infield, team owner Colonel Jacob Ruppert, during the winter, purchased the contract of a minor league phenomenon, Tony Lazzeri. Meanwhile Manager Huggins tapped another rookie, Mark Koenig, to fill the shortstop spot. While Koenig had played a few unspec-tacular games for the Yankees at the end of the 1925 season, Huggins saw something he liked in Koenig. Nevertheless, many doubted that a team, even one that boasted a healthy Babe Ruth, could survive a pennant race with two untested rookies anchoring the defense.

The 1926 New York Yankees included the charter members of "Murderer's Row."

With the exception of Babe Ruth, no player on the Yankees' 1926 roster came to spring training with more fanfare than did Tony Lazzeri. The previous season, while Yankees infielders fumbled through a lackluster summer, Lazzeri was bombarding Pacific Coast League pitching as no one ever had before. Playing for Salt Lake City he batted .355, belted out an incredible 60 home runs and drove in an equally amazing 222 runs. The figures were staggering. So impressed was Yankees owner Colonel Ruppert that he spent $50,000 to purchase Lazzeri's contract.

A self-described "tough kid," Lazzeri grew up in the Italian "Potrero" section of San Francisco. He later reminisced that his neighborhood "wasn't one in which a boy was likely to grow up a sissy, for it was always fight or get licked," and Lazzeri claimed that he rarely got licked. After being expelled from high school he went to work with his father at the Maine Iron Works in San Francisco. There young Tony labored as an apprentice to his boiler-maker father and in his spare time pursed a career as a prize fighter. Matched to box another boy from the Potrero, Lazzeri won his first and only prize fight by default.[19] Meanwhile Lazzeri also played baseball for a local semi-pro club, the Golden Gate Natives. In the field he played wherever he was needed. Some games he pitched, some games he played the outfield, but usually he could be found patrolling the left side of the diamond at either shortstop or third base.

While always a good defensive player, it was Lazzeri's prodigious power at the plate that transformed him into a local legend. Stories about his mammoth home runs and hitting prowess eventually attracted several professional baseball men. One of those interested in the youngster was Duffy Lewis, manager of the Salt Lake City club. In 1922 Lewis gave 17-year-old Lazzeri a tryout and soon after signed him to a minor league contract.

In 1923 Tony was initially assigned to Peoria, where he could get some seasoning. The next year he was brought up to the Salt Lake City club. His first year in Utah was mediocre at best but during his second season he broke many of the Pacific Coast League hitting records. News of the minor league star spread and by the end of the 1925 season he was one of the hottest properties in organized baseball.[20]

In joining the Yankees Lazzeri became the first in a string of Italian-American Yankee stars. Most notable on the list were fellow San Francisco natives Frank Crosetti and Joe DiMaggio. However, unlike Crosetti or DiMaggio, Lazzeri's trip to New York was clouded by suspicion and not so subtle racism. Immigrants, regardless of whether they were Italian, German, or from any one of more than a dozen central or eastern European countries, were targets for ethnic scorn from many Americans during the 1920s. Of course few ethnic national groups generated more animosity than did Italians.

Lazzeri's parents were among the 17.5 million Europeans who came into the United States between 1890 and the beginning of World War I. Of that number 3.8 million, or almost 22 percent, were Italians.[21] As the mass of transplanted Europeans swelled, Americans became ever more concerned. Some feared that the United States was being polluted by immigrant cultures and that the very foundation of American civilization was under attack. To fully assess the effects of unlimited immigration on the future of the nation, President Theodore Roosevelt established the Dillingham Commission. The Commission reported in 1911 that the vast majority of recent immigrants were illiterate, unskilled transients incapable of assimilating to American ways. According to the report, unless immigration limits were legislated, the newcomers would destroy the American culture, society and economy.[22]

The Dillingham Commission in many ways seemed to confirm what many Americans already suspected. Since the publication of Charles Darwin's *Origins of Species* in 1859, social philosophers had proposed that Darwin's theory of natural selection could be applied to human society.

Accordingly, certain ethnic groups were destined to lead while others would serve. To many Americans it was obvious that the illiterate, impoverished southern European was part of a genetically inferior race. Without tight controls and aggressive attempts to "Americanize" such immigrants, the newcomers would destroy American society. Italians in particular were predisposed to crime; therefore they presented a unique challenge.

Efforts to regulate and restrict immigration came in various forms. Beginning in 1913 Congress passed a series of laws that culminated in 1924 with the National Origins Quota Law which limited the number of immigrants coming into the United States on an annual basis.[23] At the same time numerous civic organizations were created to deal with local alien populations. The American Protective Society was one such organization. It was designed to purge the United States of all perceived adverse effects generated by immigration. Even more aggressive were the Immigration Restriction League and the American Super-Race Foundation, which sought rigid controls that would segregate immigrant groups from the rest of American society. Of course there were also benevolent associations such as the Young Men's Christian Association and Jane Addams' Hull House as well as other settlement houses throughout the nation that attempted to socialize immigrants through recreational and educational opportunities.[24]

Certainly *among* the most notorious anti-immigrant organization was the Ku Klux Klan. During the 1920s the Klan expanded its racist rhetoric to include recently arrived central and eastern Europeans. Encouraged by a growing nativist movement and fears of the immigrant population, the Klan resorted to terroristic methods including lynchings and nocturnal mob assaults to coerce conformity. As the American dread of a foreign-born population grew after World War I, so too did the Klan's membership. By 1926 there were more than five million Klansmen and women throughout the country.[25]

With intolerance came violence. During the last years of the nineteenth century and early years of the twentieth century there were numerous attacks on Italians. In West Virginia, Pennsylvania, Massachusetts, North Carolina, Illinois and Florida, Italians were lynched. In Louisiana five Italian shopkeepers were murdered because they had paid black employees the same wages that they had paid their white employees. In Colorado in 1914 three Italian miners were killed and eight women were burned to death when the governor ordered state troops to subdue striking miners. Six years later the Italian neighborhood in West Franklin, Illinois, was systematically burned to the ground by marauding vigilantes.[26] The anti–Italian assault reached a climax with the trial, conviction and 1927 execution of Nicola Sacco, a fishmonger, and Bartolomeo Vanzetti, a shoemaker. The two immigrants were accused of armed robbery and murder. Though eyewitnesses testified that neither of the men was anywhere near the scene of the crime, the pair were convicted. The crucial moment in the trial came when the prosecution revealed that the accused were under investigation for political radicalism. After the trial, the judge instructed jurors to disregard all eyewitness testimony which supported the two men. By the time that the verdict was rendered, the trial had attracted international attention. The convictions brought charges of racism from around the world.[27] Though these circumstances were unsettling for some Italians and infuriating to others, for most, including the Lazzeri family, such racism was merely another reality of life in the United States during the twenties.

Young Tony Lazzeri was fortunate. He had a talent that set him apart from other first generation Italian-Americans. Tony could hit home runs. As a result he was able to escape some of the most bitter prejudice. Nevertheless, fans and sportswriters regularly reminded him of his ethnic heritage. In reporting the purchase of his contract from Salt Lake City, the *New York Times* fumbled over various spellings of his name. Announcing "La Zerre, Lizzieri or Li Zerri! No, It's Not the Mussolini Yell," the Yankees' new second baseman was introduced to New Yorkers. Throughout the season he was referred to as "the noble Roman," "the swarthy Neopolitan," "Caesar's kinsman," and "the Yankee spaghetti farmer" among other sobriquets.[28]

While much was made of Lazzeri's minor league credentials, it was his keystone counterpart, Mark Koenig, who most impressed the Yankees brass during the spring. Like Lazzeri, Koenig hailed from San Francisco and his parents had emigrated to the United States. Unlike Lazzeri, his parents were of German and Swiss descent. Preferring to take a chance on baseball rather than laying bricks like his father, Mark after graduating from high school immediately agreed to play for Moose Jaw in the Western Canada League. When the club folded midway through the 1921 season, Koenig was picked up by a team in Jamestown, North Dakota. For the next two years he traveled the Great Plains in relative obscurity, playing as a utility infielder for Jamestown and Des Moines.[29]

Mark's break came in late 1924. That year his team, the St. Paul Saints of the American Association, played Baltimore in minor league's "Little World Series." Just before the opening game, the Saints' regular shortstop injured his ankle. Despite his manager's concern that the little-used utility infielder lacked experience, Koenig was penciled into the starting lineup. He went on to have such an outstanding series that at least seven major league teams reportedly sought his services for the following year.[30] However, Mark remained with the Saints and had a fine year, batting over .300. That winter St. Paul sold his contract to the Yankees for $50,000.

Few doubted Koenig's ability to hit major league pitching. As a speedy switch hitter who usually made contact with the ball, he was expected to make an excellent leadoff or second hitter in the lineup. He might also nicely complement the power hitters in the Yankees order. Where New York reporters and fans questioned their new shortstop's abilities was in the field. Koenig himself admitted that he was not a great fielder. His defensive statistics provided further evidence for his critics. Year in and year out he had ranked among the poorest infielders in whichever league he played. Though he had a strong and accurate arm, he simply was not very good at cleanly catching a baseball. Some theorized that his unusually small hands were the source of his problem. In an age when a fielder's glove was little more than a few leather straps stitched together to protect the hand rather than the specialized defensive tools they have become, the size of a player's hands, especially at a key position like shortstop, was critical. Without large, powerful hands a fielder had limited ability to catch and control a sharply hit ball. According to many of Koenig's contemporaries, Mark was proof of the theory.

One who did not completely subscribe to the "small hands" theory was Miller Huggins. While recognizing that Koenig was not a great fielding shortstop, he concluded that Mark's offensive punch would more than compensate for his defensive shortcomings. Huggins inserted Koenig as the Yankees' starting shortstop at the beginning of spring training and left no doubt the young infielder would be the team's shortstop when the season started.

Koenig was not the only Yankee to earn accolades during the spring. As always, much of the excitement swirled around Babe Ruth, who appeared ready to reclaim his place as the brightest star in the New York constellation. During the winter the Babe had trained in Artie McGovern's Manhattan gymnasium. Following McGovern's rigorous program of exercise and diet, Ruth worked himself back into playing shape. When he arrived in St. Petersburg he was almost 45 pounds lighter with a physique that resembled what it had been five years earlier. Confirming his new look, Ruth announced that he was as fit as he had ever been and ready to improve upon the 59 home runs he had hit in 1921.[31] In addition to the new and improved Ruth, third baseman Joe Dugan showed no ill effects from his off-season knee surgery. Another who shined was Lou Gehrig. Throughout the spring Gehrig demonstrated that he was ready to improve upon his rookie season. Several prodigious home runs and a slew of blistering line drives had all who watched speculating about a batting order that included both Ruth and Gehrig. The Yankees mound crew was also impressive. With three of the best pitchers in the American League — Herb Pennock, Waite Hoyt, and recently acquired Urban Shocker — the team appeared to have as good a staff as any in baseball.

There was much concern that with two rookies, Tony Lazzeri (left) and Mark Koenig (right), at second base and shortstop the Yankees could not win the pennant. Lazzeri's bat made up for his defensive lapses but Koenig's errors cost the Yankees several games during the season and an important game in the World Series.

The Yankees exhibition schedule began slowly. The team opened play by dropping three out of four to the lowly Boston Braves. However, once the Braves were out of the way, Huggins and company began to rattle off wins with remarkable regularity. Riding a Babe Ruth home run, the Yanks notched a win over the Phillies and then two more against the Reds before breaking camp for the traditional barnstorming adventure back to New York.

No team has had a better trip home from spring training than did the Yankees in 1926. The unfortunate victim of the team's success was the Brooklyn Dodgers, or Robins as they were also known, who rode north with the Yankees. The Robins boasted one of the stronger pitching staffs in the National League, but it did not take long for Yankees hitters to establish their dominance. In the initial contest between the cross-city rivals, Lou Gehrig belted two home runs and the Yankees waltzed to a 7–3 win. Two days later the Bronx Bombers smashed four round trippers, beating the

Robins 10–2. At the next stop a Tony Lazzeri grand slam propelled his club to an 11–4 win. Over the following ten days Yankees hitters devoured Brooklyn pitching. On the two occasions when the Yankees bats failed to rack up more than four runs, the Robins were tamed by Yankees pitchers. The only Brooklyn reprieve was bad weather which forced the cancellation of three games. By the end of the journey the Yankees, in a harbinger of things to come, pounded their way to a 16-game winning streak. They outscored Brooklyn 113 to 42, averaging almost ten runs per game while holding the Robins to just 3.5 runs every nine innings.

The impressive display of power and pitching excited Yankees fans. The *New York Times* cautiously proposed that "the team has tremendous potential … keep Ruth out of the hospital and the team out of the doldrums, give them a good shortstop and an efficient second baseman and we predict heaps of trouble for American League opposition."[32] Various baseball experts, including several major league managers, agreed with the *Times*. The Yankees clearly had the makings of a solid pennant contender. Not surprisingly, Wilbert Robinson, the Brooklyn manager, forecast that 1926 would be a very good year for the Yankees. After such a dismal season the year before, the predictions were sweet music to the ears of Yankees boosters.

3

The Season Begins

The Cardinals began the 1926 season at home with a four-game series against the World Champion Pittsburgh Pirates. The previous season the Pirates had won the National League pennant by 8½ games and then went on to beat the Senators in a six-game World Series. Favored to repeat as champions, no one doubted that Pittsburgh would be one of the strongest teams in the league. An early series against the Buccaneers would provide an important early-season test for the young Cardinals.

The Pirates boasted one of the more potent offensive combinations in either league. Outfielder Kiki Cuyler led the attack. The previous season his .357 batting average was the fourth-highest in the National League. Cuyler was runner-up to Hornsby for the league's Most Valuable Player award. A few years younger than the Cardinals manager, Cuyler subscribed to many of Hornsby's hitting theories. His batting stance was a mirror image of Hornsby's and, like the Cardinals manager, he neither drank nor smoked. More pleasant off the field than Hornsby, Cuyler was nevertheless an equally fierce competitor on the diamond.

Sharing the outfield duties with Cuyler were Max Carey, Clyde "Pooch" Barnhart, and rookie Paul Waner. One of the finest defensive center fielders of the era, Carey was also an excellent lead-off man. A switch-hitter, he batted .343 in 1925. Once on base he became a base stealing threat, leading the National League in that category ten times. Unfortunately Carey began the season on the bench because of an illness. His absence gave Waner a chance to play. A much touted rookie, Waner had hit .401 for the San Francisco Seals in 1925. Living up to expectations, he saw much playing time coming off the bench, often substituting for Barnhart, a .325 hitter the previous season but perhaps the slowest man on the Pirates roster. So impressive was

Waner's performance in 1926 that the following season Carey was gone and Waner was entrenched in right field. In Cuyler, Carey and Waner the 1926 Pirates had three future Hall of Famers prowling the outfield.

The Pirates infield included another future Hall of Famer: Harold "Pie" Traynor. By 1926 Traynor was considered the best all-around third baseman in the game. A consistent line drive hitter who would compile a lifetime .320 batting average, he was well suited for spacious Forbes Field. In the field he had no equal, he was simply the best. Playing alongside Traynor was young Glenn "Buckshot" Wright. In only two seasons with the Pirates, Wright had already established himself as one of the league's finest short-stops. A smooth fielder blessed with a strong, accurate arm, Wright was also a threat at the plate having hit .308 the previous season. Had it not been for an arm injury a few years later, Wright might have been another Pirate immortalized in Cooperstown.

The question mark for Pittsburgh was the pitching staff. Manager Bill McKechnie, yet another future Hall of Famer, had made no changes to the staff that the previous year had helped bring the Steel City a championship. While the mound crew had no bona fide star, it was comprised of experienced veterans who knew how to win. Nevertheless, most agreed that if the Pirates had a flaw it was on the mound.[1]

For eager Cardinals fans, opening the season by hosting the reigning world champions and that team's collection of stars was exciting enough, but there was more to celebrate. During the winter the St. Louis ballpark, Sportsman's Park, had been enlarged and updated. Phil Ball, who owned the park as well as St. Louis's American League entry, the Browns, had decided to remodel the facility after the 1925 season. Attendance at Browns games had grown each of the previous three years, as had Cardinals attendance. In addition to accommodating the growing crowds, a larger ballpark would warrant a higher rental fee for Ball's National League tenant. Likewise, a larger ballpark would justify the ten percent increase in ticket prices that Ball planned for 1926.

Sportsman's Park was one of the oldest major league parks. It had been built during the late nineteenth century and had undergone numerous renovations. Prior to the turn of the century all sorts of sporting events had been played within the ever-changing facility. At one point Sportsman's had even been transformed into a race track. However, since 1903 the park had been used primarily for baseball, serving as the home of the Browns and, since 1920, the Cardinals. Sportsman's most recent renovations had come in 1909 when a permanent double-deck grandstand was erected. Constructed of concrete and steel, the new grandstand stretched from first base around home plate to third base. Adjacent to the grandstand were two sets of bleachers that reached out along both foul lines to the home run fences. The park at that point could hold slightly more than 18,500 fans.

In expanding the park Ball spent $500,000 to continue the double-deck grandstand out along both outfield foul lines. New bleachers were also built behind both the left and right field fences. The additions added 13,500 new seats bringing the total capacity to almost 32,000. Along with expanded seating, the dimensions of the playing field were also enlarged. The right field fence was pushed back from 315 feet to 320 feet. The left field fence went from 340 to 350 feet from home plate, and the home run mark in center field swelled to 430 feet. The commodious size of the renovated park established it as one of the largest in the major leagues.

The refurbished park's first official day of business came on a chilly, mid–April afternoon when 17,000 Cardinals fans saw their team, decked out in newly designed uniforms, beat the world champions 7–6. Led by Hornsby, who had three hits, and first baseman Jim Bottomley, who hit a three-run homer, St. Louis displayed the kind of impressive offense that their fans hoped for. At the same time, the victory was tempered by several defensive lapses. In the sixth inning, with two runners on base, third baseman Les Bell booted an apparent double play ball. The next Pirates hitter smacked a hard ground ball to first which Bottomley muffed, allowing two runners to score. An inning later Bell kicked an easy roller which brought in yet another Pirates run. Meanwhile Cardinals pitcher Flint Rhem, staked to an early six-run lead, began to falter midway through the game. Fortunately for the St. Louis fans, he was able to hold off the Pittsburgh attack just long enough to register the season's first victory.

Cardinals pitching problems became the story the next afternoon. Jesse Haines, the ace of the Cardinals staff, breezed through the first seven hitters. With one out in the third, Pirates catcher Earl Smith smashed a line drive off of Haines's right foot. The Cardinals pitcher fell to the ground in obvious pain and had to be carried off the field. Though his foot was not broken as the team doctor initially feared, it was so badly bruised that Haines would be unable to pitch for at least two weeks and possibly much longer. With Haines gone Redbird relievers struggled through the last six innings, allowing nine Pirates runs. Meanwhile Cardinals hitters were able to hack out only seven hits and three runs.

The loss of Haines even for only a couple of weeks was a severe blow to the Cardinals. Manager Hornsby recognized that his pitching staff was thin long before Haines went down. Additionally, Haines was the most experienced and dependable hurler on the roster. Though he had a mediocre season in 1925, he was a veteran who had won 20 games three years earlier and could be counted on to win 12–15 games a season. He was also the kind of competitor that Hornsby liked. A crafty professional, Haines had a better than average fast ball and a good curve, but what made him exceptional was a particularly effective knuckleball. It was a pitch that he had learned from Eddie Rommel, who some credited with having invented the knuckleball. When Haines threw the pitch he actually dug his knuckles into the ball rather than gripping the ball with his finger tips as most knuckleballers did. The result was that the ball hopped up to the plate, then dived sharply down and away from right-handed hitters. Haines put so much force into his specialty pitch that he often finished games with bloody fingers. It was the knuckleball that made Haines the most successful pitcher on the Cardinals staff.

Haines was also a fierce competitor who hated to lose. Infielders who committed errors or outfielders who threw to the wrong base when Haines was on the mound often incurred the full wrath of the Cardinals pitcher.

On one occasion, after his catcher had made an errant throw that led to a 1–0 defeat, Haines became so enraged that teammates had to physically restrain him from attacking the catcher. There were other tales about the damage Haines had wreaked on various dugouts after losses. Though mild-mannered and quiet off the field, he became a raging bull when on the mound. Jesse was precisely the kind of player that Hornsby wanted on his team.

Time spent on the disabled list was sheer agony for Jesse Haines. With every game he pitched he was living out his boyhood dream. As a youngster growing up in Phillipsburg, a small farm town in western Ohio, Haines loved baseball. Neighborhood games and days spent hitting hard rub-

An eight-year veteran with almost 100 career wins, much was expected of Jesse "Pop" Haines in 1926. Despite an early-season injury he lived up to the expectations.

ber baseballs were among his earliest and fondest memories. Even when his parents prohibited him from playing Sunday games for the town team, he found a way to play. Frequently the deception involved hiding his uniform in a neighbor's corn crib and using the cornfield as his dressing room. The consequences of parental detection were worrisome but the opportunity to play baseball was worth the risk.

In 1912, at the age of 18, Jesse left Phillipsburg to play semi-pro baseball in Dayton. The following year he was invited to pitch for the Dayton Lily Brews, one of the best semi-pro teams in the area. At the same time he joined the Dayton entry in the Central League. His professional career continued a year later when he played for Saginaw (Michigan) and Springfield (Illinois). Though signed briefly by the Tigers, he saw no action in Detroit. For four years he bounced from one minor league to another except for one game with the Cincinnati Reds in 1918. His break came in 1919 when Branch Rickey purchased his contract. The following year Haines began a long, productive major league career by hurling 301 innings for the Cardinals. Over the next five seasons he became the workhorse on the St. Louis staff. His accomplishments included a 20-win season in 1923. In 1924 he threw the first Cardinals no-hitter since 1876. By 1926 Haines was the foundation upon which the Cardinals mound crew was built. With him out of action, a questionable St. Louis staff became even more suspect.[2]

Despite the loss of their ace, the Cardinals pitching staff performed surprisingly well. The day after Haines was injured, Vic Keen, a retread acquired from the Cubs the previous winter, masterfully twirled the team's first shutout of the season. In the final game of the Pittsburgh series, Si Johnson, another winter acquisition, gave up only four hits in eight innings, leading the Cardinals to a third victory over the world champions. Though he had lost his best pitcher, Hornsby was satisfied with his team's performance during their opening series.

The unexpectedly strong mound work continued against the Cubs. In the series opener, Willie Sherdel scattered eight hits in an exciting 3–2 win. The following day, after his team had again beaten the Cubs, manager Hornsby announced, "I have so many good pitchers now that I can send any one of six and get a well fought battle.... It makes a manager feel pretty chipper to know he has flingers he can rely on so early in the year."[3] The Cardinals manager was not as happy with his offense, which was hitting at a meager .182 clip, but he was certain that his "gang of sluggers" would soon live up to his expectations.

Hornsby's praise for his team proved premature. During the last two games of the home stand the Cardinals fell apart. In a frustrating 14-inning marathon that included several crucial errors, including one by Hornsby that allowed a run to score, the Cubs outlasted the home team 5–4. The results were worse the next day. St. Louis pitching was pounded for 12 hits and seven runs while Redbird hitters were shut out for the first time.

Despite two losses to the Cubs, the Cardinals' first home stand was deemed a success. Having taken three of four from one of the league's most potent attacks, Hornsby's crew could have just as easily done the same against the Cubs had it not been for a few fielding miscues. The pitching, which was expected to be the team's weakness, looked surprisingly solid. In the field, though a bit sloppy at times, the team performed adequately. Ironically, the only real soft spot was the much-touted offense. Finishing the eight-game home stand just one game out of first place, the team lived up to most expectations during the first week of the season.

A new challenge faced the team as it began its first 1926 road trip. The Cardinals' record away from home had been dismal during the previous season, with twice as many losses as wins. Hornsby and his squad would have to do much better if they were to challenge for the pennant.

The trip began on a high note in Pittsburgh. In front of 35,000 Pirates fans Flint Rhem won his third game of the season, beating the home team 5–3 in ten innings. After splitting the last two games in the series, the Cardinals moved on to Cincinnati with hopes of parlaying their fortunes into their most successful journey since 1924. Satisfied with the outcome in Pittsburgh, Hornsby took a pragmatic approach to his team's early accomplishments, proposing: "We are playing every game for what it is worth. A victory in April is worth as much as one in July or August, and a good start is a benefit to any team."[4]

The series in Cincinnati began on a bone-chilling late April afternoon. A sparse crowd of only 800 hardy souls watched a Cardinals attack that was almost as cold as the weather. Able to chip out only six hits, the Redbirds were blanked in the opener. The following day the team suffered through another punchless afternoon. Nevertheless, Hornsby's squad led by a run with one out in the bottom of the ninth. An infield hit, an error by Thevenow on a possible double play ball, and a bloop single sent the game into extra innings. In the tenth another Cardinal error sealed the victory for the Reds. After a day off because of rain, the Cardinals were able to salvage the final game of the series. A bit dispirited, the team moved on to Chicago for four games. Little did they know what awaited in the windy city.

The series with the Cubs began badly and got progressively worse. St. Louis booted away the opening contest on a crucial eighth-inning error when pitcher "Duster" Mails fielded a bunt by Cubs catcher Mike Gonzalez and heaved it into right field. One hitter later, Gonzalez scampered home with winning run. Hornsby was so upset that as soon as the game was over Mails was shipped off to Syracuse, never again to play in the Major Leagues. The following afternoon Cardinals pitcher Art Reinhart was signaled to walk Hack Wilson. Instead he got a pitch too close to the plate and Wilson poked a game-winning single into center field. The Cardinals losses continued the next day when the Cubs launched a five-run eighth inning barrage after the first two hitters were out. Grover Cleveland Alexander, aided by sloppy Cardinals fielding, finished off the sweep. A trip that had begun amidst great expectations for the Cardinals ended in sour disappointment.

As his team limped back to St. Louis, Hornsby assessed the problems. When they left home two weeks earlier they were only a game out of first place and appeared ready to challenge for a pennant. By the time of their return they had fallen to within a game of the National League cellar. Throughout most of the trip the pitching staff, even without Jesse Haines, had held up better than expected. Unfortunately the offense had not. Rarely were Cardinals hitters able to register more than five hits in any nine-inning stretch. Defensively the team performance had been unacceptable. Key errors at crucial moments had cost the team at least four games. Equally troubling was the team's inability to hold a lead. In five of the seven road losses, including three with the Cubs, St. Louis had led going into the seventh inning. If they were to contend for the league championship, the Cardinals would have to score more runs and learn how to hold a lead.

At about the same time that the Cardinals were boarding their train to go back home, another St. Louis man was preparing to take a somewhat less conventional trip back home. Two weeks earlier, 24-year-old Charles Lindbergh had climbed into a recently purchased De Haviland biplane and initiated airmail service between his hometown and Chicago. Though the flight received little attention, in fact it opened a new era in aviation history. It was also the beginning of an American legend.

Lindbergh's trip was the culmination of several years of personal preparation and several months of negotiations by his employers. Until 1925 the limited airmail service that existed within the United States was operated by the U.S. Army. However, the system ran at a substantial loss and, consequently, became the target of constant criticism. Among the most vociferous detractors were the nation's railroads. They complained that the subsidized air mail system constituted unfair competition and wasted taxpayers' money. Acceding to the complaints, the pro-business, fiscally conservative Coolidge administration in 1925 passed legislation that turned the airmail service over to the private sector.

Among those who immediately took advantage of the legislation were two brothers from St. Louis, Bill and Frank Robertson. Veteran World War I flyers, the Robertsons recognized that the legislation provided a grand opportunity for the struggling flying industry. Acting quickly, they formed a small company, established a home base at Lambert Field in St. Louis, and bid on an airmail route between St. Louis and Chicago. At the same time, they began recruiting fliers. One of the first they approached was young barnstormer/parachutist/wing-walker Charles Lindbergh.

Only 23 when he met the Robertsons, "Slim" Lindbergh already had a reputation as an exceptional pilot. Three years earlier he had dropped out of the University of Wisconsin to pursue his dream of flying. His training began at a small airfield in Nebraska where he spent more time under planes than in them. Disgruntled about his lack of air time, he went to work as a mechanic, ticket seller, publicist, and occasional wing-walker for a barnstorming pilot. After a few months he added parachutist to his resume. The trick was an especially dangerous one that few ever tried, but one that Lindbergh claimed he enjoyed. It involved strapping on two parachutes, then at a couple of thousand feet jumping out of a plane. After falling several hundred feet, the first chute was opened. When it was fully opened, the chutist cut it off, then fell another several hundred more feet before opening the second chute. The trick required careful coordination between pilot and chutist, nerves of steel, and luck. Appropriately billing himself as "Daredevil" Lindbergh, the aspiring flier joined a husband and wife team who put on air shows throughout the Midwest.

In the spring of 1923 Lindbergh bought his first plane and became a gypsy flier selling rides and doing stunts across mid–America from the Canadian border to Texas. His travels eventually brought him to St. Louis and the International Air Races at Lambert Field. Captivated by the powerful new flying machines and the skills of the aviators who flew them, he decided to enlist in the U.S. Army air corps, where he could get the best flight training available. For the next year he served as an air cadet, learning both the practical and the theoretical about flying. Studiously laboring in the classroom, he dazzled his trainers in the air. In March 1925 he graduated first in his class.[5]

With his Army wings in hand and the remains of his small Army pay in his pocket, he headed back to St. Louis. Almost as soon as he arrived he met the Robertson brothers. They told him about their plans to create an airmail service. The idea appealed to Lindbergh. A year later, with the St. Louis to Chicago contract at last in hand, the two brothers again sought out the young flier, who agreed to become the new company's chief pilot. Lindbergh quickly enlisted two of his air cadet classmates as the rest of his flying squad. Over the next few weeks the three fliers prepared what would be needed for their flights. They mapped out flight routes, arranged a string of gasoline dumps and built a series of sky lights which would allow them to fly at night. Meanwhile the Robertsons bought a small fleet of airplanes, including ten De Haviland biplanes like the ones Lindbergh had flown during his Army training. With all preparations made, the Robertson Air Company scheduled its inaugural flight. At dawn on April 15, Charles Lindbergh climbed into his De Haviland and with two refueling stops along the way flew to Chicago. Six hours later he deposited his north-bound mail and headed back to St. Louis, returning home just after dark.[6]

During the next nine months Lindbergh and his flying partners made daily round trip flights to Chicago. It was on those trips that Lindbergh began to contemplate a much longer flight — a trans–Atlantic trip. The idea was inspired by a newsreel report about a French pilot's pursuit of the Orteig Prize, a $25,000 reward to the first person able to fly non-stop across the Atlantic. Entranced by the adventure, Lindbergh began to concoct a plan for the journey. By the end of the year he had assembled a syndicate of backers, including Frank Robertson, who were willing to fund the stunt, and he had contracted with a small California aircraft manufacturing company that agreed to build a specially designed plane for him.

Of course, on that late April afternoon in 1926, as the Cardinals limped back to St. Louis from their disastrous series with the Cubs, no one could have foreseen what lay ahead for the young flier. As they bounced along the tracks, none of the Cardinals would have spotted Lindbergh's lumbering De Haviland nor could any of them have imagined that thirteen months later the plane's pilot, a man from their baseball hometown, would step out of his plane onto a Paris airfield and become an instant international hero whose renown surpassed that of even Babe Ruth.

The Yankees opened the 1926 season in Boston, where they anticipated a couple of early wins. The Red Sox were universally considered to be one of the worst teams in the major leagues. They had finished in the American League cellar three of the past four years. The previous season they had finished 27 games back of the seventh-place Yankees and 49½ games out of first place. The best that could be said for the Red Sox in 1926 was that they probably would not be as bad as they had been in 1925.[7] Aside from two capable pitchers, Howard Ehmke and Charles "Red" Ruffing, Boston was a collection of castoffs and untried rookies. For the Yankees, who were anxious to have their fans forget the previous year's problems and instead recognize the rejuvenated team as a legitimate pennant contender, there was no better opponent than the Red Sox.

The season began on a bitterly cold afternoon that the *New York Times* claimed was better suited for hockey than for baseball.[8] In front of 12,000 "blue lipped opening day customers," the Yankees wasted no time in demonstrating their offensive prowess. Leadoff hitter Mark Koenig bunted his way to first. Center fielder Earle Combs followed with a walk and Lou Gehrig loaded the bases on the inning's second bunt single. Only three batters into the season, Babe Ruth came to the plate with a chance to immediately re-establish himself as the Yankees' hero. Though he did not launch the missile that some expected, he did pound the ball into right field driving in the first New York tally of the year. Before the Yankees' half of the inning was over three more runners had crossed the plate. The Yanks went on to take a ten-run lead midway through the game, then hung on to win 12–11.

The Yankees winning streak that had grown to 16 pre-season games and their opening day victory came to an end the following afternoon. Cold weather, ineffective pitching and four errors, including a critical throwing error by Koenig, enabled the Red Sox to earn their first win of the season. Nevertheless, the Yankees again hammered out 11 hits and scored seven runs. After a day off because of cold weather, the Yankees concluded their visit to Boston on a winning note.

From their opening series against the league's worst team, the Yankees traveled to Washington for a weekend series with perhaps the league's best team. Led by their fiery young player-manager Bucky Harris, the Senators were the two-time defending league champions. In 1926 the team again appeared to be solid at every position. The pitching staff featured the incomparable Walter Johnson, who had already won 397 major league games and was coming off back-to-back 20-win seasons. Along with Johnson the Senators staff included Stan Coveleski, another 20-game winner in 1925 and future member of the Hall of Fame, and two experienced veterans, Dutch Ruether and Tom Zachary, who had won 30 games between them the previous year. Handling the Washington staff was one of the league's smartest catchers, Muddy Ruel. At the plate the team had hit at a .304 clip the previous season. The most feared hitter was Goose Goslin. Having batted over .300 for five consecutive seasons, Goslin was the team's home run threat and an especially dangerous clutch hitter. Sam Rice, who had hit .350 in 1925, teamed up with Goslin in the outfield. Both Goslin and Rice would eventually be inducted into the Hall of Fame. Smooth-fielding shortstop Roger Peckinpaugh, the league's Most Valuable Player the previous season, anchored the infield. He and Harris were considered to be the league's best double play tandem. With their championship lineup still intact and a couple of capable additions made during the off season, Washington was sure to be in the thick of the 1926 pennant race. Unlike the Red Sox, the Senators represented a true test for the optimistic Yankees.[9]

The Yankees split the first two games with the Senators, out-hitting Washington in the opener and dropping an extra-inning pitchers' duel in the second. After sitting out a day because of exceptionally cold weather, the

New Yorkers were confronted by the Senators ace, Walter Johnson. Though nearing the end of his legendary career, "Sir Walter" was still one of the most feared pitchers in the game. A week earlier, in his first outing of the season he had beaten the Philadelphia Athletics in a remarkable 1–0 16-inning shutout, one of 38 1–0 shutouts he threw in his career.

Johnson's fate on this day was in doubt only briefly. With a runner on base and two outs in the first inning, Babe Ruth began the Yankees assault by walloping a mammoth home run, his first of the season. Two innings later the New Yorkers bombarded the Senators legend with five more markers. By the end of the afternoon the visitors had banged out 22 hits, including five by Ruth, and scored 18 runs. One New York reporter claimed that Johnson had been victimized by a Yankee "homicide squad." A few days later the same reporter revised his description, referring to the New York lineup as "Murderer's Row." It was a label that came to identify Yankee hitters for years to come.[10]

While the story of the day was certainly the New York offense, for one Yankee the day was significant for another reason. For Honey Barnes, a rookie catcher, the game became both his major league debut and finale. Called on to pinch hit for catcher Pat Collins in the ninth inning, Barnes drew a base on balls. After catching the bottom of the ninth, he never again played in the major leagues. In so doing he became one of a handful of players who have recorded a perfect 1.000 career on-base percentage, though for Barnes it was done without even an official time at bat.

Buoyed by their successes in Boston and Washington, the Yankees returned home amid growing excitement. Since the end of spring training two weeks earlier, New York fans had eagerly awaited the team's home opener. The stunning performance against Walter Johnson added a few more volts of electricity to their fervor. As game time approached, 40,500 supporters scrambled into their seats while two local military bands played patriotic marches as the American flag was raised in center field (it would be 15 more years before the national anthem started every ball game). The gathering multitude then watched their popular and always controversial mayor Jimmy Walker throw out the season's first pitch "whipping a throw into (catcher) Pat Collins's glove that would have been a strike in any league."[11] Even the weather cooperated. The frosty conditions that the Yankees had endured throughout their first road trip gave way to a warm mid–April sun and balmy spring breezes. It was perfect weather for an opening day at Yankee Stadium.

With the opening day ceremonies behind them the Yankees prepared to give their fans the feast that they had long awaited. Unfortunately the day's opposition, the lowly Red Sox, was not ready to comply. Scoring two runs in the first and two more and in the second, and with their ace Howard Ehmke on the mound, Boston controlled the early innings. Then in the fourth, Yankees fans got what they had come for. Led by an Earle Combs three-run home run, the Yanks stormed back with six runs. The production was more than enough for pitcher Waite Hoyt, who breezed through the last six innings. The day ended with an 8–5 Yankee victory and 40,500 satisfied fans. The only disappointment was that Babe Ruth had not hit one out of the park.

The Yankees went on to take two of the next three games. Their only loss came in a seesaw struggle decided by a tenth-inning home run. Otherwise the New Yorkers dominated the Red Sox. New York pitchers held Boston hitters to just one run in each victory while the Yankees scored 12 times. Additionally, Ruth swatted out a home run in each of the last two games, something Yankees fans had been eagerly anticipating.

There were many reasons for Yankees fans to be excited about having their team back home. None was more compelling than the return of Babe Ruth. New York supporters were anxious to see for themselves whether their hero could still hammer the ball the way he had prior to 1925. They wanted to find out how much Ruth had benefited from his well-publicized exercise regimen during the winter. Had their champion regained his legendary power and lost his stomach? They hoped again to watch the powerful athlete who had so captivated them during his first five seasons in their city. The thought of a new and improved Babe Ruth playing alongside young power-house Lou Gehrig was equally intriguing. With two such potent bats in the lineup the Yankees might be very entertaining to watch.

Yankees fans were also curious about the relationship between Ruth and New York manager Miller Huggins. During the last weeks of the previous season the two had become embroiled in a much-reported feud. Throughout the frustrating season Huggins' patience with Ruth was repeatedly tested. The tensions finally erupted during the Yankees' last western trip of the season. Huggins hired a detective to follow Ruth during the trip. In Chicago the detective reported that Ruth had prowled saloons and brothels throughout the night. Moving on to St. Louis, Ruth's behavior continued. Armed with his evidence, the angry manager at last confronted Ruth. Reprimanding his wayward star, Huggins levied a stiff $5,000 fine and suspended Ruth until he had apologized to his teammates. The Babe was livid about the punishment. In the days that immediately followed, the volatile slugger stormed from baseball commissioner Kenesaw Landis (never a grand Babe Ruth fan) to Yankees owner Jacob Ruppert and the press, pleading his case to whoever would listen (and to many who would not). At one point Ruth spouted off that he would never again play for Huggins even if it meant leaving the Yankees. The Babe also blamed Huggins for the Yankees' 1925 failures, labeling the manager incompetent. After almost a week of thunder, Ruth cooled off, paid his fine and apologized. The Babe then quietly played out the last three weeks of the season. Though on the surface relations between the two Yankees appeared to have mended, many New Yorkers remained skeptical.[12]

Despite the truce there was good reason to expect renewed warfare between the Yankee slugger and his manager. In most ways Huggins was a complete contrast to Ruth. While the Bambino was an exceptional physical specimen, "Little Hug" was a scrawny 5' 6", 140 pounds. Ruth was driven by emotion and spontaneous energy. Huggins was contemplative and planned strategy. Ruth, who had a rudimentary education at best, often stumbled over his academic shortcomings. Huggins earned a law degree from the University of Cincinnati and was among the more scholarly men in baseball. The Babe was a larger than life personality who wallowed in his celebrity. Huggins was a quiet man who generally avoided unnecessary media attention.

Success on the ball field was another quality that separated Ruth and Huggins. For Ruth, accomplishment on the diamond came naturally. Huggins, on the other hand, spent years nurturing his baseball talents. As a youth he played ball every chance he could but despite his passion for the game, he acceded to his father's demand to pursue an education. While earning a law degree at the University of Cincinnati, which included a course taught by future President William Howard Taft, Huggins played ball for local clubs in Cincinnati. Once he graduated, the lure of baseball proved too strong. Clawing his way into professional baseball, he played for several minor league teams in the Midwest. In 1904 he joined the Reds as a second baseman. Considered a defensive specialist, Huggins worked hard to develop his hitting skills. Because he could not hit right-handed pitchers well, he taught himself to switch-hit. Lacking physical strength (reporters regularly referred to him as "diminutive"), he worked to become a bat control specialist and maximize his speed. Eventually his hard work paid off. Four times he led the league in walks, earning him the reputation as one of the better leadoff hitters in the National League.

In 1910 Huggins was traded from the Reds to the lowly St. Louis Cardinals. Three years later he replaced Roger Bresnahan as the Cardinals player-manager. Taking charge of the worst team in baseball proved a challenge, but as always Huggins combined his baseball savvy and a strong work ethic to begin building a competitive team. Among his priorities was bringing new talent to his financially strapped club. In 1915 he saw a gawky youngster in Texas who so impressed him that he repeatedly pestered the Cardinals' frugal owner, Schuyler Britton, to shell out $500 and sign the young man.

Britton balked but eventually agreed to the purchase. The new Cardinal was Rogers Hornsby. It took a year for Huggins to transform Hornsby, who Britton initially referred to as "Huggins' Folly," into a solid player and another year before he became a star.

After guiding the Cardinals for five seasons, Huggins was approached by Yankees owner Jacob Ruppert to manage the Yankees. At the time the Yankees were among the worst teams in the American League. Equally important, the team had a hard time competing with their National League neighbor, the Giants, for the hearts of New Yorkers. Impressed by Huggins' knowledge of the game as well as his quiet, methodical demeanor, Ruppert hired the Cardinals manager. The only real obstacle was Ruppert's partner, Colonel Tillinghast Huston. At the time Huggins came to the Yankees, Huston was in France serving in World War I. When he returned he vehemently opposed the hiring. Instead he wanted Wilbert Robinson, Brooklyn's popular manager. Fortunately for the Yankees, Ruppert had the support of American League president Ban Johnson. During the years that followed, Huston continued to deride Huggins despite his team's steady improvement. Finally, after the 1922 season, Ruppert bought out his disgruntled partner. Meanwhile, using Ruppert's money to buy a crew of talented players, including Babe Ruth, Huggins transformed the Yankees into a perennial pennant contender. In 1921 the team won its first pennant, and two years later they beat the Giants in the World Series.[13]

As a manager Huggins was a quiet man who preferred to remain in the shadows of the dugout rather than in the media spotlight. A true student of the game, he once claimed, "I am learning more about the game every year and expect to learn as long as I am in the game."[14] It was a quality that he instilled in his players. Physical mistakes were aggravating but mental errors were unacceptable to Huggins. In dealing with his players he could be stern when circumstances warranted but preferred quiet prodding. Among his talents was an ability to groom young players. The best example was Lou Gehrig, but there were numerous others who attributed part of their success to Huggins. On the field he was cautious leader who played percentages rather than hunches. When disciplining his players he was universally acknowledged to be a patient man who preferred psychological methods rather than physical confrontation. However, when confrontation was required, Huggins, despite his size, was ready to challenge anyone, even Babe Ruth as he had at the end of the 1925 season. Prior to the 1925 battles, a prickly relationship had developed between the two men, and while in 1926 both promised to let bygones be bygones, many Yankee fans were not convinced.

Among those most concerned about the relationship between Ruth and

Huggins was Christy Walsh. A newspaper cartoonist, writer and ad man by trade, Walsh since 1921 had operated the Christy Walsh Syndicate, the first public relations agency to represent athletes. One of Walsh's initial clients, and certainly his most popular client, was Babe Ruth. In the course of his dealings with the slugger, Walsh had become a friend and business manager for Ruth. By 1926 Huggins was another of Walsh's growing list of celebrities. An ongoing dispute between the two Yankees would put the syndicate in a difficult position and would certainly affect the services that Walsh could provide either Ruth or Huggins.

While Walsh liked both men, Ruth was obviously more important to the syndicate than was Huggins. He also considered the slugger to be a close friend. Though an avid sports fan, Walsh was not blessed with exceptional athletic abilities. Instead he used his skills to become a sports promoter and by 1926 he, like Ruth, was the best in his business. Both men came from meager backgrounds: Ruth from the docks of Baltimore and Walsh from a rough Irish neighborhood in St. Louis. Like Ruth, Walsh had used his God-given talents to pull himself out of poverty. Working his way through law school by selling his cartoons, he matured into a crafty entrepreneur with a gift for turning ideas into profits. As his relationship with Ruth grew, he became one of the Babe's regular sidekicks. Meanwhile Ruth came to trust completely Walsh's financial guidance. In time Walsh also became instrumental in tempering the Babe's behavior in personal matters.

Ruth had first committed to work with Walsh in 1921. At the time, the Babe was emerging as the most recognizable personality in the country. He was precisely the sort of celebrity that Walsh needed to get his public relations business off the ground. However, getting the Babe to become a part of the syndicate was not an easy task. Walsh literally had to camp out on the doorstep of the Astoria Hotel, where Ruth was staying. For several days he waited, but Ruth was able to dodge him. Finally, disguising himself as a beer delivery man, he sneaked into Ruth's suite and offered him a $5,000 contract for the right to use the Babe's name on a series of articles that Walsh intended to have ghost-written. The Babe agreed, the deal was cut, and with it came a long, successful business relationship and friendship.

With the Babe in his stable, Walsh signed and began promoting many more baseball stars over the next few years. Among them were Ty Cobb, Giants manager John McGraw, Rogers Hornsby, Honus Wagner, Walter Johnson and, in 1923, the year the Yankees won their first world championship, Miller Huggins. By that time Walsh had expanded his publicity agency to include celebrities in a variety of other sports as well as several silent screen movie stars. Walsh's string of ghost writers had also grown to include notable writers such as Damon Runyon and future National League president Ford Frick.

Because trouble between Huggins and Ruth might mean problems for his business, Walsh, always the wary entrepreneur, kept a close eye on Ruth. He understood as well as anyone that a cordial working relationship between Ruth and Huggins was crucial to the success of both men. Likewise, Ruth had to stay focused and self-disciplined if he were to perform again as he once had. If necessary, Walsh was ready to use his influence to pacify the Babe. However, with the Yankees winning and Ruth again hitting home runs, the chances of another blowup with his manager seemed remote.

After taking three of four from the Red Sox, the Yankees closed out their first home stand against two tough pennant contenders: the Philadelphia Athletics and the Senators. In the three games against the Athletics, New York was dominating. Yankees pitching allowed Philadelphia only 15 hits and four runs during the entire series. In the field the New Yorkers were almost flawless, and at the plate they combined timely hitting with power. Only in the last of the three games were the A's able to challenge the Yankees. Philadelphia's ace pitcher, Lefty Grove, held the New Yorkers scoreless through seven innings, striking out 11 along the way. Finally, in the eighth, the heart of the Yankees line up strung together three singles and a double to score three runs. The lead proved to be more than enough for pitcher Sam Jones, who was on his way to throwing New York's first shutout of the season. Happy to leave New York, Connie Mack, the Athletics manager, warned that the Yankees might just be the team that the rest of the league would be chasing all season.

The Senators followed Philadelphia into Yankee Stadium and did no better than the Athletics. The series featured another impressive display of power by Yankees hitters. Babe Ruth continued to shine at the plate, contributing his fourth home run of the season. New York pitching wasn't able to shut down the Washington hitters as completely as they had the Athletics, but limited the Senators to eight runs in three games. Playing before 42,000 enthusiastic fans, the Yankees closed out the season's first home stand by winning their eighth straight and climbing to a two-game lead over the rest of the league.

For the Yankees, the first three weeks of the season had been a grand success. The team ended April having won 12 of the 15 games they had played. Babe Ruth was again hitting home runs and playing right field as well as he ever had. Third baseman Joe Dugan ended the month atop American League hitters, with Gehrig and outfielders Earle Combs and Bob Meusel not far off the pace. The biggest preseason question mark, the keystone combination of Lazzeri and Koenig, looked solid in the field and at the plate. Though

Koenig's glove had cost the team one game, he had regularly contributed to the New York hitting attack. Lazzeri, after a slow start at the plate, was beginning to live up to expectations. While the team was averaging more than seven runs per game, Yankees pitchers also performed well, holding the opposition to just over four runs. Amidst such success the team looked forward to a very enjoyable summer.

4

Spring Sun, Spring Rain

The Yankees' winning streak ended abruptly. After a 15–3 exhibition game win against the Jersey City Bears, a game in which Babe Ruth pitched the ninth inning, the New Yorkers played a three-game series with the Athletics. The Philadelphia team was not the same one that just a week earlier had played so dismally in Yankee Stadium. With Lefty Grove on the mound and propelled by a four-run sixth, the A's easily won the opener 8 to 3. The following day, suffering from "excruciatingly terrible pitching and atrocious fielding," the Yankees dropped another to the Athletics, losing 10–5, the first time the team had lost two in a row.[1] In the final game of the series a key error added another one to the loss column. Aided by the Babe's fifth home run of the season, the Yankees led by a run going into the eighth. An Athletics walk, a single and an error by Ruth, another walk and a bad-hop double plated three Athletics and completed a Philadelphia sweep.

Returning home for a make-up game against the Senators, the Yankees almost lost more than just the game. Chasing a leadoff pop-up along the foul line in short right field, Ruth ran head-on into Tony Lazzeri. The slugger bounced off his teammate and tumbled across the cinder warning track, scraping his thigh and bruising his left knee. After hobbling through his turn at the plate in the bottom half of the inning he left the game amid fears that the injury might be serious.[2] Initial reports predicted that it would be several days before the slugger would again be able to play. Fortunately for the Yankees Ruth, though still hobbling, was back in the lineup the next day against the Tigers. In true Ruthian style he walloped a home run, his sixth of the season, in his first trip to the plate. The two-run blast helped his struggling mates hang on to eventually win the contest 7–6 in eleven innings.

A long-festering feud between the Yankees and the Tigers erupted in the second game of the series. Ever since Babe Ruth had emerged as the game's premier slugger and transformed his club into a regular pennant contender, there had been tensions between the two clubs. Ruth's prominence in the early 1920s came at about the same time that Ty Cobb became the Tigers manager in 1921. Of course anytime Cobb took the field there was a chance for some sort of row. Over the years his Tigers teammates had come to reflect their manager's temperament. The presence of Lou Gehrig brought additional intensity to the rivalry. During the final meeting between the two teams in 1924 Gehrig had singled to right field but rounded first base too far. Cobb rushed in, scooped up the ball and applied a hard tag to the wayward base runner. An inning later, while coaching third base, Cobb taunted Gehrig mercilessly. Finally the Yankees rookie would take no more and bounded out of the dugout to confront the Tigers leader. Before any blows could be thrown, umpire Tom Connelly interceded and banished Gehrig. However, during the following season Cobb continued to needle the young slugger whenever given a chance.[3]

The game with the Tigers began poorly for the Yankees, who found themselves down by seven runs in the bottom of the fifth. Buoyed by a three-run shot from Ruth, his seventh of the season, the New Yorkers began a comeback. In the eighth "the walloping Wop," Tony Lazzeri, added a two-run homer. An inning later, with two outs and the Yankees still trailing by a pair of runs, Tigers pitcher Earl Whitehill hit Gehrig with a high curveball that didn't break. A feisty southpaw, Whitehill often threw a sweeping side-armed curve to keep left-handed hitters back from the plate, thus carving off a bit more working room for himself on the outside. Certainly he hadn't intended to hit Gehrig and bring Babe Ruth, who had already hit one home run, to the plate with a chance to tie the game. Nevertheless, Gehrig saw it differently. Leaping to his feet the first baseman barked out a few words, then rushed the mound. Umpire Bill McGowan interceded and pushed Gehrig to the ground before he could get to Whitehill. As the Yankees slugger again got to his feet he challenged the Tigers pitcher to meet him under the stands after the game. Whitehill accepted the challenge, then quickly dispatched Ruth to end the game.

Minutes later Gehrig charged into the tunnel that led to the Tigers clubhouse and grabbed Whitehill. As the two men wrestled on the ground Babe Ruth jumped in to break up the fight. Seeing the commotion, Cobb tried to help end the melee but instead accidentally kicked Ruth, who was still sore from his collision two days earlier. Breaking free from Ruth, Gehrig turned his focus on the Tigers manager. Growling "you've been riding me a long time, now I'm going to fix you," the Yankees first baseman took a few wild swings, then slipped, hit his head on a concrete post and knocked himself out. After attending to his teammate, Ruth shoved his way into the Tigers clubhouse but was pushed back out by several Tigers, ending that day's episode.[4]

A Sunday crowd of more than 55,000 fans, the largest Yankees turnout since the 1923 World Series, was on hand the following afternoon. No doubt many expected a continuation of the previous day's battles. Instead the slugfest they saw was on the field rather than under the stands. The Tigers opened with seven runs in the first inning and the Yankees followed with seven of their own in the second. By the end of the day the two teams had banged out 26 hits, including two home runs by Cobb. When the dust finally settled the Tigers had pounded their way to a 14–10 win. The loss dropped the Yankees for the first time out of the league's lead, ½ game back of the Senators. A day later New York regained the spot atop the American League, hammering 18 hits and three home runs, including Ruth's eighth, and winning 13–9. Though again neither team sought retribution for the entanglements a couple of days earlier, the confrontation was clearly not forgotten.

The win against Detroit began a three-week streak that separated the Yankees from their American League competition. Cleveland followed the Tigers into Yankee Stadium. The Indians had finished in sixth place the previous year. Having made no significant changes during the winter, the club was picked by most baseball experts to battle Boston for the American League basement. However, the Indians had played surprisingly well during the first month of the season. Led by player-manager Tris Speaker, they came into New York tied with the Yankees for the league lead. The strength of the squad was its pitching staff. The team's ace was George Uhle, who had won 26 games three years earlier. He had already chalked up five wins in 1926 (and would win 22 more before the season ended). Rookie Emil "Dutch" Levsen had also given the staff a boost during the first four weeks. At the plate the Indians were built around Speaker, shortstop Joe Sewell and first baseman George Burns. At 38 Speaker was still one of the most feared hitters in baseball. The previous year he had hit .389, losing the batting title by four points in the last week of the season. Shortstop Joe Sewell was considered one of the best in the American League. A perennial .300 hitter, he was equally valuable defensively. His brother "Little" Luke Sewell was the team's catcher. A light hitter, the younger Sewell was a particularly perceptive backstop. Burns, who came into New York among the league's leading hitters, added punch to the lineup and like Speaker and the older Sewell was a perennial .300 hitter (in fact, Burns would win the 1926 M.V.P. award).

The series with Cleveland began amidst a bit of controversy. The day of the first game was cold and raw with rain looming. Two hours before the scheduled 3:30 start Yankees officials decided to postpone the game. Indians manager Speaker objected, complaining that the real reason for the decision was to give the battered Yankees pitching staff a day to rest. Lending credence to Speaker's claim, Yankees pitcher Bob Shawkey was diagnosed with a broken bone in his foot. A veteran hurler, Shawkey was a mainstay in the Yankees rotation. His absence further depleted the overworked pitching staff. Ed Barrow, the team's general manager, explained that the cold conditions and predicted rain would certainly limit attendance, perhaps to fewer than 300. Therefore, with the fans in mind, he chose postponement. The explanation did not satisfy Speaker.[5]

In the three games that followed, the Yankees came away victorious each time. New York pulled the first meeting out with a run in the ninth. Joe Dugan opened the inning with a triple. Speaker then ordered the next two hitters, the bottom two hitters in the Yankees order, to be walked in order to set up a force at home. The strategy almost worked. Leadoff hitter Koenig bounced into a pitcher-to-home-to-first double play. However, the next hitter, Earle Combs, rolled one down the third base line that was mishandled and allowed the winning run to score. The following day two more Babe Ruth home runs, numbers nine and ten, powered his mates to an easy 13–9 win. Ruth again came through in the final game. Though Dutch Levsen pitched brilliantly, limiting the Yankees to only two hits, one of them was yet another Ruth clout, a two-run shot in the first inning. Aided by a game-saving bare-handed grab by "Signor" Lazzeri, Yankees rookie pitcher Myles Thomas countered Levsen, holding Speaker and company to just one run.

Next up for the Yankees were the White Sox. Chicago had still not recovered from the infamous Black Sox scandal. During the five years since the eight notorious White Sox players were banished from baseball, the team had finished down in the league's second division. In 1926 hard-nosed player-manager Eddie Collins hoped to end the drought but recognized the task would be difficult. His plan was to win as much with guile as with raw talent. Combining speed on the bases with one of the best defensive teams in the league and a pitching staff that included two capable hurlers, young Ted Lyons and aging Red Faber, Collins intended to revert back to the "dead ball" tactics of the previous decade. Nevertheless, most sportswriters agreed that a pennant was more than White Sox fans could expect in 1926.

Small ball was not the way that the Yankees played baseball. Instead, home runs characterized their three games with the White Sox. In the first game Ruth hit his fourth homer in three days while Herb Pennock twirled a three-hitter. After a Sunday rain-out Bob Meusel beat the White Sox with a three-run homer. The hero of the third game was Tony Lazzeri. With the Yankees down 3 to 1 in the bottom of the eighth, "Italian" Tony came to the plate with the bases loaded and drilled "a saucy clout" to the deepest part of center field. Rounding the bases before the White Sox fielders could catch up to the ball and make the relay throw to the plate, Lazzeri added an inside the park home run to his totals and another win to New York's record.[6]

On May 18, the same day that the Yankees completed their sweep of the White Sox, 3,000 miles away in Los Angeles one of the decade's most sensational news stories was about to grip the nation. That afternoon evangelist Aimee Semple McPherson went to Venice Beach, apparently swam out into the ocean and vanished. During the next five weeks millions of Americans became engrossed in the tangled mystery of celebrity, sex, intrigue and deception that grew around McPherson's disappearance. Then, on June 23, the evangelist almost magically reappeared, adding yet another dimension to the story.

By 1926 Aimee Semple McPherson was at the forefront of a new generation of evangelists. Aided by the decade's evolving media and ever-improving communications, she became one of America's first national religious personalities. The development of the condenser microphone and electronic vacuum tube, which made amplification possible, enabled her to deliver softly spoken, impassioned sermons to thousands of listeners. Unlike the fire and brimstone tirades bellowed out by most of her contemporaries, McPherson created a gentle, almost angelic persona among her followers. The result was very effective. Likewise, the new technology was a significant step in the evolution of commercial radio broadcasting, which had begun only five years earlier. McPherson was one of the first evangelists to recognize radio's potential and use it to reach a vast new audience.

McPherson's evangelical adventures began when at 17 she married a Pentecostal minister, Robert Semple. Soon after, the two went on a mission in China during which Robert died. Upon returning to her parents' home in New York City, the young widow started giving revivals of her own. Two years later she married Robert McPherson, but within 18 months had left him behind as she set off on her own crusades. During the next eight years she crisscrossed the nation, addressing anyone who would listen. Along the way Sister Aimee developed her own unique message, the Foursquare Gospel, which promised salvation as well as her own healing powers. In 1921 her travels brought her to the burgeoning population in southern California and an audience particularly receptive to her evangelical services. Within two years Sister Aimee, who had arrived in California with little more than $100 and a broken-down car, had attracted enough followers to build her own million-dollar house of worship, the Angelis Temple. In the years that followed, McPherson's congregation grew to international proportions.

News of Sister Aimee's disappearance stunned her followers. Immediately they initiated a massive search that included the Coast Guard and local beach patrols as well as curious sight-seers who prowled the California coast-line looking for any clues to what had happened to the evangelist. Soon bits and pieces of evidence emerged that told an ever more sordid story about McPherson.

Before her disappearance there had been rumors that McPherson was having an affair with a married man — Kenneth Ormiston, an engineer who ran the radio station that broadcast Sister Aimee's sermons. During the previous February and March she traveled to Europe and the Holy Lands. At about the same time Ormiston took a leave of absence from the radio station and was not seen again until shortly after McPherson's return. Some wondered if in fact he had been with Sister Aimee on her trip. There were also eyewitnesses who reported that on numerous occasions the two, registered under assumed names, had shared local hotel rooms. A maid at the Ambassador Hotel claimed that on at least six occasions she had seen McPherson and Ormiston enter a guest room together. The story was corroborated by the Ambassador's house detective. Meanwhile a parking attendant at a Long Beach hotel, the Virginia, recounted that on three successive days when Ormiston was registered at the hotel, a car owned by McPherson had been parked in the hotel garage.

Amid the growing questions came yet another revelation. Just four days before McPherson disappeared, Ormiston, using the alias George McIntyre, paid three months' rent on a cottage up the coast in Carmel. He told the landlord that he would return in a few days with his invalid wife. Two weeks later, near Santa Barbara, an eager reporter spotted Ormiston's car traveling south with a woman passenger. When confronted, Ormiston was able to elude the reporter. Upon checking at the motel where he had seen Ormiston, the reporter discovered that he and the woman had been registered as Mr. and Mrs. Gibson and that the woman fit a description of McPherson. Later Ormiston admitted that he had briefly shared the cottage and the motel room with a woman who was not his wife, but denied that the woman was Sister Aimee. By the end of May a police dragnet, paying special attention to Ormiston, literally blanketed the state. Every train, every bus, and every highway was watched for leads.

With the intrigue growing thicker by the day, Sister Aimee made an almost miraculous reappearance. During the early hours of June 23 she stumbled out of the Mexican desert and up to a cottage in Aqua Prieta, just south of the border. Aided by a local saloonkeeper who regularly ferried Americans back and forth across the border, McPherson was taxied to officials in Douglas, Arizona.

By daybreak news of McPherson's return had been flashed across the nation, and the story she told was astonishing. She claimed that she had been kidnapped by two men whom she knew only as Jake and Steve and a woman who was called Rose. The three took her to their hideout in the Mexican desert and threatened to sell her to a prostitution ring if a $500,000 ransom was not paid. Until the day of her escape, her captors had guarded her around the clock. However, the instant she was left alone McPherson resourcefully cut the ropes that bound her, squirmed through an open window and escaped into the desert.

McPherson's followers likened her return to a second coming. The day after her reappearance, 30,000 greeted her train when it arrived in Los Angeles. Tens of thousands lined the streets and more cheered as her rose-draped limousine carried Sister Aimee back home. Another 100,000 gathered at the Angelis Temple to welcome her back home. That night more than 10,000, twice capacity, crammed into the temple to hear her preach for the first time since her disappearance.

Of course not everyone believed Sister Aimee's story. In the days and weeks following her return, law enforcement officials became increasingly suspicious. When McPherson arrived in Douglas she showed none of the normal effects of a long captivity in the desert. There were no signs of dehydration or malnutrition. She had no rope burns or bruises even though she alleged that she had been bound throughout her captivity. Her clothes were clean and shoes unmarked despite her escape and hike through the desert. Further, after an exhaustive search, investigators could not find the shack where she claimed to have been held. Likewise, not a single trace of the three kidnappers was uncovered. Meanwhile there were new accounts of the McPherson–Ormiston tryst, including eyewitnesses who put them together in the Carmel cabin. By mid–July a mountain of evidence had been gathered contradicting McPherson's story.

Through it all, Sister Aimee staunchly proclaimed that her disappearance had been just as she described it. In her sermons, newspaper articles and radio broadcasts she resolutely countered charges of deceit and fraud. Her followers rallied to her defense, insisting that Sister Aimee was being persecuted by the media, jealous religious leaders, and non-believing skeptics. Law enforcement and local political leaders, especially the Los Angeles mayor, also became primary targets of McPherson's barbs.

In late July, Los Angeles District Attorney Asa Keyes, responding to public pressure, called together a grand jury to determine whether McPherson had broken any laws. Two months later Sister Aimee was charged with obstructing justice and put on trial. The preliminary hearing and trial that followed became a scandal-driven circus. Each day for three months, a multitude of media and curious spectators packed the courtroom while scalpers outside the courthouse sold ringside seats. Once again stories of infidelity and fraud, of secret love nests, scheming and avarice swirled around McPherson. Then, in early 1927, the trial suddenly ended. Amidst rumors that he had taken a $30,000 bribe, the District Attorney moved to have all charges against McPherson dropped. (A year later Keyes was convicted of accepting a bribe to dismiss charges against an oil company.)

The dismissal did little to end the controversy. McPherson, with the unswerving support of her loyal congregation, continued to deride her critics. Law enforcement, many public officials and the general public, stunned by the strange turn of events, remained as skeptical as ever. For years afterward the saga of Aimee Semple McPherson piqued the public's curiosity, though objective observers generally concluded that the kidnapping had not occurred. Instead the popular evangelist, perhaps with Ormiston or perhaps without him, had fled on a five-week hiatus to escape the pressures and demands of her public life. Maybe it had been an act of desperation, maybe one of renewal, or maybe simply a romantic fling by a lonely woman.[7]

With the McPherson saga just beginning, St. Louis followed the White Sox into Yankee Stadium. The Browns' fate during the next four days would be no better than Chicago's had been during the previous four days. Yankees hitters remained hot, pushing across almost seven runs a game. Babe Ruth continued to hit home runs, blasting out three more which put him ahead of his 1921 pace when he set the major league mark of 59 home runs in a season. Meanwhile the pitching continued to improve, limiting St. Louis to just over three runs every nine innings. Of the four games, the only one in doubt was the final one. Down by five runs in the sixth, the Yankees chipped away at the lead, scoring single runs in the sixth and seventh and then three more the eighth. Still down by one in the ninth, New York tied the game on an infield single by Ruth and won it on a bases-loaded hit by Bob Meusel. The win was the Yankees' 11th in a row and boosted them to a five-game lead over the Indians.

Meusel's game-winner was not his first. Both he and his counterpart in center field, Earle Combs, had already made important contributions to the Yankees success. A week earlier Manager Huggins had proclaimed Meusel to be the best player in the American League. "I wouldn't trade (him) for any other outfielder in the league.... Meusel is the greatest natural player in the American League for batting, throwing, speed and fielding." [8] The Yankees manager also considered Combs to be the best leadoff hitter in baseball. It was a sentiment shared by the team's general manager. Ed Barrow bluntly stated, "I think he (Combs) is the best leadoff man of all time." Possessing a keen eye at the plate and an exceptional bunter who was fleet on the bases, Combs made the ideal set-up man for the heavy hitters who followed him in the Yankees batting order.

Blessed with arguably the strongest outfield arm in baseball, Meusel had as much talent as any of his contemporaries. Overshadowed at the plate by Ruth and later by Gehrig, he was, nevertheless, an exceptional power hitter. In 1925 he led the league in home runs and runs batted in. Only once in his first eight major league seasons did he hit under .313. During his ten years with the Yankees he also led the team in stolen bases five times. In the field he appeared effortless, loping after fly balls with long, graceful strides, and he regularly was among the league leaders in outfield putouts.

A powerfully built, brooding man of few words, Meusel's mere presence intimidated many opponents. At 6' 3" he was the tallest Yankee. Character-

An intimidating figure both on and off the field, Bob Meusel had arguably the strongest arm in baseball and was an integral part of the Yankees offensive attack.

istically unemotional, he rarely displayed the passions that fed most other players. Whether driving in a winning run or striking out with bases loaded, his demeanor changed little. Sports writer Fred Lieb once called him "the most unde-monstrative player I ever saw ... the coldest Yankee of them all." No doubt his aloofness contributed to his reputation among fans as being uncon-cerned about winning or los-ing. Miller Huggins later echoed the fan sentiment, complaining, "His attitude is just plain indifference."[9]

Meusel's older brother "Irish" may have added to Bob's dour public image. Possessing less athletic talent but a far more engaging personality, Irish became a fan favorite for the Yankees' cross-town rival Giants. The two brothers hailed from San Jose, California. Irish worked his way through vari-ous minor leagues before finally coming to the Philadel-phia Phillies in 1918. Two years later the Yankees bought Bob's contract from Vernon in the Pacific Coast League. Though Irish had less power than his brother, both were fine hitters. In the field Bob was easily the better of the two. However, he apparently lacked his brother's drive on the ball field. Off the field Irish had a pleasant, gregarious personality, while fans considered Bob unapproachable.

Earle Combs provided another contrast to Meusel. Though 6 feet tall, Combs's slender frame made him far less physically imposing than either of his two partners in the Yankees outfield. At the plate Combs understood that his job was to get on base, and he performed the task well. Eight times during his ten full seasons he collected over 180 hits and scored more than 100 runs. Seven times he also drew more than 65 base on balls. One of the fastest players in baseball, he was a threat whenever on base and able to cover a lot of ground in the outfield. His only flaw was a weak throwing arm, but with Meusel and Ruth, who had exceptional arms, on either side of him few opponents were able to take advantage of him.

Combs began his baseball career in Pebworth, a small central Kentucky farming community. Using bats his father carved from tree limbs and balls made out of worn-out shoes shaped around a slab of rubber, Combs and his four brothers played ball whenever possible. At 17 he enrolled in Eastern State Normal School (now Eastern Kentucky University) to become a teacher. Encouraged to try out for the baseball team, he became the club's star. After a year of formal training at Eastern he began teaching elementary school. At the same time he played baseball for several town teams in the Lexington area and later in eastern Kentucky. In 1922 he agreed to play for the Louisville Colonels in the American Association. Signed as a shortstop, he moved to center field where he was exceptional. At Louisville he became an outstanding line drive hitter who regularly turned singles into doubles and triples. Batting .344 in 1922 and .380 in 1923, he established himself as the Colonels' star.

In 1924 the Yankees paid Louisville $50,000 to sign Combs. A few months later he started his major league career with a flourish, batting over .400 through his first 24 games and expertly patrolling center field. Then, in a game against Cleveland, he broke his ankle sliding into home. The injury ended his season, and some, including his father, feared that his career was over. However, the following year Combs demonstrated that his ankle had fully recovered and that his career was far from over. In 1925 Combs was one of the few Yankee bright spots, batting .344. During the early weeks of the 1926 season he further established himself as the sparkplug in New York's powerful attack.

Dubbed the "Kentucky Colonel" and the "Kentucky Greyhound," Combs was an instant fan favorite. On the field he played as fiercely as any of his teammates. Off the field he was intelligent, courteous, and introspective, preferring a quiet evening with his wife, who had been his high school sweetheart, and his two young sons to a night out carousing. On a team that included several legendary revelers, Combs was recognized as a true gentleman.[10]

After dispatching the Browns, Combs, Meusel and their Yankees teammates played a five-game series with the last-place Red Sox. The series began in New York on a windy Sunday afternoon. Scoring three runs in the first inning, the New Yorkers were never challenged, winning 8–3 and stretching their win streak to 12. The two teams then traveled to Boston for the next four games.

Fenway Park had changed since the Yankees' first visit to Boston. On May 8 a three-alarm fire swept through the left field bleachers causing more than $25,000 in damages. The blaze evidently started when some brush and rubbish in the stands ignited. Fanned by a strong wind, flames jumped from the bleachers to the grandstand roof, then across the parking lot and onto several adjacent buildings. As a result, all the seating from third base to the left field fence was a charred ruin. Strapped for cash, John Quinn, the Red Sox owner, merely cleared away the debris and continued the team's schedule uninterrupted. The only beneficiaries were left fielders, who after the fire were able to run down fly balls behind the remains of the burned-out bleachers. Not until 1934 were repairs made. The improvements included concrete bleachers and a 37-foot left field fence. Two years later a 23-foot screen was added to the fence, and the famous "Green Monster" emerged a decade later when it was painted green.[11]

Fleet-footed center fielder Earle Combs was considered by many the best leadoff hitter in the American League. His ability to get on base in front of Ruth, Gehrig, Meusel, and Lazzeri ignited many Yankees rallies in 1926.

The Yankees easily won the first game in Boston, bringing their streak to 13 in a row. Wins number 14 and 15 came in the team's first doubleheader of the season. Babe Ruth was the day's story. In the first game he hammered a mammoth home run that some claimed was the longest ever hit in Fenway.[12] In the second game he did it again. This time his blast, his 16th of the season, was the margin of victory. In the final game of the series Lou Gehrig, while chasing a foul ball in the fifth inning, knocked himself out when he ran into a low-hanging concrete bullpen roof. Groggy and with a nasty gash on his forehead, he finished the half-inning but was then replaced at first by Ruth. Down by six runs, the Red Sox battled back after Gehrig's accident. The effort, however, fell a run short as New York hung on 9–8 for the team's 16th straight win.

The Yankees came home from Boston riding a 16-game winning streak, the third longest in American League history. Awaiting them were Connie Mack and his Athletics. Three weeks earlier Philadelphia had swept three games from New York. Buoyed by their streak, the high-flying Yankees were anxious to get even. The series opened with a pitching duel between Waite Hoyt, who had a personal seven-game win streak on the line, and the Athletics' Lefty Grove, arguably the league's best pitcher. Though they out-hit Philadelphia, the Yankees could only push one run across the plate while the Athletics scored three times. In the second game the visitors opened up a five-run lead in the first two innings, then hung on as the Yankees mounted an unsuccessful late-inning comeback. With the two losses the winning streak was relegated to "nothing more than a happy memory" and the pennant race was back on.[13]

Memory of the streak faded further the following day. Locked in a 2–2 tie going into the ninth inning, the Athletics scored three times. In the bottom half of the inning the Yankees scratched together three of their own on a Gehrig single, two errors, a sacrifice and a seeing-eye single by pinch hitter Ben Paschal. In the tenth Philadelphia scored two more times, but the Yankees again fought back. With two out, Gehrig on third and Ruth on second, Meusel beat out an infield single, scoring Gehrig. Trying to catch the Athletics sleeping, Ruth dashed around third and headed for the plate. The throw easily beat him but the slugger crashed hard into catcher Cochrane in an effort to knock the ball free. However, the A's catcher held fast and the game ended. In a flash, feisty Jimmy Dykes, the Athletics' diminutive second baseman, took offense to the collision and rushed Ruth to retaliate. A few shoves and some angry words later, the two were separated before either could do any real harm.

Having failed in three tries, the Yankees finally notched a convincing win against the Athletics. In front of 56,000, the season's largest crowd, New

York drilled Philadelphia 9–3. Most of the scoring came in the fifth, when 14 Yankees came to the plate and scored eight runs. The big blow was a three-run triple by Bob Meusel.

With the streak behind them the Yankees and their fans had a little time to reflect on the team's success during the previous three weeks. Some of the early questions about the team appeared to have been answered. The rookie keystone combination of Lazzeri and Koenig were playing far better than expected. Additionally, after a slow start at the plate, Lazzeri was beginning to live up to expectations. Babe Ruth was playing better than he had in several years. His 16 home runs put him ahead of his pace in 1921 when he had hit 59. Additionally, he had had no run-ins with Huggins and appeared to be a model of self-control off the field. In addition to his home runs, he, Meusel, and third baseman Joe Dugan were among the league's top five hitters, with Combs and Gehrig not far behind. The pitching staff, led by Herb Pennock, Waite Hoyt and Urban Shocker, was also doing better than expected, and rookie Myles Thomas had recently added another strong arm to the arsenal. Of course for all the satisfaction there were a few lingering concerns. During the recent winning streak the Yankees had played only one bona fide contender, the Cleveland Indians. Most of the recent wins came against the weakest teams in the league. Likewise, all but the last four of the wins came at home. To win a pennant, as many New Yorkers were boastfully predicting, the team would have to beat the best teams away from Yankee Stadium.

It was a sullen Cardinals team that slogged back into St. Louis following the club's first road trip. What had begun so successfully in Pittsburgh ended with a particularly discouraging four-game sweep by Chicago. The entire team was floundering. Cardinals hitters of whom so much was expected had yet to produce consistently. Even Hornsby was struggling at the plate. With the exceptions of Flint Rhem and Vic Keen, the team's pitchers had been unable to hold leads. In the field, errors at critical moments characterized the defense. Equally discouraging were the numerous mental errors that had already cost the team several games.

Back home in Sportsman's Park the Cardinals' first opportunity to reverse their recent fortunes came against first-place Cincinnati. The Reds had dealt St. Louis two discouraging losses a week earlier. The league leader's visit to St. Louis offered the home team an opportunity for redemption.

Most expected Cincinnati to contend for the pennant in 1926. The team was led by a veteran mound crew that included Carl Mays, Eppa Rixey, Pete Donohue and Cuban-born Adolfo "Dolf" Domingo de Guzman Luque. Mays was the best known of the Reds pitchers. A fierce competitor who combined a nasty submarine pitch with an equally nasty disposition, in 1920 he had carved out an infamous place in baseball history for himself when he fatally beaned Cleveland shortstop Ray Chapman. Many blamed the tragedy on Mays, who had a reputation for challenging hitters with high, hard inside pitches. During the five years since, he had won 20 or more games twice. Future Hall of Famer Eppa Rixey was a southpaw who featured a baffling windup and pinpoint control. He had won 21 games in 1925 and 188 in his 14 major league seasons. Off the field he was mild mannered, but on the mound he, like Mays, was a fierce competitor. Donohue was the youngest of the Reds hurlers. Since coming to the club from Texas Christian University in 1921 he had average 19 wins per season. In 1922 he led the National League with 18 wins, and in 1925 had won 21. Luque was not of the same caliber as Mays, Rixey or Donohue, but could be counted on for 12 to 15 wins a season. In 1923 he had led the National League with 27 victories. Fortified by several promising young arms, the Reds appeared to have as good a staff as any in the National League.

Edd Roush was at the core of the Reds attack. Acknowledged to be one of the best hitters in the National League, Roush had batted .321 or better for nine straight seasons. Several new faces were expected to help Roush by adding some punch to the Cincinnati lineup. Wally Pipp, who had been acquired from the Yankees over the winter, was a fine fielder and had consistently hit around the .300 mark during his 12 major league seasons. Second baseman Hughie Critz had batted .322 during his rookie season two years earlier, and if highly touted rookie outfielder Walter "Cuckoo" Christenson or rookie third baseman Chuck Dressen could live up to expectations, the Reds might win their first pennant since 1919.

For the Cardinals, the series began much as their recent games with the Cubs had ended. With a runner on first, two outs and up by a run in the sixth inning, Vic Keen walked three straight batters, forcing in the tying run. The Reds then took the lead on a rare triple steal. Critz followed with a two-run single and the Cardinals had lost their fifth in a row. The losing streak ended the following day thanks to the Cardinals' two Bells, pitcher Herman and third baseman Les. Herman pitched five scoreless innings in relief and Les drove in the tying and winning runs with a line single in the eighth. In the final game the Cards managed only five hits and one run against Red Lucas, losing 6–1.

Beginning with Brooklyn, the league's eastern teams followed the Reds into St. Louis. The Robins, as they were known in 1926, surprised many with their early-season success. When they arrived in St. Louis, Brooklyn was in first place by a game and a half and had won nine of their previous ten games. Meanwhile the Cardinals began the series without Hornsby, who was nursing a sprained back, and starting outfielders Chick Hafey and Ray Blades, who were too ill to play.

Despite the handicaps St. Louis won the first contest 3–1 thanks to three first-inning runs and another superb mound performance by Flint Rhem. However, from there circumstances for the Cardinals deteriorated steadily. The previous year, the Robins had fared especially poorly against left-handed pitching. With that in mind Manager Hornsby in the final three games started three lefties: Willie Sherdel, Art Reinhart, and Bill Hallahan. The strategy had little effect on Brooklyn's bats. The Robins took all three games, combining fine pitching, timely hitting and an exceptional defense led by shortstop Rabbit Maranville, who in the final game handled 16 chances (11 assists and five put outs) himself. The losses pushed the Cards into seventh place, just one game out of the National League cellar.

John J. McGraw and his New York Giants followed their cross-city rivals into St. Louis. Pugnacious and abrasive but a brilliant student of the game, McGraw was a living legend. During his playing days he had been an integral part of the great Baltimore teams of the 1890s. Both as a player and a manager McGraw had justly earned a reputation for doing whatever he could, whether ethical or not, to win ballgames. Players, managers, club owners, umpires and even spectators became targets for his almost insatiable need to win. As manager of the Giants since 1903 he transformed his team into a perennial pennant contender, winning nine league and three world championships by 1924. Only three times had his teams finished worse than third. However, as the deadball era ended McGraw's success began to fade. After losing the world championship in 1924 he would never again win a championship. His 1926 team reflected the decline. Few picked the Giants to win their league pennant, and by the time they arrived in St. Louis McGraw was obviously frus-

Not much was expected of Vic Keen in 1926 but his early-season victories helped keep the Cardinals in the pennant race while the team's veteran pitchers recovered from injuries.

trated. His team was in fourth place, having lost one more game than they had won. Meanwhile the other two New York clubs, the Robins and Yankees, both led their leagues, thus adding to McGraw's irritation.[14]

The series began amid rumors that McGraw was about to dump numerous players and revamp his club. The day before the Giants arrived in St. Louis, pitcher Art Nehf, who had been an integral part of the team's staff for six years, was sold to Cincinnati. In another move, veteran first baseman Bill Terry was sent to the outfield so that a promising rookie, Mel Ott, might get playing time. More moves were anticipated in the near future. Stories swirled that even Billy Southworth, one of the league's leading hitters, was on McGraw's auction block.

The first two games against the Giants went well for the Cardinals. Though out-hit in the first contest, St. Louis rode home runs by Les Bell and Ray Blades as well as another gutsy mound performance from Vic Keen to a 5–4 win. The following afternoon, aided by a Bottomley home run and another one by Blades, Flint Rhem matched Keen's effort. In trouble throughout the game, Rhem relied on his pitching guile to get outs when he most needed them. The only exception was Billy Southworth, who drove in all five Giants runs. The two wins were the team's first back-to-back victories since the first week of the season.

After defeating the Giants, Keen and Rhem had accounted for nine of the Cardinals' 12 wins. In addition to their early season successes, the two pitchers provided Cardinals fans with a study in contrasts. Keen was well educated, congenial and humble. The son of an itinerant

Flint Rhem brought a blazing fastball and excellent curve to the mound. With 21 wins he led the Cardinals staff though most of his wins came early in the season.

Methodist minister, he was dubbed "Parson" by teammates long before he joined the Cardinals. He made his major league debut late in the 1918 season when he was just 19. Pitching eight innings for the Athletics, he lost 5–3 to Walter Johnson. Soon after, despite the performance, Keen decided to leave Philadelphia and enroll in the University of Maryland's pre-med program. Over the next three years he became a campus baseball hero, at one point stringing together 34 straight victories against college and semi-pro teams. Along the way he defeated several of the best college teams in the nation. By 1921, 15 major league teams were bidding for his services (Pittsburgh was the only exception). In the end he signed with the Cubs because "I wanted to get a bunch that was congenial."[15] At the start of the 1923 season Keen joined the parent club and over the next two years won 27 games. However, in 1925, plagued by arm problems, his wins fell to two and his E.R.A. soared to 6.25. That December he was traded to the Cards. As the 1926 season began, Manager Hornsby intended to use his new pitcher in relief and as a spot starter, but the Cards' early-season mound problems pushed Keen into the starting rotation immediately.

Hailing from Rhem, South Carolina, a town named for his prominent forbearers, Flint Rhem came to the Cardinals from Clemson University where he had an outstanding college career. A formidable physical presence on the mound, he relied on a blazing fastball complemented with a hard-breaking curve. In 1924 while pitching for Fort Smith in the Western Association, he earned the title "Strikeout King" by whiffing more hitters than anyone else in professional baseball. His promotion to the Cardinals was hastened by a no-hitter he pitched for Fort Smith while Branch Rickey watched from the stands. Fun-loving and gregarious, Rhem was an immediate fan favorite who quickly earned a reputation for mischief. Coupled with a taste for whiskey, he became involved in various misadventures. The most notorious episode occurred in 1930. With the Cardinals battling the Dodgers late in the season, Rhem, who was scheduled to pitch, mysteriously disappeared from his hotel room. Two days later he reappeared, claiming that he had been kidnapped by a band of Brooklyn partisans. Most suspected that in fact he had been on a drinking binge. Thirty years later the pitcher admitted that his absence was the product of late-night drinking and carousing after which he was too sick to pitch.

An essential component of the success of Keen, Rhem and the entire Cardinals mound crew was catcher Bob O'Farrell. A steady, unflappable receiver who carefully guided his battery mates through opposing lineups, O'Farrell in 1926 was on his way to establishing himself as one of the best catchers in all of baseball. At the plate his batting average hovered around the .300 level all season, but more importantly his hits often came when the

Cardinals needed them most. Behind the plate he was superb. Manager Hornsby was so confident in O'Farrell's ability to call pitches that he often deferred to his catcher's advice, something Hornsby rarely did for anyone. In Hornsby's assessment, "There is no better catcher in baseball."[16] Even before the season started, Hornsby touted O'Farrell's abilities and predicted a great year for his team's backstop. The manager's claims became more earnest as the season proceeded. By August he was actively promoting O'Farrell as a strong candidate for the league's Most Valuable Player award. The Cardinals manager argued, "He's done more for us than any other player. You know that he's caught more games than any other catcher in either league. All the pitchers want him in there."[17]

One of the best defensive catchers in the game, Bob O'Farrell was voted the National League's Most Valuable Player in 1926. The following year he would replace Hornsby as the Cardinals' player-manager.

O'Farrell's path to stardom had not come easily. After playing semi-pro ball in Waukegan, Illinois, his hometown, he signed a professional contract with the Cubs in 1915. Used primarily as a bullpen catcher during his initial days with the Cubs, he was optioned to Peoria where he played parts of the 1916 and 1917 seasons. In 1918 the Cubs brought him back as a once-a-week replacement for the team's starting catcher, Bill Killefer. It was a role O'Farrell played for the next two years. In 1921 O'Farrell replaced the aging Killefer as the Cubs' starting catcher. The following year Killefer, who had become the team's manager, kept O'Farrell in the starting lineup. The new assignment paid off for the Cubs. O'Farrell batted over .300 in 1922 and 1923. Additionally, his defensive skills and ability to handle pitchers established him as one of Killefer's most valuable players.

In 1924 a broken catcher's mask short-circuited O'Farrell's blossoming career. During a game early in the season, a foul tip broke through his mask and knocked him unconscious. He had known that the mask needed repairs but because there was no available replacement he used it anyway. The result was a fractured skull and time on the disabled list. When he returned he was dropped to second-string status. His replacement was a hard-hitting, young catcher, Gabby Hartnett, who some in the Cubs organization were certain would become a star. As his team's starting receiver, Hartnett immediately began living up to those expectations. His batting average was better than O'Farrell's, and he hit with far more power. He was also a fiery, vocal player on the field, a sharp contrast to O'Farrell's subdued manner. By the end of the season Hartnett had established himself as a team leader both on and off the field, and O'Farrell had become expendable. The following May, despite Killefer's vehement opposition, the Cubs traded O'Farrell to the Cardinals for two part-time players: catcher-first baseman Mike Gonzalez and infielder Howard Freigau. Among those who most benefitted from the transaction were the 1926 Cardinals pitchers who came to rely on O'Farrell's skills behind the plate.[18]

After the wins by Rhem and Keen, the Cardinals dropped the last two games of the series with New York. In the third game Willie Sherdel and Giants hurler Jim Ring hooked up in a pitchers' duel. Despite a home run by Les Bell and two hits each from Hornsby and Bottomley, the Cardinals fell 2–1. With Billy Southworth again leading the way at the plate, the final game was never in doubt. The Giants scored early and often and pasted a 12–1 shellacking on the home team. Nevertheless, in three of the four games against McGraw's club, Cardinals fans had seen flashes of what they expected from Hornsby and his crew.

During the next week the team provided more satisfaction for its fans. In three games against the Boston Braves the Cardinals scored 33 runs and swept the series. While many considered the Braves to be the worst team in the National League, the sweep was particularly heartening because during the previous season Boston had won the season series against the Cardinals.

If Boston wasn't the worst team in the league, then Philadelphia was. The Phillies had finished the previous season ½ game out of last place, 27 games behind Pittsburgh. During the winter they had traded away several of their front-line players, including pitcher Jimmy Ring, who had several days earlier pitched the Giants past the Cardinals. Despite their problems, in the first meeting of the season the Phillies ended the Cardinals' brief winning streak, scoring four late runs. During the game, Hornsby was spiked by a Philadelphia base runner and had to leave the game. Most expected him to be out for the rest of the series but the following day, despite obvious pain, he was back in the lineup and helped Vic Keen win yet again. In the third game Flint Rhem kept pace with his teammate, beating the Phillies 12–4. In trouble early, Rhem became almost unhittable after the fourth. Meanwhile Cardinals batters pounded out 14 hits, including three each by Taylor Douthit and Bob O'Farrell.[19]

Several stories highlighted the fourth game of the series. Bill Sherdel, who had been the victim of a couple of one-run losses, again pitched well, holding the Phillies to just two runs. Meanwhile his mates provided him with plenty of offense, scoring nine times. What made the win particularly significant was that it brought the Cardinals to the .500 mark at 18–18 for the season.

The game was also played on "Rogers Hornsby Day" in St. Louis. The city's mayor, Victor Miller, officially set the day aside as a way to recognize Hornsby for having been named the previous year's Most Valuable Player in the National League. Never comfortable with ceremonies, Hornsby smiled through a string of tributes from Miller, owner Sam Breadon, teammates, and several opposing players. Even Branch Rickey offered a few kinds words. The celebration culminated when the Cardinals player-manager was presented with an MVP medallion and a sack containing 1,000 silver dollars. With photographers snapping away, Hornsby gratefully accepted the honors, acknowledged the day's 14,000 patrons, then hustled into the dugout and led his team to a victory.[20]

The next afternoon the Cardinals again fell below the .500 mark when they lost to the Phillies. Down by four runs after two innings, St. Louis struggled back but eventually lost 7–5.

The Cardinals ended their longest home stand of the season against Cincinnati. After leaving St. Louis almost three weeks earlier, the Reds had gone on a 13–3 tear against the same eastern opponents that the Cards were playing. The stretch included a three-game sweep of Boston and a four-game sweep of the Robins that carried Cincinnati into first place. Upon their return to St. Louis the high-flying Reds led the league by 3½ games. Meanwhile the Cardinals had climbed into fifth place but were still six games off the pace.

The three-game set against the Reds began badly for the Cardinals. Just as the Phillies had done the previous day, Cincinnati jumped to an early lead. Up six runs after the end of five innings and with Eppa Rixey perfect on the mound, it appeared that Hornsby and company were bound to drop another game back of the league leaders. Then, with one out in the bottom of the sixth, Reds shortstop Frank Emmer muffed a ground ball. A pinch single, a walk, another single and a sacrifice fly later the Cards had plated two runs. In the seventh Les Bell drilled a two-run shot over the left field fence. The blast ended the day for Rixey, who the *Cincinnati Enquirer* reported had "collapsed like a mud levee in a spring torrent."[21] Still down by two in the eighth, the Cards faced the Reds' ace pitcher, "submarine king" Carl Mays. Douthit opened with a single and Mays then walked the bases loaded. Aided by center fielder Roush's ragged play, Heinie Mueller tripled in three runs and the Cardinals stampede was on. In the inning, ten hitters came to the plate and seven runs scored. Three quick Cincinnati outs later the Cards finished off their most impressive comeback victory of the season.

Hornsby's club kept their roll going the next two days. In the second game the team, with the help of erratic pitching by Dolf Luque, scored seven runs in the opening two innings, then watched Vic Keen hold on for a 9–7 win, his seventh of the season. In the last game of the home stand Flint Rhem faltered but his mates bailed him out. The Reds scored three in the first and probably would have scored more in the second had it not been for a dazzling triple play when Hornsby speared a Curt Walker line drive and flipped the ball to Thevenow, who then fired to Bottomley at first. Meanwhile Cincinnati pitcher Red Lucas cruised through the first six innings. In the seventh an O'Farrell home run got the Cardinals on the board, but as they came to the plate in the bottom of the eighth they were was still down by four. Two Cincinnati errors, five singles, a double, a sacrifice fly and a three-run homer later, the Cardinals had duplicated their seven-run eighth-inning tally two days earlier. Three outs later the sweep was complete, pushing St. Louis into fourth place. The sweep also ended what after a frustrating start became a successful 21-game Cardinals home stand.

5

The Summer's Big Deals

As Hornsby climbed onto an eastbound train, the Cardinals manager clearly understood the importance of the trip his team was about to take. He also worried about a few holes in his roster. St. Louis would spend the next four weeks visiting every other team in the league. It was the season's first long trip and a test that would probably determine whether or not the club was a legitimate pennant contender. Concerned that his team was still not playing up to his expectations, Hornsby was searching for ways, perhaps through trades or perhaps through outright acquisitions, to beef up his pitching staff and add a bit more punch to his lineup. He was satisfied with only two of his hurlers, Flint Rhem and Vic Keen. While both were performing exceptionally well, neither had ever put together a full major league season of mound wins. Meanwhile the rest of the Cardinals arms had struggled through almost every one of their outings. At the plate the team seemed at last to be coming out of its early season slump even though injuries and illness continued to plague the outfield. Another solid bat would provide both more offense and some flexibility.

The trip began in Cincinnati. Despite the three losses in St. Louis, the Reds came home still atop the National League. In the four games that followed, the two teams reversed their recent fortunes. The Cardinals attack, which had been so potent during the previous week, struggled while Reds pitchers flourished. The series opened with a Cincinnati doubleheader sweep. The Cardinals dropped the first game 4–3 and in the second Carl Mays held Hornsby and company to a single run. The next day proved to be almost as bad. Though the Cards collected ten hits they scored only four runs. Meanwhile, the Reds, aided by 13 walks and a seven-run seventh inning, pushed 12 men across the plate. For the Cardinals the series ended with a little more than a whimper. Despite an admirable mound performance by Keen, who held the Reds to three runs, St. Louis could again only score once.

Stinging from their disappointing play in Cincinnati, Hornsby and his crew pushed off to Chicago where rookie manager Joe McCarthy and his Cubs awaited. Though they had been picked by most to finish in the bottom half of the league, the Cubs were in second place, 3½ games back of the Reds and playing surprisingly well. Led by veterans Riggs Stephenson and Charlie Grimm and youngsters Gabby Hartnett and Hack Wilson, Chicago could score runs. Their problem was on the mound. The staff included two young hurlers, Charlie Root and Guy Bush, who would have successful major league careers, but in 1926 neither had yet proven himself. Instead the anchor of the staff was the great Grover Cleveland Alexander. During the seven full seasons since his return from World War I, "Old Pete" had won 123 games for the Cubs. However, the 1926 season began badly for the ageless pitcher. During spring training on Catalina Island he sprained an ankle and missed his final pre-season assignments. Even more troubling was his increasingly edgy relationship with McCarthy. The Cubs' new manager was a disciplinarian well suited for his youthful team. Alexander, who had always carved his own path through life, did not conform well to someone else's rules regardless of whether they involved a team curfew, a physical conditioning schedule or the amount of alcohol he drank.

The series began well with Hornsby pounding out three hits, including a home run, and leading his mates to a comfortable 5–2 win. The following day the two teams split a doubleheader. Sparked by Bob O'Farrell's four hits, the Cardinals won the opener 5–3. The second game was tied at two each when the Cardinals came to the plate in the eighth. Hornsby's men scored twice but in the bottom of the inning the Cubs countered with five of their own. In the ninth the Cards again rallied but fell a run short, losing 8–7. The day after losing a one-run slugfest, the Cards rebounded in the final game, 14 to 6. The win, however, proved costly. Cubs first baseman Charlie Grimm smacked a line drive off of pitcher Vic Keen's pitching hand in the fifth, potentially sidelining the hurler. Meanwhile starting outfielder Chick Hafey, who had been struggling with various respiratory problems, was sent back to St. Louis for treatment.

Rain in Philadelphia shortened a scheduled five-game series to a Saturday doubleheader. The Cardinals won both games. Flint Rhem was the story of the first game, throwing a six-hit shutout for his ninth win of the season, the most in the National League. The win in the second game pushed the Cardinals over the .500 mark for the first time since late April.

Rain wasn't the only snag in Philadelphia. The Quaker City remained one of two major league cities that still prohibited professional baseball on

Sundays. Team owners, public officials and sabbatarian reformers had been wrestling with the issue since the late nineteenth century. At the time that the two major leagues were instituted, only five teams played Sunday home games. Of course most club owners complained that the policy cut into potential revenues and was unfair to laboring Americans who worked six days a week and could only attend games on Sundays. Opponents countered that Sunday should be a day of worship. Others warned that Sunday ballgames only encouraged gatherings of potentially rowdy gangs of laborers in general and immigrant laborers in particular.

Prior to World War I only three major league cities, Chicago, St. Louis and Cincinnati, permitted Sunday baseball on a regular basis. Several other teams, including the New York Highlanders, tried to maneuver around local limits but failed. During the following decade states began permitting local governments to determine whether or not professional baseball could be played on Sundays. By the end of World War I Cleveland, Detroit and Washington had joined the list of cities that approved of Sunday play. With help from future mayor Jimmy Walker, the three New York teams were regularly scheduling Sunday games by 1924. Walker later claimed that one of his proudest achievements as a public servant was passing the New York Sunday Baseball Bill.[1] In Boston a particularly contentious debate characterized the struggle. Amid charges of bribery and corruption, Boston, after almost a decade, finally authorized Sunday baseball in 1929. By the 1930s only Pennsylvania steadfastly rejected the change. As late as 1927 the state Supreme Court voted down Sunday baseball, contending that it was a threat to religious life within the state. Despite various maneuvers to circumvent the edict, professional baseball was not permitted in Pennsylvania's two major league cities until 1934.

Among those who opposed Sunday baseball were several prominent baseball personalities. One of the more intriguing was the Cardinals' former field manager and current business manager, Branch Rickey. A devout Methodist, he had promised his mother when he became a professional ballplayer that he would not play on Sundays. Throughout his long career in baseball, Rickey honored his promise. As a player he refused to play on Sundays, and as the Cardinals manager he had written into his contract a stipulation that allowed him to miss Sunday games. Another influential opponent was former player turned evangelist Billy Sunday. Since the end of his playing career in 1890 Sunday had built a huge following, sermonizing from coast to coast. Crusading against various social ills including demon rum and prostitution, he also railed against Sunday baseball. However, despite the sabbatarian appeals, most baseball fans by the mid–1920s not only accepted games on Sunday but expected them. According to the *New York Times*, as much as a third of team revenues came from Sunday play.[2]

After three days off in Philadelphia, the Cardinals rolled into New York rested and ready for the Giants. Mired in sixth place, McGraw's squad was off to its worst start in ten years. For several weeks the media had been speculating that an obviously disgruntled McGraw was about to make wholesale changes to his squad. The Giants manager seemed especially dissatisfied with his pitching staff, though several other players had also become targets of his wrath. Adding fervor to the rumors was an approaching June 15 deadline which required teams to cut their rosters to 25 players. If the Giants were to compete for a pennant, as their fans expected, changes seemed inevitable.

Amid the swirl of trade speculation the series began. The three games that followed only added to McGraw's frustration. In the first two, excellent pitching, timely hitting and a few crucial Giants errors earned the Cardinals a pair of wins. Hornsby, who appeared to be regaining his swing, knocked in the winning run in the first game. The story of the second game was Flint Rhem. With a pitch that moved "like a Mexican jumping bean ... and does everything but disappear," Rhem mowed down the New Yorkers 3–2 for his league-leading tenth win.[3] Hornsby again drove in the winning run. The final contest turned into a blowout. Tied at one after seven innings, the Cardinals scored four in the eighth and another four in the ninth while the Giants could put only one more marker on the board. The sweep pushed St. Louis five games above the .500 mark and into third place behind the Pirates and the Reds. Meanwhile the Giants fell deeper into the league's second division.

After yet another rainout which was followed by a scheduled day off, the Cards hiked across the East River to take on Brooklyn. Since the two teams' last meeting a month earlier, the Robins had fallen from atop the league standings into fifth place. Meanwhile the Cardinals were riding a five-game winning streak. The opening game of the series was disappointing to Hornsby and company. The usually weak-hitting Robins knocked around four Cardinals pitchers and, aided by a seventh-inning triple play, Brooklyn ended the visitors' win streak with an 8–5 victory.

The day's big news, however, happened off the field. Just hours before the June roster deadline the Giants shipped off outfielder Billy "the Kid" Southworth to the Cardinals for Clarence "Heinie" Mueller. Of German descent and a free spirit, Mueller was a fan favorite particularly with St. Louis's large German population. He was also one of Branch Rickey's favorites. On the other hand, to Hornsby Mueller and his somewhat casual approach to the game had become a challenge. The Cardinals manager complained that "Meuller has his good points ... but he has the habit of making bad plays that are disastrous in a good many instances."[4]

In Southworth Hornsby saw a solid player with a reputation as "brainy" and with potential yet to be developed. He was also one of the league's leading hitters. "The Kid" had come to the Giants from the Braves two years earlier after three .300+ years at the plate. In New York manager McGraw moved the speedy outfielder from right field to center field. Uncomfortable patrolling the Polo Grounds' cavernous outfield, Southworth's production both in the field and at the plate suffered. By 1926 he shared starting duties with Ty Tyson. Consequently, he had become expendable. Two years after the trade, McGraw claimed "I traded Southworth for Mueller because of my friendship for Rogers Hornsby. Hornsby I knew could win a pennant if he had an old head, a steadying influence, in the outfield. The Giants, I knew, did not have a

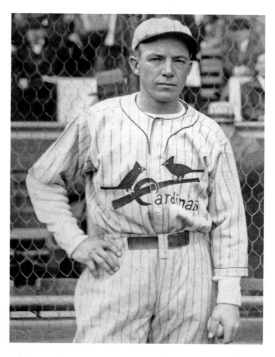

The acquisition of Billy Southworth from the Giants solidified the Cardinals both in the field and at the plate. A veteran who knew the game, Southworth provided quiet leadership to his young teammates.

chance to win, so I gave Hornsby the break and traded Southworth for Mueller."[5] The statement, however, was a bit disingenuous. At the time of the trade McGraw's team was only 3½ games out of first place and for several weeks he had been promising a shake-up that would get his squad back into the thick of the race. It's hard to believe that one of baseball's fiercest competitors would concede defeat so early in a season.

With Southworth in the starting lineup, the Cardinals finished their brief stay in Brooklyn with a dazzling shutout by Willie Sherdel. Limiting the Robins to five hits, the Cardinals hurler got all the runs he needed in the first inning. Leadoff hitter Ray Blades singled. One out later Hornsby duplicated the effort. After the two worked a double steal, Blades scored on a sacrifice fly by Bottomley. Sherdel did the rest in the 4–0 victory.

The day after Sherdel's gem, weather once again revised the Cardinals' playing schedule when New York experienced the coldest June 15 on record. With the thermometer barely climbing above the freezing point, both the

Robins and the Giants, who were scheduled to play Cincinnati, canceled their games. Two days later, rain in Boston forced yet another day off. Fortunately the Cardinals were able to chalk up a doubleheader sweep of the Braves before the rainout. Riding the success of their two pitching phenoms, Rhem and Keen, the Cardinals climbed seven games above .500. In the first game Rhem locked up in a duel with Boston's George Mogridge. The Cardinals hurler ultimately prevailed, 4–2. Keen had fewer problems in the second game. Shoddy fielding by the home team and a slew of extra base hits by the visitors enabled Keen to ring up his eighth win of the season.

After the rain day, the Cardinals duplicated their double killing of two days earlier. Jesse Haines dominated the first game. Using a baffling knuckleball he scattered seven hits in shutting out the Braves 4–0. Haines' success offered evidence that he had finally recovered from his early-season injury and was ready to rejoin the starting rotation. The second game, the Cardinals' ninth win in their last ten outings, combined another outstanding mound performance, this time by Hi Bell, and timely hitting. As Haines had in the first game, Bell limited the Braves to seven hits, though this time Boston pushed two runners across the plate. Meanwhile Hornsby, Taylor Douthit, and Tommy Thevenow scored runs for St. Louis.

Back in Brooklyn for a make-up game, the Cardinals, led by Sherdel on the mound and Southworth at the plate, drilled the Robins 9–0. Riding a six-game winning streak and having won 11 of their last 12, St. Louis headed to Pittsburgh for a single game before at last returning to St. Louis for three more games with the Pirates. The final game of the road trip became a slugfest between two of the league's most potent offenses. The Cardinals opened with one in the first and four in the second. Pittsburgh countered by knocking around Flint Rhem for three of their own in the first and four more in the third. Five Cardinals and three Pirates pitchers later, Pittsburgh had notched an 11–9 win. Though a disappointing way to end such a successful road trip, little did Hornsby know at the time that the loss would become one of the most important games in the Cardinals' season.

The ride home to St. Louis gave Hornsby some time to reflect. His team had begun its trip in fourth place, four games back of the Reds. Four weeks later St Louis returned in third place just 1½ games back. On the trip the Cardinals won 14 and dropped seven, clearly the most successful trip in several years. When the team left St. Louis, the pitching aside from Rhem and Keen was ineffective and the hitting inconsistent. By the time they returned, Sherdel and Haines were once again mowing down hitters. Meanwhile Cardinals hitters were living up to Hornsby's expectation, batting over .300 as a team during the trip. Hornsby himself had regained his eye, hitting at a .350 clip and riding a 16-game hitting streak. Over the same period Ray

Blades led the team, hitting .377, and Les Bell was second at .359. The addition of Billy Southworth in the outfield further assured the Cardinals manager that his team was a legitimate pennant contender.

The day that the Cardinals returned home was momentous, not because of their 3–1 loss to the Pirates but instead because of some off-the-field maneuvering. Soon after the game, the team added one of the greatest pitchers in baseball history, Grover Cleveland Alexander, and instantly became a favorite to win the National League pennant. On June 22 the festering relationship between Chicago manager Joe McCarthy and his disgruntled pitcher ended when the Cubs waived him. Six days earlier McCarthy had suspended Alexander indefinitely for breaking undisclosed team rules. Hornsby quickly jumped at the opportunity to add "Alex the Great" to his staff. Ironically, had St. Louis beaten the Pirates, the pick-up probably would not have happened. The Pirates,

For Grover Cleveland Alexander, coming to the Cardinals was a way to revive his career. At 39 and battling alcoholism, "Old Pete" was well past his prime but by the end of the season had become the foundation of the St. Louis staff.

hungry for pitching, would have happily claimed the veteran hurler, but because the Cardinals were lower in the league standings, Hornsby got a chance to add Alexander first. Had St Louis won the game in Pittsburgh they would have been percentage points better than the Pirates and Alexander would probably have gone to the Steel City.

At 39, Alexander was clearly in the twilight of his career. He was also epileptic and an acknowledged alcoholic. His epilepsy may have been triggered when he was hit on the side of the head by a thrown ball. Unconscious for more than two days, he suffered from blurred vision for months afterward.

Later, during World War I, he served on the front lines as an artillery sergeant. Regular exposure to the explosive concussion of heavy artillery probably aggravated the previous damage from the beaning. Suffering from frequent seizures, he was diagnosed as shell shocked. To control the seizures he drank whiskey. Upon his return to the United States the seizures continued, as did his whiskey remedy. While he eventually learned how to manage his epilepsy, he would never beat alcoholism, though he tried. Just the previous winter he had spent several weeks in a sanitarium to dry out.[6]

While some may have considered Alexander, even at the $4,000 waiver price, a risky gamble, for Hornsby the old-timer was a safe bet. The Cardinals manager knew that Old Pete was not the pitcher he had once been and had some personal problems. On the other hand, no one understood better than Hornsby, one of the best hitters in baseball, the skills that remained. Alexander's greatest asset, his control, remained as precise as ever. Hornsby once claimed, "(Alexander) had the greatest control I've ever seen. (He) could almost nick the corners of a soft drink bottle cap."[7] Likewise, Alex still had a devastating curve and a combative spirit that rivaled Hornsby's. Additionally, the Cardinals manager had Bill Killefer. A St. Louis coach in 1926, Killefer had been the Cubs catcher and then manager during Alex's eight years with Chicago. In that time the two became close friends. Hornsby expected that he and Killefer could keep Alexander sober, and when sober the hurler would be a great asset to the team.

Hornsby didn't have to wait long to collect his dividend. After splitting two games with the Pirates, the Cardinals hosted the Cubs for four games. St. Louis opened the series with a come-from-behind 8–7 win. The key blow was a seventh-inning three-run homer by Hornsby which brought his team back from an early four-run deficit. The following day the two clubs were scheduled to play a doubleheader. A record crowd of 38,000 jammed into Sportsman's Park to watch their new hurler face his former mates. Alexander did not disappoint. Limiting the Cubs to just four hits, he won a ten-inning thriller 3–2, tipping his hat to his former manager after the final out. Years later Hornsby claimed, "I don't think (Alexander) ever pitched a better game in his life."[8] While the Cardinals manager's assessment may have been overstated, certainly for Old Pete few of his 373 wins were more satisfying than his first win as a Cardinal.

In the day's second game the excitement game from the stands rather than the playing field. With two out in the Cubs half of the ninth and the visitors up by five runs, plate umpire Charley Moran waved off a third-out pop-up and awarded the hitter first base, declaring that the Cardinals' backup catcher, Bill Warwick, interfered with the batter's swing. The call was greeted with a roar of disapproval from the St. Louis partisans that shook the ball park. When a few fans in the left field bleachers jumped onto the field, the third base umpire halted the game until the recalcitrant rooters were removed from the playing field. A shower of seat cushions and straw hats immediately rained down onto the field. Glass bottles thrown from the grandstands soon followed the cushions, littering the left field foul grounds. A few police were called onto the field but the shower continued for several more minutes. Finally, after all the expendable seat cushions, straw hats and bottles had been thrown, the grounds crew cleared the debris and the game was resumed. In the end the demonstration did nothing to alter the Cubs 5–0 win.

The Cardinals ended June in second place, just four games behind Cincinnati. The month had been a good one for Hornsby and his crew. They had completed a long and very successful road trip, they were scoring runs, they had two of the winningest pitchers in the league, Flint Rhem at 11–1 and Vic Keen at 9–3, and two veteran hurlers, Willie Sherdel and Jesse Haines, who had also begun to shine. The recent acquisitions of Billy Southworth and the inimitable Grover Cleveland Alexander added experience and depth to the team. With almost half the season behind them, the Cardinals were definitely in the pennant race to stay.

June began with rain in New York. For two days the Yankees and Senators waited to begin their scheduled four-game series. When the skies finally cleared, the two teams got back to business with a mid-week doubleheader. A fifth-inning home run by Tony Lazzeri in the opener sealed a 9–5 Yankees victory. In the second game the Senators jumped to a two-run first-inning lead but four innings later New York countered with four of their own. An Earle Combs home run in the fifth added some insurance but in their next time at bat the Senators fought back with two runs. The score remained 5–4 into the ninth, when Washington got its first two hitters on base and had the heart of the order coming to the plate. Called in to relieve starter Waite Hoyt, Garland Braxton quickly ended the threat by breezing through the next three hitters and completing the day's sweep. Two Babe Ruth home runs, his first in over a week, and a win against Boston the next day reassured the Yankees and their fans that the recent losses against Philadelphia that had ended their 16-game streak had merely been a temporary lapse.

The Yankees spent the next three weeks away from home. The trip began with a western swing that took them to every American League city. The first stop was in Cleveland for three games against the Indians. On a day set aside to honor manager Tris Speaker, the Indians shelled the Yankees with 19 hits, including two Speaker singles, and 13 runs. Meanwhile New York could peck out only three runs. Adding insult to injury, the sole rally was squashed by a triple play. The only bright spot for the visitors was Babe Ruth's 19th home run.

The loss also ended Yankee pitcher Herb Pennock's personal win streak at eight. Already a ten-game winner, more than any other American League pitcher, Pennock was off to the best start in his 14 major league seasons.

Pennock came to the Yankees three years earlier after spending seven seasons with the Red Sox and four with the Athletics. A teenage phenomenon, the slender southpaw signed his first professional contract right out of high school. A friend and the catcher on one of his summer teams was Earle Mack, the son of Connie Mack. In 1911 the two were teammates on the Atlantic City Collegians. One Sunday the Collegians played the St. Louis Stars, a formidable black team. Young Pennock beat the Stars 1–0 on a no-hitter. A few days later Earle Mack's father convinced Pennock's father to allow the young pitcher to verbally commit to play for the Athletics as soon as he graduated from high school the following spring. Pennock's father was reluctant. He wanted his son to pursue an education but agreed. As promised, immediately after graduating young Herb signed a contract with Philadelphia.

Joining the A's was a dream come true for Pennock. While growing up on a farm in Kennett Square, PA, just 40 miles southwest of Philadelphia, he had been an Athletics fan. Connie Mack and pitcher Eddie Plank were his idols. Once signed, he didn't have to wait long to begin his major league career. Within days of reporting to Mack he was called on to relieve in a game against the White Sox that the A's were hopelessly losing. Over the game's final four innings he held Chicago to just one run, an impressive start for the rookie hurler. The performance, however, was not a harbinger of things to come. Mack's A's during the years that Pennock played for them had an exceptional staff that included future Hall of Famers Eddie Plank and Chief Bender. Consequently the youngster was used sparingly and almost always as a relief pitcher.

In 1915 Mack sold off many of his American League champions just as he would do again during his long career as a club owner. As part of the sale, Pennock was sent to the Red Sox. Though it took a couple of years, in Boston he worked his way into the starting rotation and began to realize his pitching potential. After coming to the Yankees in 1923, he blossomed into the staff's ace, averaging 19 wins a year during his first three summers. By 1926 he had emerged as one of the league's best pitchers. Blessed with what appeared to be an effortless windup, he was deceptively fast. However, his real weapons were stealth and control. Pennock could throw his fastball and a variety of breaking pitches from several different angles, developing near pinpoint control with each. Throughout his career he averaged slightly more than two walks every nine innings. He was also smart on the mound. A keen observer of the game, he charted each hitter and carefully plotted with his catcher how he intended to pitch to them.

Off the field Pennock earned a reputation for being even tempered, clean living and morally wholesome, no easy task on a team with explosive personalities that included his roommate on the road, Bob Meusel. Dubbed "the Squire of Kennett Square," he spent his spare time growing prize-winning chrysanthemums and breeding silver foxes on his Kennett Square estate. If the Yankees had an aristocrat in 1926 it was their ace pitcher Herb Pennock.[9]

The Yankees split the last two games in Cleveland, winning a rain-shortened contest before dropping the final game 5–2, then moved on to Detroit for more battles with Ty Cobb and his Tigers teammates. Though they were in sixth place, 11 games behind New York and struggling to stay above the .500 mark, the Tigers always played tough against the Yankees. Additionally, it was no secret that players in one dugout held long-standing grudges with their counterparts in the other dugout. From the feud between Cobb and Ruth to the recent clash between Gehrig and Earl Whitehill, the two teams simply didn't like each other.

The first two games were the kind of struggles that fans expected when New York and Detroit got together. The initial contest opened well for the Yankees. Propelled by a towering Ruth home run and another one by Meusel, New York rolled up a six-run lead after three innings. However, the next six innings belonged to the Tigers. Scratching and clawing for every run, the home team tied the score in their last at bat, sending the game into extra innings. Two Yankees lifted their team past the challenge. Pitcher Waite Hoyt relieved in the ninth and silenced the Tigers bats through the final three innings. In the 11th Babe Ruth did what he did best, smacking another home run, his 21st of the season, which proved to be the difference in the game.

The next day the two teams again locked themselves into another bitterly fought contest. This time the heroes were the keystone tandem of Lazzeri and Koenig and relief pitcher Garland Braxton. Koenig's two-run homer in the eighth tied the game at three. An inning later Lazzeri, who had already made a run-saving play at second, knocked in the winning run on an infield single. Meanwhile Braxton craftily maneuvered past Tigers hitters, holding them scoreless over the last three innings. Making the victory even sweeter, the losing pitcher was "that persistent and annoying left-hander, Mr. Earl Whitehill."[10]

The Yankees easily won the final two games. With the Tigers out of capable pitchers and the Yankees bats pounding away, New York scored a total of 17 runs in the two games. Meanwhile the Tigers could plate only four runs against the Yankees moundmen. The only unpleasantry was a warrant issued for Babe Ruth for fishing out of season. At dawn on the day of the final game Ruth wandered off to a lake near Howell, Michigan, about 15 miles northwest of Detroit and caught "only a few scrawny blue gills."[11] Unfortunately he caught them five days before fishing season opened.

With Ruth's fishing misadventure behind them, the Yankees rolled into St. Louis. The Browns were already cemented into seventh place with little hope of improving their standing but little fear that the lowly Red Sox might catch them. The two teams split the four games that followed. St. Louis notched wins in the first and third while New York took the second and the fourth. In each game the Yankees knocked out at least one home run, an awesome display of power in a year when combined the other seven American League teams averaged just two round trippers a day. By the end of the season the Yankees had four of the league's eight players with more than ten home runs. Of course Ruth would easily lead the league, hitting more home runs (47) in the season than did five of the other seven teams in the American League. While home runs flew out of National League parks at a slightly greater rate, no team came close to the power of the Yankees. During their four days in St. Louis Gehrig and Lazzeri each smacked out two while Meusel and Ruth hit one apiece. Ruth's was his 22nd and came in a losing effort on a day when he sprained his knee chasing a fly ball. Yet another nagging injury for the Babe, it kept him out of the series finale.

Though they lost two of four to the Browns, the Yankees came out of St. Louis better off than when they went in. Second-place Philadelphia had just dropped three of four to Cleveland, creating a knot of three teams — the Athletics, the Indians and the surprising White Sox — in a virtual tie. The combination of Yankees wins and Athletics losses pushed New York's league lead to ten games, a margin that in light of the way the Yankees were playing seemed almost insurmountable to some.[12]

During the previous month the White Sox had been playing better than any team in the league except the Yankees. The source of the team's success was their offense. With a team batting average over .300, again second only to the Yankees, the White Sox were scoring runs in bunches. The pitching staff, aside from Ted Lyons, whose 11 wins tied him with Pennock as the league's leader, had not performed as well but was winning the close games. With its victories mounting, the team and its fans eagerly anticipated the Yankees' visit.

The four-game series started on a chilly Thursday afternoon with 12,000 fans on hand. The story of the day was White Sox pitcher Ted Blankenship, who held New York to just three hits. Aside from the return of a heavily bandaged Babe Ruth, the only Yankee excitement came in the second inning when Lazzeri legged out an inside the park home run. The next day, in front of 25,000 Chicagoans, the Yankees made up for their previous game's lack of punch. Rattling out 16 hits, including four by Combs and three by Koenig, the team cruised to a 10–2 win. The beneficiary of the attack was Herb Pennock, who won for the 12th time. An even bigger crowd packed into Comiskey Park for the Saturday game. Among the 32,000 spectators was Cardinal Patrick O'Donnell, the primate of Ireland, who threw out the first pitch. The day was also Eddie Collins Day in Chicago. However, despite the crowd, the Cardinal, and the Collins gala, the Yankees slipped past the White Sox 6–5 by scoring five runs in the fifth inning. In the finale, 40,000, some standing on the field along the two foul lines, watched Blankenship come in to pitch in relief and once again tame Yankees bats. In the sixth, with the score tied at two, one out, runners on second and third and Babe Ruth at the plate, Blankenship was summoned from the bullpen. After walking Ruth to load the bases, the White Sox hurler ended the threat by getting Meusel and Lazzeri to ground out. An inning later, Chicago took advantage of some sloppy play to plate the winning run.

During the series a total of more than 109,000 fans watched the two teams do battle. The four-day figure accounted for more than 15 percent of the 710,339 who watched the White Sox in all of their 77 home games. It was an extraordinary showing.

After a travel day the Yankees made a brief stop in Washington for a doubleheader. In the first game, despite some sloppy play, New York cruised into the last half of the ninth up by five runs. The Senators combined a double and two singles to plate a run. A Yankees double play seemed to end the threat but, following a walk, Koenig booted a routine play that would have ended the game. Three more singles and one more error, this one by Meusel which allowed the winning run to score, gave Washington an exciting come from behind victory and the Yankees an ugly loss. The second game turned out better for New York. Waite Hoyt, who hadn't won in two weeks, baffled Senators hitters. Babe Ruth belted a tape measure home run while his teammates added a slew of extra-base hits on their way to an easy 9–1 victory and a bit of redemption.

Two days later the Yankees made their last trip of the season to Boston. In the first game New York once again went into the bottom of the ninth with a lead. This time they were up by a run, 5–4. A muffed foul fly ball followed immediately by a poorly played ball that got past center fielder Ben Paschal for an inside-the-park home run tied the game. Two innings later Boston scored the winning run when Gehrig flubbed a ground ball.

The Yankees pounded out 30 runs in the three remaining games. Ruth added his 24th and 25th home runs and Lazzeri hit two of his own. However, despite the impressive wins the Yankees lost a critical part of their attack. The day after the extra inning loss, Bob Meusel twisted a foot while sliding into second base on the back end of a double steal. With Meusel writhing in obvious pain and unable to walk off the field, it was clear immediately that the injury was serious. The official diagnosis confirmed Yankees' worries. Meusel had broken a bone in his left foot and would be out of the lineup for at least four weeks. The fourth-leading hitter in the American League, he had been hammering pitchers as well as anyone in the league during the previous ten days. With Ruth still hobbling on two sore legs and often playing only part time, Meusel's bat had become an even more important part of the Yankees offense. The thought of a Yankees lineup for a month or longer without the slugging left fielder in it worried manager Huggins.

The Yankees ended their long road trip with three games in Philadelphia. Waiting there was Lefty Grove. In the opener Grove dominated New York hitters as no other pitcher had, whiffing ten hitters. "His fastball came up hopping like a kangaroo; his curve had the blind staggers: it whirled and sagged and took unique angles and his control was so perfect that he tossed no more than two bad balls to any hitter."[13] Meanwhile Waite Hoyt had another disappointing outing, lasting only five innings in the 7–1 drubbing. The following day the Yankees' star southpaw, Herb Pennock, who was far less dominating than Grove had been, maneuvered through the Athletics lineup. Spreading around 11 hits, Pennock was aided by home runs from Gehrig and Ruth, beating the Athletics 7–5. The final game went to Philadelphia. With his team down a run in the bottom of the ninth, A's first baseman Jim Poole doubled in two runs to hand yet another last-inning loss to the Yankees.

June ended with the Yankees comfortably ahead of their American League competition. The White Sox sat nine games back. Cleveland was another 1½ games behind, while Philadelphia and Detroit were 11 games off the pace. Almost at the season's halfway point, many considered the Yankees' lead too big to overcome. Miller Huggins was not one of them. With Meusel gone for the next month and Ruth still hobbling, the Yankees manager knew that there were still a lot of games left in the season. His pitching staff had performed well but he was concerned about Hoyt's recent ineffectiveness. Likewise, Urban Shocker, the third man in the rotation, had a history of fading in the late months of the season. Huggins was also worried about his rookie shortstop. Always suspect defensively, Koenig was in the lineup because of his hitting. However, over the past ten days his bat had been relatively silent and his glove had contributed to a couple of the Yankees losses. On a positive note, Koenig's keystone partner, Tony Lazzeri, was beginning to pound the ball and his play in the field had at times been spectacular. Nevertheless, Huggins knew that if Koenig continued to slump, if another starter was hurt, or the pitching fell off, that ten-game lead could easily slip away.

6

The Summer Gets Hot

On a blazing hot July 1 afternoon the Yankees briefly interrupted their long road trip to play a home doubleheader with the Senators. Just a quick stop before heading south to play three more in Washington, Yankees players were glad to be back in their Bronx home. In the opener Urban Shocker hooked up in a duel with Walter Johnson. Tied at two going into the bottom of the ninth, the Senators manager-second baseman Bucky Harris bobbled Earle Combs's leadoff ground ball. Mark Koenig followed with a triple, earning Shocker his 11th victory of the season. Feeding on weak pitching, Washington handed the home team an embarrassing 12–5 loss in the second game.

After the game manager Huggins made two bold decisions. He first announced that Babe Ruth would be taken out of the starting lineup indefinitely. For several weeks the Babe had been playing through pain and had been limited to part-time duty in many games. When he did play, his inability to chase balls down had contributed to several Yankees losses. After the Washington doubleheader the team doctor reported that blood clots had formed in Ruth's right leg. The Babe could continue playing but to do so might cause permanent damage. The only sure cure was a long rest. Huggins also decided to send pitcher Waite Hoyt to get treatment on his pitching arm. Clearly struggling, Hoyt was too important to the team to risk possible season-ending injury. The Yankees manager scheduled his pitcher for X-rays the following day. When the results came back, Hoyt was diagnosed with a strained ligament and bone fragments in his elbow. Treatment would take several weeks and keep him off the mound until the end of July.

In addition to his two injured stars, Huggins had another dilemma. Since the beginning of the season he had not been completely satisfied with his two catchers, Benny Bengough and Pat Collins. Bengough had done a good job as the starting catcher during the last half of the previous season. Solid defensively, an adequate hitter and a smart receiver, he was a team favorite. Unfortunately he came to spring training with an arm that was so sore he could barely throw to second base. Midway through the season his arm had not improved. Collins was a better hitter but not as good defensively. His arm was obviously stronger than Bengough's but it could be erratic. From time to time his pegs to second or third ended up in the outfield. He also occasionally dropped popups, including one that almost cost the Yankees a game. With the heat of the summer looming Huggins contemplated finding another reliable backstop.[1]

Ruth's replacement was Roy Carlyle, who had been sharing time in the outfield with Ben Paschal since Meusel broke his foot. In their first game together in Washington, the two substitutes combined for five hits. However, despite their efforts the Yankees dropped the game. With Ruth watching from the bench, Paschal, Carlyle and their teammates marched out to a three-run lead. All was going well until the seventh. A five-run Senators burst gave the home team a lead that they did not relinquish. The following day the Yankees again jumped out to an early five-run lead, then hung on as the Senators pulled to within a run in the seventh. In the eighth Washington loaded the bases with one out but was unable to score. An inning later the home team again filled the bases but this time was foiled by a game-ending double play.

The Fourth of July, the 150th anniversary of the Declaration of Independence, was a muggy, sweltering day in Washington. A light rain fell throughout the night, transforming the playing field into a soggy quagmire. The infield dirt was thick and slippery and there were shallow puddles in the outfield. Nevertheless the game was begun as scheduled. The starting pitchers for the day, Urban Shocker and Stan Coveleski, added a unique quality to the game. They were among the last legal spitball pitchers in baseball and one of the last pairs to start a game against each other.

The spitball was first thrown sometime in the early twentieth century. Elmer Stricklett is usually given credit for introducing the pitch to the major leagues. Stricklett learned it from minor league teammate George Hildebrand who, along with teammate Frank Corridon, claimed to have devised the pitch. Each pitcher who threw the spitball had his own method, but the basic tactic was to moisten the ball with saliva. Some simply licked their fingers, then gripped the ball, while others actually licked or spat directly onto the ball. Fortunately for hitters the pitch was almost as difficult to throw as it was to hit, and consequently few regularly threw it. Those who did master the spitball were often very successful. Among the best was Jack Chesbro, who won 41 games for the New York Highlanders in 1904. That same year, despite the amazing number of games he won, Chesbro was also remembered for flinging a spitter over his catcher's head which allowed the winning run to score in the game that decided the American League pennant. Arguably the best spitballer was Ed Walsh, who won 40 games in 1908 and 195 in a career shortened by arm problems.

The spitball, along with any other substance-altered pitch, was banned from professional baseball in 1920. Many argued that the spitball gave pitchers an unfair advantage and, because the ball became harder to control when loaded up with a foreign material, it was dangerous. Nevertheless, 17 pitchers whose repertoire featured the pitch were permitted to continue throwing it beyond 1920. By 1926 only seven remained. Two of them were Urban Shocker and Stan Coveleski. Of the others, only Brooklyn's Burleigh Grimes and Red Faber of the White Sox were starting pitchers. Grimes would be the last of the legal spitballers. When he retired in 1934 the pitch was officially gone from major leagues.[2]

In 1926 the spitball was no longer a controversial issue. Instead resin was. At its meeting in January the major league rules committee agreed to allow pitchers, under the supervision of umpires, to use small bags of resin to dry their hands between pitches. It was the first time since 1920 that a foreign substance was permitted on baseballs. The ruling set off a storm of opposition. Leading the charge against use of a resin bag was American League President Ban Johnson. On the other side were baseball Commissioner Kenesaw Landis and several National League owners. The resin bag debate quickly became part of an often acrimonious seven-year power struggle between Johnson and Landis.

Prior to 1920 the major leagues were guided by the National Commission of Baseball. Dubbed the Supreme Court of the major leagues, the three-man Commission was comprised of the two league presidents and chaired by a club owner. As president of the American League, Ban Johnson was a member of the Commission from its inception in 1903 until its demise 17 years later. Johnson used the Commission as his base of power from which he attempted to direct major league baseball. In 1920, after the Black Sox scandal, team presidents decided to replace the commission with a powerful commissioner. Not particularly happy about the change, Johnson accepted the concept but vehemently opposed the choice of Judge Kenesaw Landis as the commissioner. During the next six years Johnson regularly challenged Landis's authority. However, his efforts often backfired and instead, slowly but steadily, he lost power. His last real hope to supplant his rival would come at the end of the 1926 season when Landis's contract came up for renewal. The resin bag dispute became a part Johnson's final campaign to wrestle support away from the commissioner.[3]

Johnson and several American League managers argued that pitchers who used a resin bag would easily be able to apply resin dust onto the ball, thus affecting the flight of the ball. So adamant was Johnson that he hired umpire George Moriarty to investigate the possibilities. Moriarty reported that with just a little resin on his fingers a pitcher "...can do things with (the ball) that will bring back and equal every trick that has been complained about and legislated against for years."[4] Browns player-manager George Sisler lamented that making resin available to pitchers gave them an unfair advantage over hitters. Another outspoken opponent of the new rule, Athletics owner-manager Connie Mack, simply forbade his pitchers from using a resin bag.[5] Johnson, as league president, went a step further by contemplating sanctions against any pitcher in his league who used a resin bag.

Despite the American League opposition, Commissioner Landis decreed that use of a resin bag was not optional. Both leagues were required to supply them at every game, and pitchers, under the supervision of an umpire, were free to use them while on the mound. Landis contended that the rule didn't create a new problem but solved an old one. Pitchers were already using resin in their dugouts between innings. The new rule merely "brings the resin bag from the players' bench out into the open. It legalizes a practice that pitchers in all leagues ... have pursued surreptitiously for years." Further, because it was contained in a small meshed bag, it would be a fine resin dust that would actually be used. Therefore, the new rule would make it more difficult for a pitcher to doctor a ball with resin. Additionally, allowing pitchers to dry their hands with resin was no different from allowing pitchers to dry their hands with dirt which was universally permitted.[6] Though the edict remained controversial it was implemented in both leagues throughout the 1926 season.

The resin bag issue was not a subject of debate in Washington on July 4. With two spitball pitchers facing each other, neither particularly cared about keeping his hands dry between pitches. However, they both cared about playing on a dry field. Soon after the game started, a light rain began to fall, transforming a field that was already slippery into one that was treacherous. By the fifth inning hitters and fielders alike were having a hard time with their footing. An inning later, with the score tied at 4, the skies finally opened up and washed the contest away.

The next day in Philadelphia the Yankees again faced their left-handed nemesis, Lefty Grove. In the first game of a doubleheader Grove throttled the New Yorkers. Striking out 12 and allowing only four hits, he held the Yankees to a single run. Meanwhile Yankees hurler Bob Shawkey for six innings was even better Grove, shutting out the home team. Then, with two outs in the seventh, Koenig made a wild throw to first on a routine ground ball. Two batters later the A's tied the score. Koenig's problems continued an inning later. Philadelphia's leadoff hitter popped one up to the Yankees shortstop. Koenig again muffed the play, allowing what became the winning run to get on base. In the second game Koenig was benched. Manager Huggins moved Lazzeri to shortstop and penciled Aaron Ward in at second. The change had little effect on the game's outcome. The Athletics went up 5–1 through six. When the Yankees began to mount a comeback in the seventh, Lefty Grove was called on to shut down the New Yorkers one more time. Pitching the final three innings, the Philadelphia ace gave up one run but the final outcome was never in doubt once he came to the mound.

After his play in Washington, Koenig's problems in the field had become intolerable to Huggins. With 33 errors so far, the Yankees shortstop had more than twice as many as any teammate. Though Koenig was the team's only bona fide shortstop, Huggins was so impressed with Lazzeri's recent defensive play that he decided to keep Lazzeri at short and Aaron Ward at second for a while. A seasoned veteran, Ward had been the team's regular second baseman during the past six seasons. At the plate he was not Koenig's equal, but in a lineup with the Yankees' run-scoring potential, Huggins was willing to give up a bit of offense if it would shore up the defense.

Finally back home after more than a month on the road, New York began a three-week stand against the league's four western teams. With the exception of the recent doubleheader against the Senators, the Yankees had played 28 games since leaving home back in early June. Though they won only two more times than they lost while on their trip, the team had added a game to their league lead. At home they had so far been a different team, winning almost three out of every four times they played. Huggins and his crew expected that the last three weeks of July would be equally productive. The visit would also provide a bit of time for the team's ailing stars to get regular treatment.

The Yankees opened the home stand with a five-game series against the Indians. One of four teams locked in a battle for second place, the Indians hoped the stop in New York would be a step toward catching up with the Yankees. In the first game the Huggins experiment proved costly. With two outs in the third inning and bases loaded, Lazzeri fumbled a routine ground ball allowing a run to score and opening the door for three more Cleveland markers. Staked to an early four-run lead, Cleveland pitcher George Uhle easily cruised through the last six innings, winning 6–1. The following day Babe Ruth, still a bit gimpy but back in the lineup, drilled his 27th home run of the year to lead the Yankees to an easy win.

Lou Gehrig went from goat to hero in a soggy game three. In the eighth he misplayed a popup that allowed the go-ahead run to score. In the bottom of the inning the Yankees pushed the tying run across the plate. Four innings later Gehrig's single drove in the winning run. Played under stormy skies and delayed twice by rain, the seesaw contest included several defensive gems by the Yankees. In the fourth Joe Dugan speared a blistering shot down the third base line. Two innings later, Lazzeri made a leaping catch on another line drive, and in the tenth with the bases loaded Earle Combs made a spectacular one-handed, over-the-shoulder catch. Each of the catches kept Indians runs off the scoreboard and the Yankees in the game. While the two teams battled back and forth there was excitement off the field as well. Midway through the game police rounded up 16 gamblers in the right field stands and ushered them out of the stadium.

In the years following the Black Sox scandal, baseball zealously, sometimes over-zealously, tried to rid itself of gambling. Just months after the eight Chicago players were banned, a utility infielder for the Phillies, Gene Paulette, was accused of conniving with gamblers to recruit teammates to throw games. In a letter to Commissioner Landis Paulette admitted taking a loan from a pair of St Louis gamblers, including Carl Zork who allegedly was part of the Black Sox fix, but denied ever throwing a game. For Landis the loan was incriminating enough, and he banished Paulette for life. Pitcher Carl Mays, one of the most vilified players in baseball, narrowly escaped a similar fate. Amidst rumors that Mays intentionally lost the fourth game of the 1921 World Series, detectives were hired to follow him. However, the detectives found no proof that the rumors were true, and Mays remained in baseball. On three other occasions accused players were not so lucky. Benny Kauff, Phil Douglas and Rube Benton were each allegedly tied to gamblers. Landis expelled all three based on flimsy accusations and even flimsier evidence.[7]

While Landis could be severe when dealing with marginal players, his tact with prominent figures differed. In 1924 Giants outfielder Jimmy O'Connell described a gambling scheme that included three of his team's stars, Frankie Frisch, Ross Youngs, and George Kelly as well as the Giants' famous manager, John McGraw. According to O'Connell, during a late-season game with Philadelphia a Giants coach, Al "Cozy" Dolan, told him to offer $500 to one of the Phillies to throw the game. Dolan, in turn, was taking orders from McGraw, who had a long list of professional gambler friends. Frisch, Youngs and Kelly, according to O'Connell, encouraged him to do what his coach had told him to do. After a hasty investigation, Landis banned O'Connell and Dolan but exonerated McGraw and his three players.[8]

Another episode during the 1926 season further demonstrated the prevalence of gambling in the game as well as Landis's double standard. Two of baseball's biggest stars, Ty Cobb and Tris Speaker, were accused of fixing a game seven years earlier. Dutch Leonard, who pitched for Detroit in 1919, claimed that the two players, along with himself and pitcher-outfielder "Smokey" Joe Wood, had concocted a plot to throw a late-season game that would help the Tigers earn the league's third place bonus money. Confident of the game's outcome, Cobb also placed a personal bet on the game on behalf of the four co-conspirators. As evidence, Leonard produced letters from Wood and Cobb discussing the deal. While a six-game Yankees win streak kept the Tigers in fourth place, Cobb's bet paid off for all but Leonard, who claimed to have been cut out of the deal at the last minute.

The evidence against Cobb and Speaker, the only two of the four still in baseball, was so compelling that Ban Johnson, in an effort to avoid a scandal, quietly bought the incriminating letters from Leonard and pressured Cobb and Speaker to announce their retirements at the conclusion of the 1926 season. When in December the story finally broke, Landis was livid about what Johnson had done. Concerned that the affair might again rip baseball apart, the Commissioner ordered his own investigation. Meanwhile, with the assistance of the media, he tried to protect the game's public image. A month later he exonerated the two players though they were prohibited from ever coaching or managing again. Clearly Landis knew that Cobb and Speaker were guilty but he chose to overlook their transgressions rather than again scar the game. The following season, Cobb played for the Athletics and Speaker for Washington.[9]

Of course gambling was not limited to baseball. In a decade of excesses, betting on everything from stocks and real estate to sports became almost a national obsession. Riding a booming economy, Americans had extra cash and free time. They were surrounded by examples of successful speculators who were making fortunes playing the stock market. Bucket shops and neighborhood brokerage houses brought maximized returns on minimum outlays. For those who preferred sports to stocks there were just as many opportunities. If there was a game being played or a race being run, there were people making wagers. Horse racing, which reformers condemned ten years earlier, made a strong comeback in the 1920s. At least 15 major race tracks were built during the decade. Boxing matches provided another regular haunt for gamblers. In fact, many boxers were financed by gamblers. The growing popularity of golf and tennis offered additional opportunities. During the decade, gamblers discovered collegiate football even though the game was still in its adolescence. Likewise, more and more bettors patronized bicycle and auto races. In the 1920s, just about any game or contest from badminton to horseshoes provided an opportunity to make a wager.

Gambling was so prevalent that along with a growing defiance of Prohibition it became a central element in an evolving American subculture.

In cities of all sizes gambling webs or syndicates flourished. At the heart of these organizations were local gambling halls, pool halls, and parlors. Just as speakeasies became the secret hideaway for a growing number of "wets," hidden gambling parlors served those ready to make illegal bets. Further encouraging bettors, most gambling parlors had access to a sophisticated network of communications. Much like what the stock ticker did for investors, betting lines provided up-to-the-minute information about sports contests throughout the nation. For those unable to visit a gambling hall, there were bookmakers. In all big cities small armies of "bookies" operated as agents of the local gambling syndicate. Bookies were so ubiquitous in New York City that some claimed there was one on every corner.[10]

The evolving subculture also produced a host of intriguing personalities who in some cases became household names. Just as each city had its own crime organization, each city had its own kingpin. Many remained hidden in the shadows of their operations but a few became celebrities. None was more prominent than Al Capone, whose Chicago empire included just about anything a person could not get legally. Bootleg alcohol and gambling were easily Capone's two most important endeavors. Though he was a ruthless gangster, his sins were generally overlooked in lieu of the products and services his organization provided. Arnold Rothstein was another counterculture personality whose adventures eventually became legend. A gambler by trade, Rothstein was credited with having organized and participated in some of the biggest gambling encounters during the decade. He was also acknowledged to have been the brains behind the Black Sox conspiracy.

Despite Commissioner Landis's efforts, gambling was too deeply entrenched in the game and in American society to eliminate it altogether. There were too many stars, like Cobb, Hornsby, and McGraw, who bet too often to banish all players who wagered on games. Friendships between gamblers and ball players were common and well publicized. Likewise, despite officially opposing betting on games, at least some clubs quietly tolerated it. There were sections in many ballparks where bookies took bets during games. Outside parks before ballgames, gamblers regularly wagered with eager patrons. Major newspapers typically printed daily gambling lines on the same page where they reported play from the previous day. Gambling was so thoroughly a part of American society in general and baseball specifically that a few token raids, like the one in Yankee Stadium the day that the Yankees played the Indians, were about as much as Landis could do to rid the game of gambling.

Cleveland dominated the final two games of the series. The day after Yankees officials expelled the gamblers, Myles Thomas and Emil Levsen, who had hooked up in a nail-biting duel two months earlier, again went at each other. This time Levsen waltzed away with an easy 8–3 victory. For the Yankees "the pitching was bad, and so was the hitting, the base running, some of the thinking and a portion of the fielding."[11] It was not one of their better games. The following day was almost as bad. George Uhle closed out the series the way he began it with an impressive four-hit 6–2 win. In addition to dropping three of the five games, Huggins' experiment with Lazzeri at shortstop was not going well. During the series Lazzeri committed four errors and looked befuddled several times. On the bright side, Babe Ruth was back in the Yankees lineup full time and appeared to be healthy again.

Koenig was back at shortstop when the Tigers came to New York. The change, however, was of little importance in the series opener. Good pitching and hitting by the Tigers and two key Yankees errors, neither of which was committed by Koenig, led to a 5–4 Tigers victory. The following day started even worse. Tigers pitcher Earl Whitehill breezed through the first eight innings giving up just three hits. Then in the bottom of the ninth, down by five with two outs and a runner on first, the Yankees launched a comeback. Four singles and a walk brought in three runs and loaded the bases for the Yankees' recently reinstated rookie shortstop. Koenig immediately smacked a sharp single to left that tied the game. Three innings later Gehrig tripled Ruth home, completing yet another Yankees comeback win. After a rainy loss the next day, New York again excited their fans with yet another ninth-inning assault. Limited to just one hit through the first eight innings, the Yankees were down by two in the ninth. Ruth led off with a single. One out later Combs twisted a line drive into left field. With the tying run on second Lazzeri drilled a double to right and then scored the winning run on a single by Dugan.

By mid–July the Yankees' inconsistent play had given a couple of rivals a chance to whittle down New York's once comfortable lead. Since the beginning of the month the Athletics had caught fire, winning 13, including two against the Yankees, of 15 games. Combining good pitching and timely hitting, Philadelphia had won eight one-run games in the two-week stretch. Four of the wins were credited to rookie relief pitcher Joe Pate. A left-handed knuckleballer, Pate was having the best three weeks in his two-year major league career. After sweeping the Browns while the Yankees were splitting four with Detroit, the Athletics climbed to within 5½ games of the leader. Since the beginning of the month Cleveland, led by hurler George Uhle, had also pulled two games closer to New York.

With their lead steadily shrinking, the Yankees hosted the Browns for four games. In the opener, "one of the quietest and most placid games of the season," Pennock masterfully held St. Louis to just six singles.[12] Meanwhile his mates lashed out only six hits of their own. The difference was a fourth-inning triple by Lazzeri and sacrifice by Dugan. The next day, New York knocked out three more hits than they had in the opener but for the first time all season they were shut out. Aided by four double plays and several dazzling defensive plays, Browns pitcher Tom Zachary weaved his way through several jams enroute to the win. As they had throughout the month, the Yankees followed the loss with a win, this time a convincing one. Scoring eight first-inning runs that pitcher Urban Shocker protected with an outstanding mound performance, New York danced to an easy 11–2 victory. The series ended with another loss. Staked to a two-run lead thanks to Babe Ruth's first home run in almost two weeks, Yankees pitcher Walter Beall was unable to hold the advantage. Down by three runs in the bottom of the ninth, the Yankees rallied for two and had the tying run on base but were unable to pull off another last-inning miracle.

The home stand ended amid a sweltering heat wave with a five-day visit from the White Sox. Unlike Cleveland and Philadelphia, the White Sox had not been able to gain ground on the Yankees during the previous three weeks. Instead the club had fallen from second to fourth place. The series began on a scorching afternoon with a doubleheader. Though they lost the opener 4–3, the Yankees were encouraged by the results. Most importantly, Waite Hoyt was healthy enough to pitch the full nine innings. Scattering eight hits, Hoyt appeared to be back in mid-season shape. Babe Ruth, who swatted his second home run in two days, also seemed to have regained his stroke. In the second game Herb Pennock sailed through the White Sox until an eighth-inning error by Lazzeri tipped off a four-run Chicago barrage. In their half of the inning the Yankees recaptured the lead with a four-run barrage of their own. The win was Pennock's 16th of the season. The next three games were never in doubt. The Yankees pounded White Sox pitchers for 31 runs while holding the visitors to half that many markers. Gehrig was especially productive during the three games, knocking out seven hits, including three doubles, a triple and his eighth home run of the season. The final game belonged to Babe Ruth and his sidekick Waite Hoyt. A sixth-inning two-run "herculean sock" by the Bambino provided Hoyt all the runs he needed for his first win in more than a month.[13]

On Monday, June 29 the Cardinals left on a brief five-day trip to Pittsburgh. However, their player-manager remained behind in St. Louis. For two weeks Hornsby had been battling an increasingly painful right thigh. Finally, after the eventful Saturday doubleheader against the Cubs that started with Alexander's revenge and ended with a field covered by seat cushions and straw hats, the pain became so severe that he could hardly stoop to field ground balls. Warned by team physician Dr. Robert Hyland that without immediate attention he might be forced to miss several weeks, Hornsby reluctantly agreed to surgery. Two days later, as his team prepared to take on the Pirates, their leader was admitted to St. John's Hospital in St. Louis to have an infected carbuncle surgically removed. The operation went well but afterward Hornsby was confined to his bed indefinitely. Stubborn as ever, the ailing Cardinal, despite his doctor's doubts, pledged to rejoin his squad when it returned home the following Sunday.

With Hornsby gone, Bill Killefer filled in as manager and George Toporcer took over at second base. Killefer had five years' experience managing the Cubs but more importantly he had the confidence of Hornsby. Like Hornsby, he treated his players as skilled professionals. On the field he insisted that they perform as instructed. Off the field he recognized that his players were capable of making their own decisions. In both cases he expected that the success of the team should be his players' chief concern. Killefer's players in Chicago appreciated his methods even though his teams had never finished better than fourth. After half a season in St. Louis the interim manager had already established himself as a fair-minded leader.

Hornsby's replacement at second base was a skinny and apparently frail kid who since childhood had worn thick, wire-rimmed glasses. Signed right off of the sandlots of Manhattan's Lower East Side, George Toporcer was dubbed "Specs" by schoolmates and carried that name for the rest of his life. Passed over by neighborhood teams because of his vision problems, he nevertheless developed into a flawless infielder and dependable hitter once given a chance to play. In 1921, immediately after signing with the Cardinals, Specs was added to the team's starting lineup, making him the first infielder in major league history to wear glasses. To create a spot for him Hornsby was briefly moved to third base and then to the outfield. However, the experiment failed. For Specs the failure meant that his overnight trip from amateur sandlot teams to the Cardinals' starting lineup was temporary. By the end of the season he was playing for the St. Louis affiliate in Syracuse.

The following year Specs was back in St. Louis. Though he would never be an everyday player, he proved to be an excellent pinch hitter and reliable substitute for Hornsby on the rare occasions that the Cardinals star was unable to play. He also brought a degree of leadership to the team. On the field Toporcer compensated for his physical shortcomings with grit and savvy, two qualities that his manager particularly valued. Off the field he proved to be a true student of the game, again a characteristic that Hornsby respected.[14]

Since playing the Pirates a week earlier, the Cardinals had moved into second place, 1½ games ahead of Pittsburgh. Meanwhile Pirates pitching had given up more than nine runs a game in Cincinnati and dropped all five against the league leaders. In the opening game with the Cardinals, pitching again plagued Pittsburgh. A three-run homer by Les Bell and a solo shot by Ray Blades provided more than enough punch for Jesse Haines, who held the home team to just seven hits and two runs. The rest of the visit did not go as well for the Cardinals. The Pirates decisively ended their seven-game skid the next day. Ahead by a run in the seventh inning, the top of the Pittsburgh lineup knocked around Flint Rhem for five runs which sealed a 7–3 win. The third game was a pitchers' duel between Grover Cleveland Alexander, who was making his second start for the Cardinals, and the Pirates ace, Ray Kremer. Alexander had always given the Pirates problems and this game was no different. Old Pete limited the home team to just three runs. However, Kremer did even better, scattering seven hits and holding the Cardinals scoreless until the ninth when they scored twice. In the final game the Cardinals' hopes of salvaging a series split ended in the bottom of the fourth inning. Tied at two apiece, the Pirates launched an eight-run barrage that enabled them to coast to an easy 12–3 victory. The win also pushed Pittsburgh past St. Louis back into second place.

Despite his promise, Rogers Hornsby did not return to the Cardinals lineup in the opener against Cincinnati. Nor did he play in any of the five games with the league leader. Making matters worse, Vic Keen, who two days earlier had missed his scheduled start in Pittsburgh, was listed with a sore arm and his return to the rotation was uncertain. Already a nine-game winner, Keen was one of the keys to the Cardinals success thus far in the season. The loss of one of the league's most effective pitchers just as the pennant race was heating up did not bode well for the Cardinals. Fortunately Haines and Sherdel were again pitching well, and the addition of Alexander appeared promising.

Back in St. Louis, the league-leading Cincinnati Reds came to town to celebrate Independence Day week with a five-game series. At the season's traditional midpoint the Reds were clearly the team to beat in the National League. Despite having just lost four of six to Chicago, Cincinnati remained where they had been since early May: perched atop the National League. When they arrived they were three games up on the Pirates, four ahead of the Cardinals and six up on the Cubs. Of the four eastern teams only the Giants and Brooklyn Robins appeared to have a shot at the Reds though their chances seemed remote. The Reds were playing especially well against the other three western teams, winning games at almost a .600 clip. Meanwhile the Pirates and Cardinals were both playing well under .500 against western teams. Against the four eastern teams it was a different story. The Cardinals had the best record, and some projected that if during the second half of the season St. Louis could continue their pace against the east and match the Reds against western teams, they would win their first pennant. The time to start would be the upcoming series with the Reds.

In the Independence Day opener the Cardinals gave the ball to "Wee" Willie Sherdel. The previous season the little lefty had befuddled the Reds with an assortment of curves and off-speed pitches and pinpoint control. Beating them twice, he had given up only one run in more than 18 innings on the mound. Sherdel's mastery, however, did not continue into 1926. Spurred by Edd Roush's two-run homer, the Reds tripled their entire 1925 run production against Sherdel in just the first inning. In all Cincinnati pounded out 17 hits on their way to a comfortable 7–2 win. It was a disappointing start for St. Louis.

Having now lost four in a row, the Cardinals hoped to reverse their recent fortunes with a Monday doubleheader. In the opener Cincinnati pitcher Pete Donahue shut out the home team on just six hits. The second game began almost as badly for the Cardinals. The Reds' big lefty, Eppa Rixey, powered his way through the first four innings while his mates pecked out a four-run lead. In the fifth, St. Louis hitters finally woke up. Scoring three in the fifth and two more in the sixth, the Cardinals scratched out a one-run lead. An inning later the Reds battled back to tie the score. With the scored still knotted at five in the eighth, Billy Southworth became the game's hero. Sent in as a pinch hitter he blasted the first pitch he saw into the right field bleachers for a two-run homer that ended the Cardinals' skid.

The two teams split the last two games of the series. In the first Alexander masterfully cut through Cincinnati for eight innings, holding them scoreless on just two hits. Meanwhile his hurling counterpart, Carl Mays, had done almost as well, giving up only four hits and two runs. Cruising into the ninth, Alexander's fate changed. With a man on, the Reds first baseman, Wally Pipp, took advantage of one of the few bad pitches Alexander had thrown all day, driving a two-run shot over the right field fence to tie the game. The two pitchers continued to dominate through the tenth but in the 11th Alexander finally weakened. Cincinnati scored three times to notch another win. The Cardinals earned a bit of consolation the following day when their bats finally awakened. Led by Specs Torporcer's three hits, St. Louis outscored the league leaders 11–2.

Winning two of the last three against Cincinnati provided the Cardinals some solace. The series had begun poorly and could have turned into a disaster. Nevertheless, the three losses dropped the Cardinals yet another game back of Cincinnati and assured that the Reds would win their season series against St. Louis. The two teams were scheduled to play each other only four more times, making the Cardinals' task of catching the league leaders even more daunting. On a positive note, Manager Hornsby was again healthy and ready to play. Likewise, for the next five weeks the Cardinals would be playing only the league's four eastern teams whom they had done so well against.

With Hornsby back in the lineup, Cardinals bats continued to produce. The Boston Braves were in last place and had not beaten the Cardinals in 1926 when they arrived in St. Louis. In the opener the Cardinals rode a home run by Les Bell, a run-scoring double by Bob O'Farrell, and Sherdel's crafty pitching to a 2–1. In the second game Jesse Haines, who had quietly won six in a row, became the beneficiary of his teammates' offensive barrage. Scoring in all but the fourth inning, St. Louis tallied 18 runs. In addition to a Hornsby home run, Bell's five RBI's and four more from Southworth, the Cardinals were aided by five Boston errors. The Cardinals made it ten in a row over the Braves in the first game of a doubleheader the next day. However, in the second game their mastery over Boston abruptly ended. On a sweltering afternoon, Flint Rhem failed to make it past the third inning, giving up six runs. An eight-run eighth further propelled the visitors to a 19–5 drubbing. Boston closed out the series with another win. Rhem again started but this time lasted less than two innings. It was the fifth unsuccessful start in a row for Rhem. Down by four, St. Louis battled back to tie the score in the seventh. In the eighth Vic Keen, who was pitching for the first time in almost two weeks, became the fifth Cardinals pitcher called upon to hold off the Braves. Instead he served up a two-out ninth-inning home run and lost the game.

Brooklyn continued the assault on Cardinals pitching. In the four games between the two teams the Robins averaged seven runs and 12 hits a game. Sherdel and Haines, the two most effective hurlers during the previous month, were both rocked by Brooklyn hitters. Sherdel surrendered ten runs in the opener, and the next day Haines's winning streak ended with a 5–2 loss. Fortunately Cardinals hitters were up to the challenge. Despite his weak performance, Sherdel earned a complete game win thanks to a 12-run assault by St. Louis hitters. An 11-run outburst two days later enabled the Cardinals to chalk up another win and split the series.

Though much media attention focused on the return of Hornsby's bat to the lineup, Billy Southworth and third baseman Les Bell led the Cardinals' recent offensive flurry. From the moment he was acquired two months earlier Southworth was expected to add some clout at the plate. By mid–July he was fulfilling all expectations. On the other hand, Bell's play was a surprise. In the field he established himself as a reliable addition to an excellent defensive infield. At the plate, after a slow start he became one of the hottest hitters in the National League. Since late June, when Hornsby went on the disabled list, Bell was hitting at over a .400 clip, bringing his average up from the mid–.280s in late May to almost .350 by the end of July (easily the best six weeks in his entire ten-year career). He was also amongst the league's home run and RBI leaders. He was especially tough when a game was on the line, knocking in at least three game-winning runs during Hornsby's absence.

One of the Cardinals' young stars, Les Bell led his team with a .325 batting average in 1926. A shoulder injury the following year shortened what might have been a stellar career.

His play was so impressive that a few sports writers began mentioning him as a potential Most Valuable Player.[15]

Bell had become the Cardinals' regular third baseman the previous year after two solid seasons in the Cardinals farm system. In 1923 at Houston, his last minor league stop, some considered him to be the best player in the Texas League. Surprisingly fast and blessed with a strong, accurate arm, he was well suited for a middle infield position. At the plate he seemed to possess all the qualities of an outstanding hitter. He rarely struck out and could hit for average and with power. During his first season with Houston his batting average led the Texas League. However, the transition to the Cardinals included some growing pains for Bell. Moved from shortstop to third base he had a difficult year in the field, committing 36 errors. Meanwhile at the plate his batting average dipped to .285, respectable for a rookie but not what was expected of a full time major leaguer.

Bell's professional baseball career began ten years earlier when he was

16, playing for a dollar a game with semi-pro team in his hometown, Harrisburg, PA. The team's manager, Jimmy Sheckard, had played professionally for 17 years with teams including the famous (or infamous) 1899 Baltimore Orioles for whom he had been the regular right fielder. Sheckard became Bell's mentor in Harrisburg. In 1921 a scout for the Tigers signed Bell to a contract with a team in Bristol, Tennessee. Three weeks later he was back in Harrisburg, playing for Sheckard. However, the following year he joined a minor league team in Lansing, Michigan. Later that season a scout for the Cardinals was impressed enough with the young shortstop that he purchased Bell's contract. From Lansing, Bell went to Houston and from Houston to St. Louis.

Seventh-place Philadelphia was the next team to visit Bell and his mates. With Cardinals hitters on track and the pennant race tightening a bit, the team intended to sweep the lowly Phillies. All went well in the first game. St. Louis hammered out 19 hits and scored 13 times. The beneficiary of the assault was Flint Rhem, who hadn't won a game in a month. His fastball again hopping, Rhem held the Phillies to just eight hits and five runs. The following day Southworth's bat led the way to another win. Down by a run in the seventh, the Cardinals tied the game on a Southworth double. Two innings later, with the score still tied, the St. Louis right fielder launched his ninth home run of the season. Philadelphia avoided the sweep in the final game, squeaking out a ten-inning 4–3 victory. Though the Cardinals smacked 12 hits they were unable to string them together into runs. On the bright side, like Flint Rhem two days earlier, pitcher Vic Keen, who threw all ten innings, appeared to have regained his mound magic. Only a bumbled fly ball that led to a pair of runs in the first inning separated Keen from his first win since mid–June.

After the Phillies' departure, the Cardinals had two days to rest and recuperate while their next visitors, the Giants, finished up a series in Chicago. No one needed the time off more than Hornsby. Since his return he had had been hitting at a .350 clip, which for any other player would have been exceptional. For Hornsby, who had hit over .400 three of the previous four seasons, a .350 average was sub-par. Additionally, of his 16 hits since returning only three had been for extra bases, and even though he was batting third he had driven in only five runs. During the previous four years almost 40 percent of Hornsby's hits were for extra bases (39 of them in 1925 were home runs) and he had averaged just under one run batted in per game. Clearly the Cardinals manager still had his batting eye but not his usual strength.

Of more concern to Cardinals fans was their team's inconsistency. Still in third place just 2½ games behind Cincinnati, the Cards seemed unable to string wins together. If they could put together a nice eight- to ten-game winning streak or two they would be well in front of the league. Some speculated that the source of the problems was behavior off the field. Players were accused of spending too much time celebrating. The St. Louis Post Dispatch was more direct, affirming that "Disquieting reports have come out recently that some of the boys are doing a little fudging on the Eighteenth Amendment." There were also rumors that Cardinals management, probably vice president and teetotaler Branch Rickey, was fuming about Hornsby's lack of control over his players. It wasn't difficult to find tangible evidence to support the claims. Grover Cleveland Alexander was a known alcoholic. When released by the Cubs, one of the reasons given was Alexander's drinking problem. Flint Rhem was another suspected of imbibing excessively. Rhem's mysterious losing streak seemed likely to be in part alcohol related. The *Dispatch* acknowledged that the problem was probably not pervasive but that there were several Cardinals who needed to sever their relations with "friendly bootleggers" because "booze does not go along with baseball efficiency and the better chances of the Cardinals for the pennant."[16]

Even though the sale of alcohol was illegal, the drinking habits of the Cardinals players were no different from those of many other Americans. Since enacted in January, 1920, the Volstead Act had been a source of passionate debate throughout the nation. The Act implemented the Eighteenth Amendment to the Constitution and began the era of Prohibition in the United States. Promoted by a diverse collection of national organizations, zealous reformers and politicians, much of the support for Prohibition came from rural, Bible-belt areas in the South and Midwest where rigid anti-alcohol legislation was passed even before World War I. Advocates claimed that alcohol threatened the moral fiber of American society. The family was especially vulnerable to the evils of alcohol. However, from the outset many questioned whether the benefits of the "noble experiment" were worth the costs. On one hand, enforcement was expensive. Likewise, the legislation spawned a drinking subculture that included speakeasies, toxic home-brewed alcohol and organized crime. As a result, millions of otherwise law-abiding Americans openly disobeyed the act. The defiance generated fierce support on both sides. By 1926 the debate about Prohibition had polarized the nation into two camps: "Drys" who supported the law and "Wets" who opposed it.

Almost as soon as Prohibition began, supporters labeled it a spectacular success. Citing government statistics, testimonials and anecdotal evidence, they proclaimed that the immediate results of the new law were dramatic. In 1920 the per capita consumption of alcohol dropped by as much as 80 percent. Likewise, alcohol-related deaths declined from just over two per 100,000 to one per 100,000 Americans, and arrests for drunkenness fell sharply in 1920.[17] Illnesses associated with alcohol psychoses also appeared to be in decline. Consequently state budgets were spared significant enforcement and medical costs. Some business leaders, most notably J.D. Rockefeller and Henry Ford, who were both major contributors to the Anti-Saloon League, claimed that absenteeism had fallen and production was soaring since Prohibition began. Some "drys" went a step farther, arguing that the decade's booming economy was a direct consequence of the new law. Since Americans were no longer spending money on alcohol and alcohol-related activities, they were instead buying new consumer goods ranging from automobiles to toasters.[18]

Opponents built an equally convincing case challenging the apparent successes of prohibition by gathering their own data. Their statistics showed that while deaths from alcohol-related circumstances fell initially, the numbers began to rise steadily after 1920. Likewise within five years arrests for drunkenness had reached levels close to those from before Prohibition began, and the consumption of alcohol by Americans climbed back to approximately 70 percent of what it had been prior to Prohibition.[19] By 1926 the federal government's expense of enforcing the law had grown by at least 50 percent but fell far short of the mushrooming costs that full enforcement required. "Wets" argued that open disregard for the law permeated American society. Violators could be found everywhere. Even Congressmen were known to keep large stocks of liquor in the cellars of the House of Representatives and the Senate.

More troubling was the obvious connection between Prohibition and an evolving criminal underworld. While Prohibition was intended to fortify the nation's moral fiber, it also created vast new opportunities for crime. Local gangs fed by bootlegging profits grew into well organized crime syndicates in cities throughout the nation. Violent crime bosses became prominent and often popular local personalities. None was better known than Chicago's Alphonse Capone, who employed a small army of thugs to carry out his orders. Like his gangland contemporaries, Capone stopped at nothing to eliminate competition and neutralize law enforcement. Operating an extensive network that included "speakeasies" and glamorous nightclubs, Capone annually raked in more than $60 million. As his crime empire grew so too did the brazen tactics he used to maintain his power. During the 1920s in Chicago alone there were at least 550 known gangland killings (and no doubt many, many more that went unreported). By 1926 it was obvious that law enforcement was losing its battle against organized crime.

In April, 1926, with the nation at a crossroads in the prohibition experiment, Senator William Cabell Bruce, a Democrat from Maryland, organized a Congressional hearing to assess the Volstead Act. A sharp critic of Prohibition, Bruce intended to give opponents of the law a formal opportunity to be heard. He opened the hearing with his own scathing assessment of the law. He began by proposing that "prohibition in the United States ... has proved to be a disastrous, tragic failure." The only effects of the law were "...that of blighting human happiness, debasing human morals, and discrediting human laws." Citing files full of government statistics, he argued that consumption of alcohol had grown steadily since 1920 and that enforcement had become impossible. Massachusetts attorney Julien Codman reinforced Bruce's assessment. Codman, who represented several labor and constitutional rights organizations, claimed that "(Prohibition) has done incredible harm instead of good." He called the law "a pitiable failure" that rather than decreasing drinking and crime had increased both and transformed law breakers into local heroes. He further lamented that in addition to exorbitant manpower costs, enforcement was monopolizing the federal courts.[20] The most colorful of Bruce's witnesses was New York Congressman Fiorella LaGuardia, who calculated that "a million dollars a day is paid in graft and corruption to Federal, State, and local officers."[21]

Bruce's hearings proved to be an early salvo in an increasingly confrontational campaign against Prohibition. The hearings encouraged various "wet" organizations to work together toward Congressional repeal of the Volstead Act. These groups were composed of middle class Americans— lawyers, businessmen, teachers and laborers— who, like Senator Bruce, had become completely disillusioned with the "noble experiment." After the Bruce hearings a number of states' bar associations as well as the powerful American Bar Association also aggressively stepped up legal challenges of the Volstead Act. Veterans groups added yet another dimension to the campaign. Though it would take another eight years before the law was repealed, change was in the air throughout 1926. Even in places that had discouraged consumption of alcohol, like major league ball parks, new tolerance was emerging. However, despite the loosening attitudes, there were still Americans who steadfastly continued to worry that alcohol was undermining the moral fiber of the nation, just as there were some Cardinals fans who worried that a few hard-drinking players were ruining their team's otherwise exceptional season.

The Cardinals ended their July home stand with a four-game series against the Giants. Since their last encounter with St. Louis, McGraw's crew had been quietly slipping out of the pennant race. Still only seven games back of league leading Cincinnati and three behind the Cards, New York had sputtered around the .500 mark all season. However, a sweep of St. Louis would help to revive the Giants' hopes. Meanwhile, the Cardinals were anxious to add a few more wins to their home record. Since returning home the team had run up a mediocre record of nine wins and eight losses. Three or four more wins would add a degree of respectability to the home stand. To drop three or four to the league's sixth-place team would be devastating.

The opening game was Heinie Mueller Day. Always popular in St. Louis, the Giants' new center fielder remained a crowd favorite even after being traded to New York six weeks earlier. After some preliminary welcome home gifts and speeches, the day turned serious. The Giants jumped out to an early two-run lead but in the fourth back-to-back home runs by Billy Southworth, Mueller's replacement in the Cardinals lineup, and hot-hitting Les Bell tied the score. With the score tied in the top of the ninth, the bases empty and two outs, Cardinals catcher Bob O'Farrell dropped a third strike that would have ended the Giants half of the inning. Given a reprieve, Irish Meusel lashed the next pitch for a double to left. The throw back into the infield took a bad hop and hit Hornsby, who was covering second, in the right eye and knocked him to the ground. Groggy and with blurred vision, the Cardinals manager had to leave the game. He later reported that he felt like he had been hit in the eye by heavyweight champion Jack Dempsey. With Meusel now on second, the next hitter, "Long" George Kelly, worked Alexander for a walk. Travis Jackson then slapped a single to left, scoring Meusel with the winning run. The loss was doubly disheartening for the Cardinals. Not only had they lost a bit more ground to the Reds but Hornsby's eye swelled shut, making him doubtful for perhaps the rest of the series.

The following day proved to be much better for the Cardinals and their fans. Hornsby, shiner and all, was back in the lineup despite the team doctor's advice. Again Billy Southworth and Les Bell pounded away at the plate, driving in six runs between them. Meanwhile "Wee" Willie Sherdel mystified Giants hitters all day. Additionally the Braves walloped the Reds enabling St. Louis to get back the game they had lost the day before.

The last two games of the series were hard-fought extra-inning struggles. The day after Sherdel's easy win, Flint Rhem tried to duplicate the effort. Instead the game began much as the first game had except that this time the Cardinals jumped out to an early three-run lead. In the eighth, aided by a St. Louis error, the Giants evened the score at three. The score was still tied in the 11th when the first two New York hitters singled. As everyone in the park expected, the next hitter, light hitting Hugh McMullen, attempted to bunt the two runners up a base. Poorly placed, the bunt bounded straight back to Rhem. However, Rhem, hungry for the force out at third and possibly a double play, rushed the throw, uncorking "one of the wildest, woolliest and most costly throws in the history of St. Louis baseball."[22] The ball went well over Bell's head, caromed along the stands and ended up all the way down at the left field wall. By the time the ball was finally returned both runners had scored, McMullen was on third and the Cardinals had another loss.

Like two of the previous three games, the finale was a thriller. The Cardinals struck first with a run in the opening frame but the Giants scored twice in the second. Through the next eight innings the lead bounced back and forth four more times. For the Cardinals it was the bats of Bell and Southworth that again kept them in the game. Both homered, and Bell finished a single short of hitting for the cycle. Going into the bottom of the ninth the Giants held a one-run lead, but a Thevenow single pushed the game into extra innings. After the two teams each added a run in the tenth, Cardinals center fielder Taylor Douthit finally ended the afternoon with a run-scoring single to left in the 11th.

Douthit's single enabled the Cardinals to salvage a series split and finish their home stand with a winning record. However, for a team with a reputation for playing well at home the previous three weeks had not been particularly successful. Fortunately league leading Cincinnati had played even worse, winning ten while dropping 12. Additionally, the Cardinals were only 2½ games out of first place and comfortably above the .500 mark. On the other hand, the club was also only 2½ games ahead of the fifth-place Brooklyn Robins and had the toughest part of its season still ahead. As their train chugged east, Hornsby and his players all realized that while a string of wins on their journey might push them even closer to the league's top spot, a string of losses could effectively end the team's hunt for its first National League crown.

7

Dog Day Races

Rogers Hornsby arrived in Philadelphia exhausted and with an ailing back. Since the beginning of the season he had been plagued by minor lower back problems. After his thigh operation in early July the pain became increasingly intense, no doubt because he was trying to protect his slowly healing thigh. By the end of the Cardinals' July home stand Hornsby's back was clearly affecting his play. On several occasions during the previous week he had taken himself out of the lineup late in games. It had also been ten days since he had an extra base hit. Hornsby admitted that "I have been feeling weak for several weeks ... for several days I have had trouble knocking the ball out of the infield." Enduring the 23-hour train ride east, Hornsby was barely able to bend by the time he reached Philadelphia.[1]

When the series with the Phillies started, manager Hornsby was in a coat and tie rather than his playing uniform. Finally complying with the team doctor's advice, the Cardinals slugger decided to rest himself until his back was better and he felt stronger. On the mound for St. Louis that day was Grover Cleveland Alexander. The tiny Baker Bowl, where the Phillies played their home games, held many good memories for the Cardinals pitcher. He spent his first seven major league seasons in Philadelphia. It was in the Baker Bowl that Alex was appropriately dubbed "Alex the Great" and put together the best four-year record of any pitcher in baseball history. Between 1914 and 1917, his last year with the Phillies, he won 121 games, averaging more than 30 wins a season while giving up just 1.74 earned runs per game. In 1915 his mighty arm led his team to its first National League championship (and the last Phillies pennant until 1950). Though the years since had taken an obvious toll on Old Pete, for many Phillies fans his mere presence rekindled images of earlier glory days just as the Baker Bowl did for Alexander.

While there were glimmers of Alex the Great during the opening game, for most of the afternoon it was Old Pete who battled the Phillies. Gone were the blistering fastball and the unhittable curve, but Alexander still had near pinpoint control and remained a crafty mound man. Scattering 15 hits, he held the Phillies to five runs. Meanwhile his teammates, led again by Billy Southworth, banged out one less hit but scored nine times. The win was Alexander's sixth of the season and got the important Cardinals road trip off well.

The following day had become oppressively hot and humid by the time the two teams squared off for a doubleheader. Willie Sherdel started the first game for the Cardinals. The most effective St. Louis pitcher during the previous six weeks, Sherdel only made it to the sixth inning, yielding six runs and 11 hits along the way. In a reversal of the previous day's outcome, the Phillies, though out-hit by the visitors, easily outscored them 6–3. In the second game Vic Keen was on the mound for the Cardinals. Since early June Keen had been struggling, but on this day through eight innings he kept the Phillies in check. However, the ninth inning started poorly. Up by a pair of runs, Keen walked the leadoff hitter, then gave up a triple. With the tying run on third and nobody out he now faced pinch hitter Oscar Grimes, a .297 hitter, leadoff man Heinie Sand, who already had three hits in the game, and Cy Williams, who was on his way to a .345 season. Normally manager Hornsby would have lifted Keen but instead he relied on his instincts and left his starter on the mound. It turned out to be the right decision. With his father watching in the stands, Keen skillfully mowed down the three Phillies, getting each one to dribble an easy ground ball to the infield.

After a day off, the Cardinals traveled to New York City and games with the Giants and Brooklyn Robins. A week earlier the Cardinals and Giants had split four of the season's most exciting games. The five games that followed in New York included few of the previous week's thrills but instead a lot of disappointment for the Cardinals. Aside from Flint Rhem's masterful effort in the opening game, the Cardinals floundered through the series. In each of the last four games they took an early lead but were unable to hold it. In the doubleheader that followed Rhem's win St. Louis jumped out to a quick six-run lead, then watched as Giants hitters, led by Frankie Frisch, hammered away scoring eight unanswered runs while two Giants pitchers shut the door on Cardinals hitters. In the nightcap New York replicated the early game's pattern. After going down by a run, Frisch and company settled any doubts about the final outcome by scoring six times in the sixth inning. Meanwhile Giants pitchers Virgil Barnes and Chick Davies limited the visitors to just six hits and a single run.

The final two games were no better for the Cardinals. In the first, the

Giants knocked out three home runs against Alexander and easily won 7–2. Vic Keen was the victim in the finale. The Cardinals pitcher cruised through the first five innings. Then with two outs in the sixth he beaned Giants left fielder Ty Tyson. On the ground for several minutes, Tyson required medical attention before his head cleared. When play resumed Keen was a different pitcher. He gave up a run-scoring single to the next hitter and would have given up more had center fielder Taylor Douthit not made a brilliant running catch to end the inning. The Giants resumed their assault in the seventh, banging Keen around for three more runs before manager Hornsby lifted him.

For the Cardinals the four losses to the Giants were distressing. Falling 4½ games back of the league leader with just 52 games left in the season, Hornsby and his crew understood that if they were to win the pennant there was very little room for mistakes. In 1925 the league champion Pirates had won 95 games. Though no team was winning as often in 1926 as the Pirates had a year earlier it seemed likely that to win the pennant a team would have to win about 90 games. After the Giants series the Cardinals had won 53 games. To get to 90 wins they would have to win 71 percent of their 52 remaining games. Adding to the task, 33 of those games would be played away from home. On the road the Cardinals had lost two more games than they had won. While the club's first championship was still a possibility, Hornsby and his players realized that they would have to start stringing wins together immediately.

For Les Bell the Giants series was doubly disappointing. On one hand it marked the end of the longest hitting streak in his career. Against New York in the opener he had pushed his streak to 21 games, but the following afternoon failed to get a hit for the first time in almost four weeks. The end of the streak also began Bell's slow decline from brilliance to mediocrity. For six weeks he had been one of the best hitters in baseball, batting over .400, driving in runs and raising his average to .357, second highest in the National League. It would easily be the best six weeks in his nine-year career. Once past his streak Bell hit .285 through August and September while his season average, though remaining high enough to lead the Cardinals, slid back to .325. In the years that followed he would never again reach the .300 plateau, instead batting at a .280 clip through his last six seasons.

Hornsby was back in the lineup when the Cardinals began six games with the Robins. In the first inning the St. Louis manager demonstrated the resolve he expected of his team throughout the rest of the season. Batting in his usual third position, Hornsby came to the plate with two out and lined the first pitch he saw for a single. A double and two singles later the Cards had put two runs on the scoreboard. Unlike the previous four games, this time St. Louis held that early lead. Throughout the rest of the afternoon, whenever the Robins got close the Cardinals countered with runs of their own. Even Cardinals pitcher Sherdel contributed to the offense with a triple and a rare home run. "Wee Willie" was so surprised by his home run that he stopped at second, assuming the ball had bounced over the fence. On the mound Sherdel was clearly in control. Aside from weathering a three-run storm in the fifth he twirled past the Robins as he had twice before earlier in the season.

The Cardinals' new resolve was on display again the following day. The game started well for St. Louis. With Flint Rhem slicing through the Robins lineup, the Cardinals rolled into the sixth up by five. Seven Brooklyn runs later, the Cardinals were having flashbacks of the Giants series. This time, though, Hornsby and company fought back with a run in the seventh and then tied the score in their half of the ninth. In the tenth, fueled by a three-run Jim Bottomley double, St. Louis scored four times. In the bottom of the inning the Robins launched their own comeback. Zack Wheat homered and another run scored after a walk and a pair of singles. With the potential tying run on base and winning run at the plate, manager Hornsby called Alexander in from the bullpen to get the final out. The fifth Cardinal pitcher of the day, Old Pete did what was he was called in to do, saving a hard-earned victory for his team.

St. Louis easily won the next three games. At the plate Cardinals out-fielders took turns leading the offense. In the first game center fielder Taylor Douthit collected three hits and scored three of his team's seven runs while pitcher Art Reinhart held the Robins to just three markers. The following afternoon Douthit knocked out two more hits and right fielder Southworth drove in four runs, two of which were scored by left fielder Ray Blades. The story of the third game was Alexander, who shut out the Robins on four hits. At the plate Southworth again drove in two of his team's three runs while Douthit scored one of them.

Pitching was the difference in the final game of the series. This time Sherdel stymied the Robins in a ten-inning thriller. Baffling Brooklyn hitters with his assortment of pitches, the little lefty gave up a run in each of the first two innings but then shut the door on the Robins. Meanwhile Cardinals hitters fought back with two runs in the fourth to tie the game. Still tied in the tenth, Blades led off with a single, went to second on an error and scored the winning run on a double by Hornsby. The win completed an impressive six-game sweep and erased some of the doubts that arose after the four straight losses to the Giants. Still aware that they had a tough challenge ahead of them, Cardinals players left Brooklyn clearly more confident than they were when they arrived. Additionally, they had picked up two important games on the Pirates, who had forged ahead of Cincinnati during the previous week, and moved into second place, nine percentage points ahead of the slumping Reds.

While the Cardinals were dispatching Brooklyn, on the other side of the Atlantic a young American woman was making international news of her own. During the early morning of August 6th, 18-year-old Gertrude Ederle splashed into the English Channel at Cap Gris-Nez, France. For 14 hours and 31 minutes she churned through cold choppy waters, rain, and a fierce tide. When she finally climbed onto the rocky beach at Kingsdown, England, just north of Dover, she had become the first woman to swim the Channel. Ederle also made the crossing faster than any of the five men who had previously done the swim. News of the accomplishment was flashed back to the United States and immediately propelled Ederle to celebrity status. Upon her return home, her new status was further confirmed by a ticker-tape parade through New York City.

Ederle's accomplishment was another indication that the place of women in American society was changing. Ederle was one of a relatively small but growing group of notable women athletes. Like Ederle, several woman swimmers, including Aileen Riggin and Sybil Bauer, built international reputations particularly after the 1924 Olympics in Paris. Tennis star Helen Wills, perhaps the best known woman athlete of the era, became the darling of sports columnists everywhere. In 1926 she played a much publicized match against her French counterpart, Suzanne Lenglen, that generated international coverage. Though she lost to Lenglen, Wills eventually won 31 Grand Slam events. In golf Glenna Collett (Vare), winner of four U.S. Women's Amateur Championships, established herself as "The Queen of American Golf." At a more local level, elementary and secondary schools throughout the nation began including girls' athletics as part of their regular curriculum. By the mid–1920s more than 25 percent of American universities offered women varsity sports programs.

The most visible example of the "new" American woman and an icon of the era was the flapper. In *The Crack-Up* F. Scott Fitzgerald describes a flapper as "lovely and expensive and about nineteen." These jazz age women discarded the methods and standards of their mothers in favor of a fun-loving pose. Assumed to be sexually active and coyly submissive, the flapper symbolized the new morality associated with the Roaring Twenties. She was young, had an adventurous spirit and flaunted the conventional. She smoked cigarettes in public, drank bootleg liquor and hung out unescorted in speakeasies. Almost boyish in appearance, her look was her most distinguishing characteristic. She bobbed and often colored her hair, used lipstick and cheek rouge, and wore provocatively short, loose-fitting and almost shapeless attire.

Most importantly, she appeared ready to enjoy the present with little regard for the past or the future.

While only a small percentage embraced the flapper lifestyle, a growing number of women redefined themselves in other ways. During the decade about three million women joined the work force. For some a job outside the home was a financial necessity. For others it was a way to supplement the family income and afford a new house outside the city, an automobile, a radio, an icebox, or a whole array of other consumer goods that first became available during the decade. These working women generally found "female jobs" like schoolteachers, nurses, office workers, and sales clerks that generally did not compete with the jobs men held and paid significantly less than men were paid. Post-secondary education was another avenue women increasingly pursued. By the end of the decade more women than men were enrolled in colleges. Likewise, women were awarded about one-third of all the graduate degrees handed out during the decade (though only a very small percentage of women were able to use those degrees for career purposes).[2]

Of course the vast majority of women during the decade remained traditional housewives. Their lives focused on home and family. For some, particularly those in metropolitan areas, the new affluence, mobility, and labor-saving devices transformed their domestic responsibilities. The time saved when doing basic household tasks was often redirected to child rearing. A measuring stick for families in general and for mothers in particular was the development of their children. As a result, families became ever more child-focused thus promoting a twenties youth culture. For many women in the heartland, the new appliances and labor-saving devices were neither available nor affordable. For these women chores still required dawn-to-dusk, physically demanding labor and family roles that generally remained unchanged.

The Cardinals ended their trip in Boston. Despite the Braves' seventh-place standing the team had been playing well before the Cards arrived. Against the other three western teams, Chicago, Cincinnati and Pittsburgh, who preceded St. Louis into Boston, the Braves had won seven of 12. Most recently they had split a six-game series with the league leading Pirates. Sitting in second place and eager to continue their climb, Hornsby and company recognized that the Braves would pose a challenge.

In the first game the Cardinals' six-game streak ended with a 5–0 loss. Braves pitcher Larry Benton completely dominated the visitors, limiting them to just five hits. The Cardinals reversed the results the next two days. Both Flint Rhem and Jesse Haines shut down Boston on five hits. In the first game Rhem gave up a single run, winning 3–1. In the rubber game Haines locked up in a duel with Johnny Wertz. Through seven innings neither team had scored. In the eighth, after Bottomley and Douthit singled, Bob O'Farrell doubled them both in. The tallies were enough for Haines. The only real scare for Hornsby came in the fifth when first baseman Bottomley chased a foul ball into a concrete dugout wall and was knocked out. Revived after a few minutes, three innings later "Sunny Jim" scored the winning run.

Aside from the four straight losses to the Giants, the trip had been a success. The Cardinals won 11 while dropping six. If the team could maintain that pace they would certainly remain a major factor in the pennant race. When they left home they were in third place. They returned in second, two games back of the Pirates. During the upcoming home stand, their last of the season, the Cardinals would play every team in the league except Cincinnati. The last five games would be against the Pirates.

The Cardinals headed back to St. Louis in two shifts. Several of the starters went directly home. The rest of the squad stopped in Erie, PA, to play an exhibition game. Hornsby was no fan of exhibition games during the season, especially with his team in the middle of a pennant race. However, to generate much-needed cash Branch Rickey and owner Sam Breadon, like most other owners, scheduled a number of exhibitions during the last two months of the season. Initially Hornsby grumbled about the plans but as the pennant race tightened he became more strident, demanding that the games be cancelled. Breadon agreed to consider the request but ultimately chose to play the games. Success had made the team a hot commodity and the potential revenues were too fat for Breadon to pass up.

The decision infuriated Hornsby, who saw it as a burden to his players and a challenge to his authority. A month later in early September, amidst growing tension between Hornsby and the Breadon/Rickey management team, Breadon uncharacteristically came into the Cardinals dugout to reinforce his decision to play a pair of exhibition games. With his team preparing to leave on its final trip of the season, he informed his players that the exhibition games were still on. The team would stop in Syracuse and Buffalo on their way to Boston. Hornsby was livid. Years later he claimed that Breadon and Rickey almost cost the Cardinals the pennant because they wanted to make a few extra dollars playing exhibition games. In open defiance, he again split his squad. This time he and his starters went to New York and watched the Yankees play the Red Sox. Meanwhile, the rest of the squad played the exhibition games. Of course, without the team's marquee players gate receipts were much smaller than expected and the windfall that Breaden and Rickey anticipated was lost.[3]

The Cardinals opened their last home stand of the season with three games against the Cubs. For much of the season Chicago had played surprisingly well. Many attributed the team's success to their new manager, Joe McCarthy, a low-keyed student of the game. However, by the time his team arrived in St. Louis it was tied for fourth place with the Giants and slowly falling out of contention for the pennant. A sweep of the Cardinals would at least temporarily revive Chicago's hopes.

The series started badly for the Cardinals. Staked to a two-run lead, "Old Pete" Alexander gave up two runs in the sixth and then committed a costly error in the seventh which allowed another run to score. Meanwhile his mates were unable to do any more damage and St. Louis lost 3–2. The next day the Cardinals evened the score with a 7–2 victory. On the mound Flint Rhem was at his best. In the field the Cardinals were flawless, making several outstanding plays including a couple of acrobatic stops by Thevenow. At the plate Jim Bottomley led the way with three hits including a triple and home run. He also scored three times. "Sunny" Jim came through again the following day. With score tied at four in the bottom of the ninth, the Cardinals had two men on base and Hornsby at the plate. Playing the percentages, Manager McCarthy instructed his pitcher, a southpaw, to walk Hornsby thus loading the bases, and pitch to left-handed hitting Bottomley. "Sunny" Jim lined the first pitch he saw into right field, driving in the winning run. The win pulled the Cardinals to just 1½ games back of the Pirates.

Bottomley's game-winner was yet another example of his late-season resurgence. Before the season started, many expected that Hornsby and Bottomley would be the most potent 3–4 hitting combination in the league. During his first three full seasons as the Cardinals first baseman, "Sunny" Jim had driven in 333 runs, including 128 in 1925, and carried a .350 lifetime batting average. However, in 1926 he got of to a slow start. His batting average in mid–May dipped to .231 and his power production lagged as well. During the next four weeks he slowly but steadily climbed out of his slump, and by mid–August was back up over the .290 mark. Just as importantly, he was again banging in runs the way he had during the previous three seasons. With Hornsby healed and Bottomley out of his slump the Cardinals attack was as lethal as any in the National League.

The path to the Cardinals had been a relatively short one for Bottomley. The son of an Illinois coal miner, he had briefly joined his father in the mines. After a younger brother died in a mine accident Jim traded his pick and shovel for a bat and ball. In 1919, Bottomley's high school principal pestered Branch Rickey to take a look at the school's baseball star. Rickey eventually obliged. Though Bottomley stumbled through his tryout in a pair of floppy, oversized baseball spikes, he nevertheless impressed Rickey enough to be offered a contract. The long, lanky kid with oversized shoes proved to be both graceful in the field and powerful at the plate. During his first two years as a professional, the young slugger had varying success on four minor league clubs. Late in the 1922 season Rickey decided to bring him up to the Cardinals. One of the first products of Rickey's innovative farm system, Bottomley lived up to all expectations. By the beginning of the following season he was entrenched as the Cardinals starting first baseman. That season he hit a career-high .371and drove in 94 runs for the fifth-place Cardinals. During the next two seasons he continued driving in runs and also established himself as one of the best fielding first basemen in all of baseball. When the 1926 season started there was little doubt that Bottomley would be a key to the Cardinals' success.[4]

By 1926 "Sunny" Jim Bottomley had become one of the most feared RBI men in the National League. Though he started slowly, by mid-season he had regained his batting eye and was living up to manager Hornsby's expectations.

Though he was a fierce competitor Bottomley had an easy-going personality. His perpetual smile earned him the sobriquet "Sunny Jim." Teammates as well as opposing players considered him one of the most genial players in the game. In addition to his cheery countenance, his trademark was the way he wore the brim of his cap down a bit and pushed back over his left eye. He was also a quiet leader whom younger teammates looked to for support. Les Bell claimed that after a particularly bad game early in his career, Bottomley put his arm around Bell's shoulder, told him to forget the game and gently assured him that better days would follow.[5] The quiet counseling worked for Bell.

Brooklyn followed the Cubs into Sportsman's Park for three games. On the mound for the Cardinals in the first game was Robins-killer Willie Sherdel. Only once in six tries had the Robins been able to get to Sherdel, but even on that occasion the Cardinals won the game. On the other hand, Sherdel had twice shut out the Robins and twice had allowed them only two runs. This time, however, "Wee Willie" was out of magic. The Robins jumped on him for a run in the second and three more in the third. Fortunately, Cardinals hitters plated three of their own. Down by just a run in the third, Hornsby had seen enough of his lefty and brought in Herman Bell to relieve. The change did little to stop the Robins. By the sixth they had scored three more times. However in the seventh the Cardinals launched a comeback. Stringing together three singles and a double, they scored a pair of runs and had runners on first and second with two outs when Billy Southworth came to the plate. Southworth had already homered but the Robins chose to pitch to him rather than face Hornsby with the bases loaded. It proved to be a bad choice. Swinging at the first pitch, Southworth belted a shot over the right field pavilion and out onto Grant Street. Now up by a run, Hornsby called in Alexander to hold the Robins. Once again the veteran hurler did what he was asked to do and the Cardinals picked up yet another half-game on the idle Pirates.

The Cardinals easily stretched their streak to nine over the Robins the next two days. In the second game St. Louis built up a quick four-run lead, then held it to beat Brooklyn 6–2. Having pitched little more than two innings in the first game, Sherdel was tabbed by Hornsby to close the series. This time "Wee Willie" was back in control of the visitors. Scattering eight hits, he gave up only two runs. In the field his teammates' sloppy play accounted for both of the runs, but at the plate the Cardinals lashed out 14 hits and scored six times. The win, the Cardinals' fifth in a row, pushed them into a virtual tie for first place with the Pirates, who had split a doubleheader with Philadelphia.

By the time the Giants got to St. Louis a palpable excitement about the Cardinals' recent success filled the city. For the first time in club history, the Cardinals stood atop the National League at such a late date in the season. Banners and signs were beginning to appear throughout the city. Street corner conversations more and more turned to the fate of the team. Pennant fever was beginning to infect the city. Of course just two weeks earlier the Giants had embarrassed the Cardinals in New York. Another drubbing would no doubt cost the Cards their lofty standing and, with the Reds rebounding from their two-week slide, three losses to the Giants could easily sink Hornsby and company back into third place.

The series started with 15-game winner Flint Rhem on the mound for the Cardinals. Through the first three innings he easily sliced through the visitors, but in the fourth New York got to him for four hits and two runs. In the bottom of the inning the Cards retaliated. Southworth led off with a single to center. Hornsby followed with a bloop single to center and when

Southworth tried to leg it out to third Heinie Mueller threw the ball into the Cardinals dugout, allowing Southworth to score and Hornsby to take third. Bottomley then popped out and Bell grounded to second baseman Frankie Frisch, who caught Hornsby at the plate. Three straight singles by Douthit, O'Farrell and Thevenow drove in two more runs, giving the Cards a 3–2 lead. It was all Rhem needed. Through the last five innings he shut out the Giants while his mates added three more markers. The win pushed St. Louis half a game ahead of the Pirates, who had the day off.

Though no one suspected it at the time, the game had far-reaching implications and became the nexus of an off-season blockbuster trade between the two teams. After the loss, Giants manager McGraw was livid at his team's sloppy play. His particular target was team captain Frankie Frisch. Though Frisch had a couple of hits and made several nice plays in the field, he missed a McGraw signal in the seventh that cost his team a run. After the game, in front of the team, McGraw ripped into their captain. The tirade was more than Frisch would tolerate. That night he packed his bag, bought a train ticket back to New York and left the team, promising never to play for McGraw again. The manager retaliated, fining Frisch $500 and again lambasting him, this time in front of the press. Finally, after sitting out for more than a week, Frisch rejoined the team, but his days with the Giants were numbered. By the start of the 1927 season he would be wearing a Cardinals uniform.

Cardinals pitching and defense dominated the last two games with the Giants. The second game was played in front of 25,000 raucous Cardinals fans, and Alexander the Great was at his best. Holding New York to just five hits and one run, he twice escaped trouble on outstanding, run-saving plays. In the third, with runners on second and third and one out, left fielder Wattie Holm, who was substituting for Ray Blades, made a running shoestring catch, then doubled the Giants runner off second to end the inning. Five innings later a diving Les Bell speared a line shot just inside the foul line, then, still on his knees, rifled a throw to first to double up the runner. Bell also delivered the Cardinals' big hit of the day as well. In the second, with a runner on first, he lashed out a triple and then scored what proved to be the winning run on an O'Farrell single. The Cardinals won their eighth straight and 16th out of 18 tries in the final game. This time, in front of 26,000 cheering supporters, it was Jesse Haines who tamed the Giants on five hits. Again solid defensive play and timely hitting combined for 4–2 win. The wins enabled the Cardinals to end the week still half a game ahead of the Pirates.

Three games each with the league's two cellar dwellers, the Phillies and Braves, were next on the surging Cardinals schedule. Most expected Hornsby and company to throttle both teams easily. Neither of the visitors, however, was ready to give up without a battle. All three games against the Braves were settled by a single run, twice in favor of the Cardinals and one that went to the Braves. The Phillies were even tougher, taking two of the three. The three losses dropped the Cardinals into third place a game back of both the Pirates and the red hot Reds, who had won 13 out of their last 14.

With the worst two teams in the National League gone, the Cardinals geared up for five games that their fans had been anticipating for weeks. In what local sports writers dubbed "the little world series," the world champion and league leading Pittsburgh Pirates came to St. Louis for the Cardinals' last home series and perhaps the most important series the team would play all season. By the time that the Pirates arrived not only was the city in a baseball frenzy, but so too was much of the Midwest. Locals camped out overnight, hoping to get bleacher seats. Scalpers hawked tickets for more than ten times their original price. Boosters from as far away as St. Paul, Minnesota, paraded into the city to watch a game or two. Thousands packed onto trains headed for St. Louis. One group of 300 from Omaha, Nebraska, rode a train all night to get to St. Louis in time for the opening game. Various civic organizations scheduled to meet in other cities during the series, like the Knights of Columbus of Missouri, which had planned their annual gathering for Kansas City, moved their meetings to St. Louis. Meanwhile merchants in St. Louis tried to entice new business by promising tickets to a game. One enterprise, The Merchant's Exchange, a local grain broker, provided more than 1200 customers with tickets but was unable to fill another 200 requests.[6]

Pittsburgh arrived racked by internal divisions. Two weeks earlier, team captain Max Carey, outfielder Carson "Skeeter" Bigbee and pitcher Babe Adams had been waived by manager Bill McKechnie for insubordination. Carey and company were accused of leading a player revolt against club vice president and assistant manager Fred Clarke. A former Pirates outfielder and manager, Clarke had a long-time friendship with Pirates owner Barney Dreyfuss. As a manager Clarke had led the team to four pennants and a world championship. As a manager, he demanded absolute discipline from his players. Those players who challenged his authority were labeled disruptive and a threat to team unity. Despite Dreyfuss's pleas, Clarke retired from baseball in 1915 to pursue various business ventures and spend more time with his family. Ten years later, with the Pirates fighting for a championship, Dreyfuss convinced his friend and former manager, now a successful entrepreneur, to return to the Pirates bench and instill the combative spirit that the Pirates would need to win the pennant. After the team won the 1925 World Series, Dreyfuss credited Clarke with transforming the club into the world champion team it had become.[7]

Despite the team's success the previous year many Pirates players resented Clarke's methods. Through the first four months of the 1926 season relations between Clarke and Pirates players smoldered. The tensions finally came to a head on August 7. Between games of a doubleheader with the Braves, Clarke moaned that "Max (Carey) is having a hard time of it." He advised McKechnie that someone else should play center field in the second game. When McKechnie said he had no other outfielders, Clarke sharply replied, "Put someone out there even if it is a pitcher."[8] After the game Carey heard about Clarke's remarks and as team captain called a secret meeting. Carey wanted Clarke banned from the team's dugout bench. Though only six players endorsed the idea, Carey, Bigbee and Adams confronted McKechnie with the proposal.

Rather than try to mediate the problems, McKechnie reported the demands to Clarke. A day later, probably on orders from Clarke, the three players were waived. For Bigbee and Adams it was the end of their major league careers. Future Hall of Famer, Carey, on the other hand, was quickly claimed by Brooklyn and within the week was prowling center field for the Robins. Carey's departure did not sit well with Pirates fans. He was the team's leadoff hitter, superb defensively and a favorite in Pittsburgh. Carey was also a team leader both on and off the field. So angry were Pirates supporters that throughout the home stand fans booed the team even though they were in first place.

The first game between the Cardinals and the Pirates was a classic. In front of more than 36,000 delirious fans, the second largest crowd in St. Louis history, the home team started strong. In the first inning Les Bell looped a two-run double into right field. Boisterous Cardinals supporters demonstrated their joy by launching a shower of straw hats onto the field. Half an inning later a torrential downpour halted the game for more than two hours. The rain came so hard and so quickly that the grounds crew was unable to cover the field completely. When play resumed the infield was a sloppy mess but the umpires deemed it playable. After another scoreless inning the rains came again, this time delaying the game for almost an hour. Just an inning short of an official game and up by two runs, the Cardinals anxiously continued play despite deteriorating field conditions. Through the first four innings Alexander tamed the Pirates bats, but in the fifth Pittsburgh evened the score at two. During the next four innings both teams threatened to take the lead but each time the defense stepped up to the challenge. Twice the Cardinals were denied the go-ahead run by center fielder Kiki Cuyler's perfect throws, and twice Paul Waner made game-saving catches. The Pirates were also thwarted by defensive gems. In the eighth with two men on, Cardinals left fielder Wattie Holm made a fingertip catch that robbed Pie Traynor of an extra-base hit. An inning later the Pirates again put the go-ahead runner on second base with just one out and the heart of their order coming to the plate. This time Alexander struck out Cuyler and got Traynor on a feeble ground out. Finally, after ten innings, almost five hours since the game had begun and with darkness descending, the umpires stopped play for the day. The game was declared a tie, which meant that the two teams would have to play back-to-back doubleheaders the next two days.

The first of the twin bills was dominated by pitching. In front of almost 30,000 rabid Redbird fans, the largest weekday crowd in National League history, the Pirates opened with a quick first-inning run. That was all their ace, Ray Kremer, needed. Pitching his best game of the season, he blanked the home team on just two singles. In the second game the Cardinals evened the ledger. Down by a run in the first, the Cards' leadoff hitter, Taylor Douthit, opened with a double and came home four batters later when Les Bell slashed one off pitcher Joe Bush's glove. The score stayed knotted until the fifth, when Cardinals hitters combined three singles with a crucial Pirates error to score three times. Les Bell's eighth-inning home run provided a bit more cushion. Meanwhile veteran hurler Jesse Haines time and again maneuvered through the visitors' lineup, holding them to three runs on seven hits.

Another packed, raucous crowd came to root for the Cardinals in the second doubleheader. More than 23,000 loyal fans watched Willie Sherdel masterfully cut through Pirates hitters. The little lefty was at his best, giving up just one run and seven hits. At the plate his teammates staked him to an early four-run lead, scoring once in the second and three times in the third. The big blow was a two-run homer by Les Bell.

In the second game manager Hornsby played a hunch. In a surprise move, he called on pitcher Allan Sothoron to make a rare start. A spitball pitcher who relied on deception and guile, Sothoron won 20 games for the Browns in 1919. However, since then he had bounced around with several teams, never again coming close to the 20-win mark. By 1926 his days as a major league pitcher were numbered. Early in the season, with the Cardinals' front-line pitchers ailing, Hornsby had given him a couple of starts. The experiment failed. On each occasion he was knocked out of the game early. The Cardinals manager had also dangled Sothoron on the waiver wire but instead pulled him back (perhaps because there were no takers) for spot relief work.

After watching Sherdel weave his assortment of off-speed pitches and breaking balls past Pirates hitters, Hornsby decided to start Sothoron in the nightcap. Initially it looked as if the Cardinals manager had made a bad bet. With leadoff hitter Paul Waner on first, Sothoron struggled with the number two hitter, Hal Rhyne. On the verge of walking Rhyne, Sothoron fought back, striking him out, and on the third strike O'Farrell threw out Waner trying to steal second. Sothoron then got Traynor on a fly ball. The next eight innings belonged to the Cardinals' journeyman pitcher. With the fans roaring on every pitch, Sothoron, like Sherdel in the first game, baffled Pirates hitters the rest of the afternoon, surrendering a single unearned run in the fourth and just three hits. Nevertheless, despite the brilliant performance the Cardinals were down a run through the sixth and it looked as if Sothoron might be saddled with another loss. Then in the seventh his mates scratched out two runs on three seeing-eye singles. It was all that was needed. In front of 23,000 delirious fans, Sothoron finished off the day's sweep. Adding to the celebration, the wins, coupled with a Cincinnati loss in Chicago, propelled St. Louis back into first place a half-game ahead of the Reds and a full game over the Pirates.

The Cardinals' last home game of the season was played on a sunny, early September afternoon. Another 20,000 crazed Cardinals devotees crowded into Sportsman's Park, bringing the four-day total to more than 110,000, easily a St. Louis record. The Pirates, desperate to salvage a win, put Ray Kremer back on the mound with only two days' rest. Manager McKechnie hoped that his ace could duplicate his two-hit win despite the short rest. For five innings it looked as if he might. Although the Cardinals hit Kremer better than they had the first time around, they were unable to score any runs. Then, down by a run in the sixth, they finally broke through. Amidst cow bells clanging and horns blaring in the stands, Bell laced a single to left field. Hafey walked and O'Farrell lined a pitch over second to score Bell. After Thevenow popped out, Cardinals pitcher Art Reinhart tapped a ball to the Pirates' second baseman that was misplayed, allowing Hafey to score the go-ahead run. An inning later the Cardinals added three more to their lead on two singles, a double and a towering Hornsby home run. The Pirates tallied once more in the ninth but never threatened the lead.

The win closed out an extremely successful Cardinals home stand. Since returning to St. Louis the club had won 15 of 20, including sweeps against Brooklyn and the Giants. The four straight over the Pirates established the Cardinals as the team to beat in the pennant race. During the three weeks, the team had played all phases of the game like champions. Hornsby was finally back in shape, Bottomley, who had struggled with leg problems, was again completely healthy, and the pitching staff, with the exception of Vic Keen, was throwing better than it had all season. The Cardinals left home a game up on the Reds and two ahead of the Pirates. Of course, the challenge for Hornsby and company would be to maintain their momentum during the next four weeks on the road. It would be a tall order.

With their July stay at home ended, the Yankees climbed onto a west-bound train for a 25-hour ride to St. Louis. Along the way Babe Ruth strayed into yet another misadventure. About halfway into the journey the Babe, who had been unable to bathe prior to the team's departure, quietly confiscated a trainer's tub, filled it with water and, as the train passed through Terre Haute, Indiana, he took a bath. When several team members discovered him suds up and soaking they were appalled. Coach Fred Merkle snarled, "the big bimbo is turning out to be a terrible mug." By indulging in a luxury that none of his teammates could share, "the slugger has violated one of the cardinal rules of baseball." Another coach, Charlie O'Leary, agreed that Ruth had insulted the entire team and seriously threatened the club's esprit de corps. For his part, Ruth acknowledged that "maybe I did pull a boner ... but I was hot and maybe the heat went to my head."[9]

The Yankees brought another traveler along with them on the western swing. Three days earlier Manager Huggins had attempted to solve his dilemma behind the plate by picking up Hank Severeid, a journeyman catcher who had been waived by the Senators the previous day. A 15-year veteran, Severeid spent most of his career with the Browns but in 1925 was traded to the Senators. With the Browns he had caught over 100 games in seven different seasons, earning him a reputation as one of the strongest and most durable backstops in the game. He also had several good offensive years with the Browns, batting over .300 five times. Though

Hank Severeid was a veteran catcher who was acquired mid-season to plug the Yankees hole behind the plate. Though he played exceptionally well during his brief stay with the Yankees, he retired immediately after the season.

he was clearly on the downhill side of his career, Severeid was still a capable catcher with an accurate arm. Huggins was confident that the acquisition had solved the team's problems behind the plate.

Huggins did not have to wait long for his investment to pay off. In the opening game against the Browns Severeid knocked out a single and two doubles, scoring two runs and driving in another in a 6–5 victory. The following day he was reunited with his old battery mate, Urban Shocker. The two had spent seven years together in St. Louis before Shocker went to New York and Severeid to Washington. There was probably no catcher who knew how to handle Shocker's spitball better than Severeid. With him once again calling the pitches, Shocker locked up in a duel with Browns hurler Ernie Wingard. Through seven innings the score stood at one run apiece. In the eighth Yankees right fielder Ben Paschal slammed a drive over the left field wall to give Shocker all the runs he needed for the win. After a sloppy 10–7 win in which the Browns committed five errors and the Yankees two, Shocker and Paschal again came through in the final game of the series. Aided by another Paschal round tripper, the Yankees were able to push the game into extra innings. In the tenth a Gehrig double broke the tie. Shocker was then called upon to put down the Browns for the win. The four-game sweep brought New York's current run to nine wins in a row and stretched the lead over Cleveland back out to nine games. With 100 games behind them (including one tie) and 55 to go, the Yankees appeared to be back on track for the American League pennant.

Intense and unemotional on the mound, Urban Shocker was the foundation of the Yankees pitching staff. Although he shared starting duties with two future Hall of Fame hurlers, Herb Pennock and Waite Hoyt, as 1926 began Shocker had 45 more career wins than Pennock and 65 more than Hoyt. He also had four 20-win seasons, three more than his two contemporaries combined. Since 1919 he had averaged 19 wins a season, again far more than either Pennock or Hoyt. Additionally, most of his wins had come while he was toiling for the also-ran St. Louis Browns. When opposing teams in 1926 looked at the Yankees staff it was Shocker they most feared. Had it not been for his early death from heart disease (diagnosed as "athlete's heart") two years later, Shocker might very well have joined his two teammates in Cooperstown.

Shocker broke into professional baseball in 1913 with Windsor in the Border League. Playing semi-pro ball in and around his hometown of Cleveland he had been a catcher, the position he intended to play professionally. However, the Windsor manager recognized Shocker's strong arm and accuracy and used him on the mound instead. The following year Shocker moved on to Ottawa in the Canadian League where he won 39 games during his two-year stay. Late in his second season with Ottawa, the Yankees purchased his contract and brought him to New York. Shocker began the 1916 campaign with the Yankees, though he almost ended up back in Cleveland. Before the season started the Yankees put him on waivers and the Indians quickly attempted to snap him up. New York then withdrew the waivers, much to the anger of the Indians. League president Ban Johnson, called in to mediate the dispute, ruled that Shocker was in fact still a Yankee. Splitting the 1916 season between New York and Toronto, he established himself as the International League's best pitcher.[10]

In 1917 Shocker finally landed in the major leagues for good. Used sparingly by manager Bill Donovan, the following winter he became part of a trade with the Browns, one of the few trades Miller Huggins ever regretted. In St. Louis Shocker blossomed. During his seven years with the Browns he became one of the league's best pitchers. A spitballer

A tough competitor who some considered the ace of the Yankees staff, much was expected of Urban Shocker in 1926. Sadly his life would come to a tragic end two years later.

with a nasty curve and pinpoint accuracy, Shocker, attributed much of his mound success to an injury during his time as a catcher. One day while behind the plate he broke the ring finger on his throwing hand. The finger healed crooked and "hooks over a baseball just right so that I can get a fine break on my slow ball.... I can get a slow ball to drop just like a spitter." He also carefully studied hitters, using information — from box scores to scouting reports and observation — to devise a strategy for each batter he faced. He claimed that "you can very often tell what is in a batter's mind by the way he shifts his feet or hitches his belt or wiggles his bat."[11]

In 1925 Huggins got an opportunity to make up for his earlier mistake. Shocker got into a nasty argument with Browns owner Phil Ball. During the team's final road trip the previous year Shocker had asked to take his wife along on the trip. Since other wives had been taken on other trips, Shocker thought it a reasonable request. When he was denied permission, he took her anyway. Immediately Ball fined him $1000. Angry, the pitcher hired a lawyer and appealed the fine to baseball Commissioner Landis. Ultimately the Commissioner, in consultation with league president Ban Johnson, ruled against Shocker, claiming that the club had a right to enforce its own rules. The episode soured relations between the pitcher and the Browns. Feeling personally challenged, Ball put his star pitcher on the trading block. Huggins quickly responded, offering the Browns three players, including "Bullet" Joe Bush. By the start of the 1925 season the deal was done, and Urban Shocker was again a Yankee. Although Shocker's first year back in New York was the worst of his career, Huggins knew his potential and was happy to have him back. In 1926 the Yankees manager counted on Shocker to win games.[12]

Bad weather stamped the Yankees' first two games in Chicago. In the opener a blustery wind blowing in off Lake Michigan made scoring runs particularly difficult. The home team struck first with a tally in the second. Two innings later the Yankees evened the count. In the fourth a sensational leaping catch by Earle Combs up against the right-center field fence helped to keep the score knotted. The Yankees broke the tie in the eighth when Babe Ruth walloped his 33rd home run through the wind and into the center field bleachers. An inning later the White Sox mounted a final threat when the first three hitters reached base. Having dodged disaster all afternoon, Yankees pitcher "Sad Sam" Jones reached back one more time. A force out at the plate and two strikeouts later, Jones had his win and New York's streak was at ten. A light rain, more wind and dark clouds marked the second game. However, despite the conditions, the Yankees had few problems with the White Sox. In a workmanlike effort Herb Pennock notched his 17th victory and Yankees hitters doubled the Chicago run output, winning 8–4.

Red Faber ended the Yankees streak at 11 the following afternoon. Locked in a duel with Urban Shocker, Faber deftly twirled the ball past Yankees hitters inning after inning. Only a tally in the fourth marred his effort. Meanwhile Shocker matched the White Sox hurler pitch for pitch. He too ran into a bit of trouble in the fourth but for Shocker the damage cost two runs. In the end Chicago's fourth-inning runs were enough. After losing seven straight to the New Yorkers, Chicago finally beat them 2–1.

The final game of the series was a thriller. Chicago opened the scoring with runs in the first and second innings. In the fourth Ruth lashed a single to right that drove in the Yankees' first run. Ben Paschall followed with a double to plate Ruth. Lazzeri then closed the inning with his 14th home run of the season, a two-run shot that gave the Yankees a two-run lead. The White Sox got the lead back an inning later on three singles and a sacrifice fly. Again down by two, New York fought back in the seventh. With a runner on second Combs knocked out his fourth hit of the day, driving in a run. Koenig followed with a double off the top of the left field fence to once again tie the game. The Yankees scored the winning run in the ninth. Combs collected his fifth hit and one out later scored on Gehrig's triple. Having taken three of the four in Chicago, the Yankees eagerly headed to Cleveland for three games with the second-place Indians.

By the time that the Yankees arrived in Cleveland their league lead had again swelled to ten games over the second-place Indians. Not since the 1923 Yankees did a team have as big a lead entering August. With New York playing as well as it had during the previous two weeks, some were already conceding the pennant to the Yankees. Team business manager Ed Barrow reported that by August 10 he had already received more than 1,000 World Series ticket requests. His boss, owner Jake Ruppert, was more cautious, warning that "accidents may happen ... wait until our boys are under the wire."[13] Miller Huggins agreed with Ruppert but admitted that his team was playing like a championship club. His front-line pitchers were at top form and several backups like Sam Jones and Dutch Ruether had been pitching unexpectedly well in recent weeks. At the plate Ruth was popping home runs again. Hank Severeid had plugged the hole behind the plate, and the team anxiously awaited the return of slugger Bob Meusel in a week or two though his replacement, Ben Paschal, had filled in exceptionally well. While Huggins was not ready to look too far into the future, his April prediction that the Yankees would win the pennant seemed safer almost every day.

Tris Speaker and his crew were not among those ready to crown the Yankees champions. The Indians still had 11 games to play against New York, including a six-game series in late September. With a few breaks along the way, Speaker was confident that his team could catch the front runner.

One reason for Speaker's confidence was pitcher George Uhle, who was having the best season in his career. He had already beaten the Yankees three times, giving up a total of just six runs. Speaker tabbed Uhle to open the current series. The Cleveland ace got off to a shaky start. Struggling with his control, he walked three and gave up five hits in the first three innings. In the second, after two runs had already scored, he dodged a disaster by striking out Ruth with the bases loaded. Surviving into the fourth, Uhle settled down, giving up just two more hits during the last six innings. Meanwhile his counterpart, Waite Hoyt, also started slowly. He walked the leadoff hitter, gave up a double to the second hitter and then watched both score on a single by Speaker. Back-to-back errors to the next two hitters loaded the bases. Down by two runs with the bases loaded and no one out, Hoyt seemed destined for a short afternoon. However, he was rescued by a line drive double play and was able to get out of the inning with no more damage done. A crucial Yankees error in the fourth led to another pair of Indians runs. From that point on Hoyt pitched well but not as well as Uhle, who won his fourth in a row against the Yankees.

The Yankees made up for their first-game problems during the next two days. Powered by Babe Ruth's 34th home run, the Yankees drubbed the Indians 8–2 the day after Uhle's win. Highlighting a first-inning barrage, Ruth's blast landed on the roof of a house well beyond the right field wall. On the mound, rejuvenated "Sad" Sam Jones turned in another outstanding performance, limiting the Indians to just seven hits. The Yankees win in the final game did not come as easily. The Huggins crew jumped out to a two-run lead in the first and then pushed it to four before the Indians began chipping away. By the ninth Cleveland had narrowed the lead to a single run and had the tying run on second base. Called on to relieve, Waite Hoyt struck out pinch hitter Pat McNulty, saving the day for his mates. The one-run margin came as a result of Babe Ruth's fifth-inning, bases-empty home run. Another mammoth shot, this time the ball hit a telephone pole just in front of the roof that he had hit the day before. The win added another game to the Yankees' league lead, stretching it to 11 games.

The trip to Detroit included a bit of peril for Babe Ruth. Three days after arriving in the Motor City he was scheduled to appear in the Brighton, Michigan court to answer for his fishing violation earlier in the summer. Rumors swirled that the court might require him to spend a day or two in jail. Certainly an excessive consequence should it happen, but there were some who thought the fix was in and that the local court would keep Ruth out of the lineup for the last two games of the series. Fortunately for the Yankees Ruth appeared in court as scheduled, paid a $15 fine and celebrated by hitting a game-winning home run.

Since the last time they had seen the Yankees, the Tigers had fallen to seventh place and completely out of pennant contention. While the offense, led by Harry Heilmann and Heinie Manush, was still potent, the pitching staff was struggling. During the previous three weeks Tigers pitchers had given up an average of almost 7.5 runs per game. Ty Cobb was also struggling. He was no longer playing regularly and in fact would appear only once as a pinch hitter in the four games against the Yankees. There were also reports that his six-year tenure as the Tigers' field general was about over which probably meant that his 21 years in Detroit would also soon end. However, despite Detroit's problems the rivalry between the Tigers and the Yankees guaranteed that the four games would be hard-fought contests.

The Tigers played as expected, bouncing their visitors three times in the next four days. During the first two games the Yankees' only lead came on a Mark Koenig three-run homer in the second inning of the opener.

Aided by sloppy Yankees infield play, Detroit tied the game two innings later and pushed across the winning runs in the seventh. The second game turned into a nightmare for the Yankees. Their old nemesis Earl Whitehill was on the mound and at his best. Striking out 12, his only mistake was a two-run shot by Ben Paschal. Meanwhile, the Yankees in the field were even less effective than they were at the plate. In all the team committed five errors, a season high, which the Tigers used to score half of their eight runs. Frustrated and ineffective, Waite Hoyt struggled through only four innings, yielding six runs.

Babe Ruth won the third game for his mates. On the same day that he appeared before the Brighton Police Court, his three-run homer in the seventh enabled New York to squeak out a narrow 9–8 win. For the Yankees the game started much as the previous day's game had ended. The Tigers jumped out to a two-run lead in the first inning but the Yankees began chipping away in the second. Scoring another run in the third, one in the fourth and three more in the fifth, the Yankees appeared in control of the game. Ruth's 36th home run of the season pushed his team out to what appeared to be an insurmountable six-run lead. However, the Tigers refused to concede. They scored once in the seventh and then in the ninth, with two outs and no one on base, they launched a rally. The assault started when shortstop Koenig muffed a routine popup that would have ended the game. Four batters later, with the tying run on first base, the Yankees' third pitcher in the inning, Bob Shawkey, finally got the last out.

The Yankees travel schedule may have cost them the final game against the Tigers. Down 3–2 in the seventh inning, Detroit jumped on relief pitcher Shawkey for three runs. The key blow was a run-scoring single up the middle by Ty Cobb, his only plate appearance during the series. Once the inning was over, a decision was made to call the game so that the Yankees could catch a train to Washington, where they were scheduled to play a double-header the following day. Immediately whisked off in cabs, the team spent the next 15 hours rushing east. They arrived just before dawn and slumped off to catch a few hours of sleep.

It was a weary crew of Yankees that took the field for the twin bill against the Senators. Oppressively hot and humid weather, conditions that typify late summer in the nation's capital, only added to the team's fatigue. Despite it all the Yankees got off to a fast start, scoring three times in the second. However, by the sixth circumstances began to catch up with the visitors. Starter Pennock, who was completely drained by the heat, failed to make it through the sixth. In the same inning Babe Ruth was struck by leg cramps while chasing a fly ball. The ball fell in for a single that pushed in the tying run. An inning later the Senators scored the winning run when a ball down the third base line got past an exhausted Joe Dugan. The second game began almost three hours after the day's first pitch. Again the Yankees jumped out in front with two first-inning markers, and again the Senators caught them quickly, this time with four in the third. Holding the Senators in check, the Yankees scored again in the seventh on Ruth's 37th home run. In the ninth Tony Lazzeri led off with a single and three batters later scampered in with the tying run. The long afternoon ended ingloriously for the Yankees in the 11th with Ruth hobbling after a ball to deep right center that became an inside-the-park home run.

For Waite Hoyt the afternoon included additional frustration. Called upon to start the second game, he was lifted after surrendering four runs in the third. Angered by his manager's decision, Hoyt, when asked to hand over the ball, instead fired it into the backstop and stomped off the field. Huggins punished the pitcher with a $200 fine. Two days later the recalcitrant hurler redeemed himself. After dropping a third game to the Senators, New York's fourth loss in a row, the Yankees ended their long road trip facing Walter Johnson. Originally Huggins had planned to start someone else but instead gave Hoyt the assignment. Battling through another oppressively hot and humid afternoon, the Yankees pitcher, assisted by two Gehrig home runs, ended Washington's run with a 7–5 victory.

Heading back home after almost three weeks on the road, Miller Huggins was satisfied with the results of the trip. His only concern was his pitching staff. Hoyt had been inconsistent and Shocker seemed to be drained by the August heat. On the other hand, veteran Sam Jones, who had lost 21 games the previous year, won four of the road games. At the plate Huggins's "Murderer's Row" was living up to its name. Along with Ruth, whose 38 home runs easily led the majors, Lazzeri and Gehrig were also among the league leaders. Additionally, the team's .300 batting average was ten points better than any team in either league. Bob Meusel's imminent return to the lineup would add even more punch to the powerful Yankees attack. Although the recent trip ended with a string of losses, on the whole Huggins considered it a success. When his team left New York it was nine games ahead of the Indians. When the team returned it still had an 8½-game lead. With 40 games left in the season, if the Yankees played just .500 baseball the Indians would have to win 28 of their remaining 39 games.[14]

More than 40,000 fans trooped into Yankee Stadium to greet their team back home. On deck was a pair of doubleheaders, the first against the Senators and one the following day against the Red Sox. In both, New York remained true to recent form. In the first game against the Senators, Sam Jones had another outstanding performance, limiting the visitors to just six hits and two runs. Meanwhile Ruth and Gehrig each hammered a home run, leading their mates to a 4–2 win. The second game had a much different outcome. Once again Urban Shocker was unable to complete what he started. This time he gave up five runs in less than two innings. The two relievers who followed didn't do much better, giving up five more runs. Yankees bats kept the game close for a couple of innings but by the end of the day the Senators had pulled away to a comfortable 10–5 win.

In front of another 40,000 fans the next afternoon, the hot and cold Yankees continued their inconsistent play. This time in the opener Herb Pennock throttled the Red Sox on six hits, giving up just two runs. At the plate Ruth again led the way, drilling another home run, his 39th, and scoring three of the Yankees' four runs. The second game went better than the previous day but the end result was the same. Pitcher Myles Thomas lasted five innings before falling apart. His relief man gave up one more tally over the final four innings. This time Yankees hitters, with the exception of Ruth who had three hits, could only push three runs across the plate, losing the game 5–3.

The same day that the Yankees split their doubleheader with the Red Sox, one of America's leading movie stars, Rudolph Valentino, was rushed to Polyclinic Hospital in the Lower East Side for an emergency operation. Valentino was in New York for the opening of his new film "Son of the Sheik," the sequel to "The Sheik" which five years earlier had established him as America's first male sex star. For several months the actor had been suffering from stomach pains but refused to see a doctor. On Sunday morning the 15th, while leaving his suite at the Ambassador Hotel, he collapsed. That afternoon doctors successfully operated on a gastric ulcer and removed his appendix. By all accounts the two surgeries went well and Valentino was expected to make a full recovery.

For five days reports from the hospital remained encouraging. The movie star's three doctors agreed that Valentino, despite some discomfort, was improving as expected and should be released within a few days. They were so confident that they discontinued issuing updates on their patient's status. Meanwhile Valentino spent his time reading some of the thousands of telegrams, notes and letters sent to him by his many fans. Then, six days after the operations, Valentino's condition took a serious turn for the worse. After two hours of consultation his doctors announced that their patient had developed pleurisy and fluid was dangerously collecting in his lungs. By the next day the film star, described as "a very, very sick man," was fighting for his life. Manning an around-the-clock bedside vigil, his doctors watched helplessly as their patient steadily deteriorated. A day later, August 23, Valentino died.

Almost as soon as the film star's body was moved to Campbell's Funeral

Home at 69th and Broadway, distraught fans began to gather. The morning after Valentino's death hundreds tried to push their way into the funeral home to get a quick glimpse of the body. By noon the throng had grown to 10,000, and during the next couple of hours it ballooned to more than 30,000, stretching three blocks, spilling out onto Broadway and blocking traffic. At 2 P.M., when the funeral home doors were finally opened for a viewing, "the crowd rushed forward bowling the police aside and threatening ... to wreck the inside of Campbell's place."[15] As the numbers swelled, police were called in to maintain order but were quickly overwhelmed. Pushing and shoving escalated into a small riot. Frenzied fans, many of them women using umbrellas, hats, walking sticks, and whatever they could get into their hands, tried to jostle their way into the funeral home and past Valentino's body. Time and time again the police charged into the crowd to restore order but with minimal success. Throughout the afternoon the melee continued. During one police surge, the mob countered, pushing the police into two of the funeral home's plate glass windows, shattering them both. By early evening a makeshift emergency room had been set up to treat the more than 100 who were injured. The skirmish continued until midnight when the funeral home, assisted by the police, finally closed its doors.

When the funeral parlor opened the next morning, a crowd estimated at 10,000 awaited. This time, however, the police were more prepared. A force of 150, including 20 mounted officers, was assigned to direct the mourners. During the night, barricades snaking through three blocks were set up to channel the crowd past the body. Nevertheless, constant scuffling marked the crowd as it grew to more than 75,000. As mourners shuffled through the funeral parlor, some grabbed onto whatever memento they could carry out. A few even tried to get buttons and threads off of Valentino's suit coat. Another ominous element further threatened to disrupt the delicate order. Amidst the previous day's fracas, ten black-shirted members of the Fascisti League of North America arrived. Claiming that Valentino was one of them and that they had been sent by Italian Premier Benito Mussolini, they posted a four-man guard around the dead star's coffin. A short time later, members from the Anti-Fascisti Alliance of North America appeared. Insisting that Valentino never supported the fascists or Mussolini, they demanded that the black shirts be removed from around the coffin. If not, they warned that an ugly confrontation loomed. Fortunately the immediate problem was solved when police escorted the fascist guards back out onto the street and refused to allow them back in. Again the day ended with a minor riot at midnight when a hundred or so were told that the funeral parlor was closing and that they would not be permitted in.

Two days of unruly mourners were as many as the funeral parlor and

Valentino's friend and business manager, S. George Ullman, would tolerate. On the third day Ullman lamented, "I am greatly disappointed at the way the men and women acted when they were allowed to see Valentino's body.... They showed the most gross irreverence."[16] He announced that during the four days remaining before the funeral, Campbell's would only allow selected friends and family to view the body. Of course the proclamation did not end efforts by some to get inside. Packs of fans continued to roam up and down the street in front of the funeral parlor, looking for an opportunity to sneak in. More than 200 police were also on hand to control the crowds and to patrol the streets and side streets in area. Finally, four days later, with a massive but subdued crowd waiting outside, a funeral mass was held for the star at St. Malachy's Roman Catholic Church on West 49th Street. Afterward the body was shipped off to Hollywood for burial.

Rudolph Valentino was part of a new category of celebrity that had been spawned by the film industry. Just 23 years earlier, *The Great Train Robbery* introduced the world to the movies. Overnight thousands of storefront nickelodeons combined short films with live vaudeville performances to draw ever larger audiences. By 1910 there were more than 9,000 nickelodeons operating throughout the United States.[17] Maneuvering around patent restrictions, small, independent companies of performers, speculators, technicians, writers and directors feverishly cranked out dozens of "shorts" to satisfy the almost insatiable demand for motion pictures. Within a decade the upstart film companies provided exciting, inexpensive entertainment for millions of Americans.

The success of full-length feature films in the mid 1910s transformed the new industry and ended the brief but significant nickelodeon era. No longer was live performance coupled with five- to ten-minute "shorts." Instead, "picture shows" were stretched to as long as three hours and told well developed stories. The viewing public thoroughly embraced the innovations. Swelling profits generated intense competition which, in turn, led to the construction of grand, luxurious movie theatres that brought an air of elegance to the viewing experience. New revenues also encouraged consolidation. After World War I various film makers merged into a handful of large movie companies, including Warner Brothers, Metro-Goldwyn-Mayer, Twentieth Century–Fox and Paramount, that were able to control theatres in major cities as well as production and talent. Feeding on the new industry's ever-growing popularity, movie makers mounted lavish productions on a majestic scale and dazzled patrons with cinematic magic. By the mid–1920s movie-goers lined up at more than 18,000 theatres throughout the nation to watch lavish productions that spared no costs.[18]

Consolidation also gave rise to the "studio system." Movie companies fiercely competed for talent that could be parlayed into ticket sales. After signing actors, actresses, writers, and directors to long-term contracts, the companies promoted their new talent to the point of iconic status. Public appearances, newspaper ads, gossip columns and stunts were used to keep the new celebrities in front of their public. Along with Charlie Chaplin, Mary Pickford, Douglas Fairbanks, Buster Keaton and a host of others, Rudolph Valentino became one the most recognizable people in America. Wherever he went during the 1920s he was followed by press and fans. As with his contemporaries, his life became an ongoing, and at times a fictionalized, saga followed by millions.[19] By 1926 Valentino and his colorful, sultry, exciting, innocent celluloid counterparts became as much a part of main street America's daily conversation as was Babe Ruth or Rogers Hornsby.

While the last chapter of the Valentino saga was being written, the Yankees were a mile away battling their American League competition. The day after splitting a doubleheader with Boston they dropped a rain-shortened makeup game with the White Sox. It started with Waite Hoyt giving up four runs in just one-third of an inning, included five Chicago stolen bases in five innings, and ended after a late-summer deluge. Yankees fans went home both soggy and disappointed. Two days later was Boys' Day, a promotion started by league president Ban Johnson. Prior to the start of the 1925 season, Johnson decreed that all eight American League teams would have a day when they admitted local youths for free. On the second Boys' Day, more than 10,000 boys crowded into the Yankee Stadium right field bleachers to watch the league-leading Yankees play the Browns. What the boys saw they liked. The home team pounded out three runs in the first inning and, aided by five St. Louis errors, cruised to an easy 10 to 4 victory. The day after Boys' Day, Herb Pennock was the story. For eight innings he and Browns pitcher Elam Vangilder were locked up in a 1–1 pitchers' duel. The duel ended in the Yankees half of the eighth. With two out and a runner on first, Bob Meusel banged out a double to left. Lazzeri followed with a single up the middle that drove both runners home. Now up by two, Pennock breezed through the ninth to collect his 20th win of the season.

The Yankees wins against the Browns pushed their league lead back to ten games. Boasting a double-digit lead, the home team began to display a bit of swagger by the time the second-place Indians arrived in town for a three-game set. With just a month left in the season it would almost take a miracle for anyone to catch them. Of course miracles had happened before. Twelve years earlier the Boston Braves were in the National League cellar, 11½ games behind the Giants, on July 15th. During the last half of the season the Braves caught fire, winning almost eight out of every ten games they played, and amazingly won the National League pennant by 10½ games. Huggins and his team no doubt remembered the 1914 Braves, but with just four weeks left to play rather than half the season they seemed to be a sure bet to win the American League pennant. One of the few to challenge that conclusion was Tris Speaker. The Cleveland manager remained confident that with a little luck his squad could still catch the leaders.

The games that followed were dominated by pitching. In the first, Urban Shocker finally returned to his early season form. Scattering seven hits, he limited the Indians to just two unearned runs. Meanwhile Yankees hitters struggled behind him. Cleveland pitcher Emil Levsen was even more effective than Shocker, giving up only five hits. Fortunately for New York three of their hits came in the fifth inning and accounted for two runs. Coupled with an unearned run the previous inning, the tallies were all Shocker needed. Rain washed out the second game, forcing a doubleheader the following day. The twin bill started well for the Indians. Under a steady drizzle, Yankees nemesis George Uhle was at his best, easily mowing down hitters all afternoon. His counterpart, Sam Jones, looked almost as effective until the eighth inning, when the Indians, already up by a run, strung together five hits with a walk and a Yankees error. The combination accounted for a five-run cushion that guaranteed Uhle his fifth win of the season over the Yankees. With rain falling throughout the game, the field had become a quagmire by the late innings. Several players slipped in the mud while rounding bases or chasing balls. At least two of the Indians' eighth-inning runs could be attributed to the field conditions. So when the umpires called off the second game, no one questioned the decision.

The Yankees swagger continued through the last six games in the home stand. They took two of three against the Tigers, including gems by Pennock and Shocker. In a makeup game against the Senators, Yankees bats pounded Walter Johnson for 11 hits and six runs. Unfortunately Senators hitters drilled Sam Jones for eight runs in the first three innings, smoothing the way to an easy 12–6 win. The last two games were against the third-place Athletics. The A's had been a problem for New York all season and, because they were the only team other than the Indians with a realistic chance to catch the frontrunners, the two-game series was an important one. In the first game Mack's men jumped on Pennock for six early runs and knocked off the Yankees 8–6. In the second the Yankees reversed the assault, scoring six in the first three innings, then coasted to a 6–4 win and a series split.

With the season in its final weeks and a comfortable lead on the board, the Yankees and their fans began looking past the American League. While the players were still a bit wary, their faithful were less constrained. New Yorkers began wondering which National League team they would see in October and speculating about a World Series rotation. Wouldn't it be fun to see Ruth and Hornsby on the same field? Or watch the Yankees' "Murderer's Row" shred the flimsy Pirates staff? Should "Sad" Sam Jones, who recently had been surprisingly effective, start in front of Hoyt? Or maybe a three-man rotation would be best, especially if the Series were faraway Cincinnati or St. Louis. Few fans, however, anticipated the scare that awaited in the coming weeks.

8

Winning Pennants

A quirk in the schedule had the Yankees and Athletics following their two late–August games traveling together to Philadelphia to play three games. Then, following a day off, the two teams returned to Yankee Stadium for a twin bill that would finish the seven-game series.

After splitting the two games in New York, the teams opened in Philadelphia with a doubleheader. Playing under an overcast sky, the Athletics began the day steadily pecking away at Urban Shocker. They scored single runs in the second, fourth, and sixth and added three more in the seventh. Meanwhile A's pitcher Howard Ehmke breezed through the Yankees lineup, surrendering only six hits and coasting to an easy win. In the second game the Athletics again jumped off to a quick lead, scoring three times in the opening frame. Their victim was "Sad" Sam Jones, who for the fourth time in a row failed to finish the game he started. During the stretch, Jones had clearly lost his mid-season magic, giving up 24 runs in just 8⅔ innings. Against Philadelphia he didn't make it out of the first inning. With Lefty Grove on the mound for the Athletics, the Yankees seemed destined for a very unsuccessful afternoon. However, Grove was pitching with just two days' rest and by the fourth he was spent. His backup, Jack Quinn, tamed the Yankees for two more innings but with two outs in the seventh he walked his mound counterpart, Bob Shawkey. Four hits and two walks later the Yankees had hung a "5" up on the scoreboard. The big blows came from Bob Meusel, who contributed a three-run single, and a two-run single by Tony Lazzeri. Up by four, Shawkey held off the home team to earn a much-needed split.

The following day Herb Pennock blanked the Athletics, his first shutout and 22nd win of the season. All afternoon the Yankee southpaw was dazzling.

133

Only in the ninth did he encounter any problems. Aided by a Koenig error, Philadelphia loaded the bases with one out. However, Pennock coolly coaxed the next hitter to tap a ball back to the mound which he turned it into a game-ending double play. The win put the Yankees up a game in their strange series with the Athletics as the two teams headed back to Yankee Stadium for their final two games of the season against each other.

The Yankees took a detour on their way back to New York. With a day off, the team's business manager, Ed Barrow, scheduled an exhibition game in Baltimore against the Orioles, who played in the International League. Of course Baltimore was Babe Ruth's hometown and he was still the city's favorite son. A game against the Orioles was sure to bring out a big crowd and some extra cash. Two rarely used pitchers, Herb McQuaid and Walter Beall, pitched for the Yankees. The team's makeshift lineup included Babe Ruth at first base and Lou Gehrig, briefly, in right field. Of the starters, only Ruth was around for the final out. The game, which the Orioles won 18–9, was purely for show and rolled right along until a bizarre brawl in the seventh. From the first pitch of the game Ruth had been needling his shortstop, Mark Koenig. Among the barbs, the Bambino teased the rookie about his inconsistent fielding and erratic arm. Finally, after seven innings, Koenig could take no more. As his team came into the dugout at the end of the seventh inning he jumped in front of the Babe and hit him with several punches. Teammates quickly grabbed Koenig while Ruth, perhaps a bit stunned or perhaps a bit amused, shuffled away to the other end of the dugout. In a scrap, the rookie shortstop presented no real threat to the powerful Babe Ruth. However, several fans, anxious to defend their hero, leaped out of the stands and onto the field, ready to continue what Ruth had just walked away from. Fortunately police interceded immediately, restoring order and escorting Koenig out of the park.

Back in New York, the Yankees and Athletics finished off their week-long series with a doubleheader. Ignoring dark, ominous clouds, 60,000 fans, the largest crowd of the season, packed into Yankee Stadium to watch. Just eighteen hours earlier, the worst thunderstorms in years had rumbled through the city, flooding the entire metropolitan area. Streets were inundated, a building was washed away and tens of thousands of vacationers returning from Labor Day festivities were stranded without transportation. In Brooklyn two men died when they jumped from their subway car to escape a mud slide. However, by game time the field had dried out enough to play ball.

Ignoring the threatening weather, ticket holders were treated to what the *New York Times* a bit overzealously labeled "one of the greatest demonstrations in the history of New York baseball."[1] Both teams sparkled in the field, playing errorless ball. The day's moundsmen were also at the top of their game. Timely hitting and shrewd base running proved to be the difference between victory and defeat. The opener included several minor rhubarbs, a couple of outstanding catches and scrappy play by both clubs. Through six innings a pair of Athletics pitchers throttled the home team while their mates backed them with a pair of runs. In the seventh the Yankees scored twice without getting a hit to tie the score. The A's scratched back with a run of their own, then added two more in the ninth to win 5–2. Waite Hoyt's strong right arm carried the home team through the second game. Down 1–0 in the eighth, New York, to the delight of a stadium full of effusive patrons, pushed across the two runs they needed to win the game and earn the doubleheader split.

The Yankees' last three home games of the season were against the Red Sox, the same team that had opened their home schedule five months earlier. Since then the two teams had traveled in opposite directions. The Yankees, of course, were riding comfortably atop of the league. At the other extreme, the Red Sox were in last place, 42½ games behind the leaders, 13½ behind the seventh-place Browns and on their way to losing 107 games. The 1926 season would be the second of six consecutive last-place finishes for Boston. Few teams in baseball history have ever put together a string of failure as did the Red Sox in the late 1920s. The Red Sox were also the Yankees' favorite opponents in 1926, losing 17 of the 22 games the two teams played, more than any other team in the league.

In the club's last home games of the season, the Yankees sandwiched two more triumphs over the Red Sox around a loss. In the first game Urban Shocker turned in another stellar performance, the third in his last four outings. While Boston chipped out ten singles and a double, Shocker was in control throughout, surrendering only two runs. Among the spectators the next day were eight members of the Cardinals. After finishing a series in Pittsburgh, St. Louis had two days off before playing the Braves in Boston. On their way Hornsby, catcher Bob O'Farrell and the team's six best pitchers stopped over in New York to watch the Yankees play the last two games against the Red Sox. What they saw was Harold Wiltse, a little left-handed pitcher in the mold of the Cardinals' lefty Willie Sherdel, baffle "Murderer's Row" with an assortment of off-speed pitches, limiting the Yankees sluggers to just five hits and two runs. It was a lesson that Hornsby tucked away for possible future consideration.

The next day, the St. Louis visitors saw the Yankees at their best. Against four Boston hurlers Yankees hitters smacked 12 hits and scored ten runs. In the field they played flawlessly, including a gem by third baseman Joe Dugan. Meanwhile pitcher Bob Shawkey pitched perhaps his best game of the season, shutting out the hapless Red Sox on four hits. Unlike the previous day, it was a performance worthy of a league champion.

Dugan's play against the Red Sox was typical of his play throughout the summer. Coming into the season Dugan had been one of the question marks on the Yankees roster. During the previous winter he had extensive surgery on his left knee. However, aside from a few weeks on the disabled list early in the season, he was putting together a solid year both in the field and at the plate. Though his batting average had slipped to the .300 mark in recent weeks, through the first half of the season he had been among the league's leading hitters. Quick, sure-handed and blessed with a strong throwing arm, his prowess in the field was obvious. On numerous occasions Manager Huggins had confirmed to reporters that there was no one he would rather have at third base than "Jumping" Joe.[2]

Now in his tenth major league season, Dugan began his career with Connie Mack's Athletics. When he arrived he was scheduled to replace fan favorite Frank "Home Run" Baker, whom Mack had sold a year earlier. Just 20 years old and with no previous professional experience, Dugan had a difficult time adjusting to big league pitching and an even harder time putting up with life in Philadelphia. During his first two seasons his sub-.200 batting average and sporadic play in the field made him a regular target for arguably the nastiest fans in baseball. So affected was he that he regularly begged Mack to be traded. When his pleas failed, he periodically left the team, threatening never to return. Of course after a few days away he always returned. In reaction, some of the spiteful Philadelphians dubbed "Home Run" Baker's replacement "Run Home" Dugan. Others simply called him "Jumping Joe," a moniker that he carried the rest of his life.

As a schoolboy Dugan attracted interest from several major league teams. One winter evening during his junior year in high school, his baseball destiny was set by an unannounced visit from Connie Mack. Neither of Dugan's parents knew who Mack was, but when he offered them $500 for a promise that when their son was ready to play professionally it would be with the A's, Dugan's father, an Irish immigrant who worked the docks in New Haven, happily took the money, telling Mack that for $500 he could take all ten Dugan children if he wanted. Two years after Mack's visit and following an outstanding freshman season at Holy Cross College, Joe made the journey to Philadelphia. Six difficult years later he happily left the not so friendly Quaker City for New York.[3]

In New York Dugan found a city he loved and a gang of fun-loving sidekicks. His two favorites were Babe Ruth and Waite Hoyt. Often gallivanting together, their escapades became legendary. Most included long nights and plenty of alcohol. On one occasion in a Chicago restaurant operated by Al Capone, Dugan asked the waiter to see "Big Al." Minutes later he, Hoyt and two other Yankees were patted down and ushered into Capone's office.[4] Another time he and Ruth were playing golf at a posh club near Dugan's Scarsdale home. Sipping whiskey as they went, Ruth blamed his poor play on pesky squirrels. At the 14th tee the frustrated Bambino told the caddy to get him a gun. Minutes later, armed with a .22 rifle, Ruth began shooting squirrels. The afternoon ended soon after when the two Yankees were thrown off the course.[5]

During the season Dugan and a teammate rented an apartment next to Ruth's in the Astoria Hotel. Always stocked with a case of bootleg whiskey and a keg of beer, Ruth's apartment was a regular hangout for Dugan. Many nights when not out on the town Jumping Joe and a few teammates caroused into the early morning hours with Ruth and female admirers at Ruth's apartment.

"Jumping" Joe Dugan was considered the best defensive third baseman in the American League. One of Babe Ruth's regular sidekicks, Dugan had a colorful career with the Yankees both on and off the field.

Usually the parties ended when Babe invited one of the women "guests" to stay while Dugan was given the task of sending everyone else (or almost everyone else) home. Dugan ultimately paid for his reveling in 1931 when his wife sued for divorce. His lawyer called sidekick Waite Hoyt as a character witness, and when Hoyt's wife, who had become close friends with Dugan's wife, was told what her husband planned to do she too sued for divorce.

Though Dugan's off-the-field exploits were taxing, he rarely let them affect his play. When acquired in 1922 he was hailed as a crucial piece for future Yankees championships. In 1926 Dugan was finally fulfilling that prediction. The only veteran infielder starting for the team, he brought stability and experience onto the field. His low-keyed demeanor and consistent play helped to ease the nerves of his rookie counterparts, particularly shortstop Koenig. Along with Dugan's playing abilities, manager Huggins considered him one of his most savvy players and the captain of the infield.[6]

After dispatching the Red Sox, Jumping Joe and his teammates went back on the road for the final time during the regular season. The team's last 17 games would be played against the league's four western teams, and as they rolled toward Detroit Yankees players were certain that after one of those games the American League championship would be theirs. It probably wouldn't happen for another week or so, but it was going to happen. Though they had played better early in the season, the team left New York with an eight-game lead over the second-place Indians. To lose the pennant now was simply inconceivable.

Babe Ruth was the hero of the opening game in Detroit. With two outs and down by four runs in the top of the ninth, the Yankees pushed a run across and had men on second and third when Ruth came to the plate. Most expected that with first base open Tigers manager Ty Cobb would order his pitcher, right-hander Lil Stoner, who after eight innings had obviously lost some of his steam, to walk the Bambino. Instead Cobb instructed Stoner to pitch to the Yankees slugger. On the fourth offering Ruth drilled a line drive way over the left center field fence, his 42nd home run of the season, to put New York ahead by a run. Despite the blast, Cobb left Stoner on the mound and the Yankees tacked on yet another run before their half of the inning ended. In the bottom half of the inning Urban Shocker, the Yankees' fifth pitcher of the day, finished off the Tigers and put his team one game closer to its goal.

Light snow, rain and cold weather the next day forced the two clubs to end their season's play with a doubleheader. It was a day that started badly for the Yankees and got worse. Detroit pitcher Earl Whitehill and reliever George Dauss tamed Murderer's Row in the first game, winning 4–3. In the second game Sam Gibson handled the job himself, mowing down Yankees hitters as well as anyone had all year. Giving up just three hits, Gibson and his mates were further aided by shoddy Yankee fielding and Waite Hoyt's poor mound work. Adding to New York's woes, the Indians completed a four-game sweep of the Senators which cut the Yankees lead to 5½ games. If Cleveland could sweep the upcoming six-game series with the Yankees, what had been unimaginable just a week earlier would become a reality. The Indians could push Ruth and company out of first place.

The most important series of the Yankees' season began on a gloomy afternoon in Cleveland. On the mound for Cleveland was George Uhle, who had beaten the New Yorkers in dominating fashion five times already during the season. In three of those games the Yankees had only been able to score twice. They had done even worse in the other two outings, scoring a single run in one and being shut out in the other. Apparently making matters worse, instead of using well-rested Yankees ace Herb Pennock, Manager Huggins assigned "Sad" Sam Jones to oppose Uhle. Some Yankees fans complained that Huggins's choice was a sign that he had already conceded the opener to the Indians.

After waiting through a 50-minute rain delay, the Yankees opened the game by loading the bases. However, Uhle was up to the task. Bearing down, he limited the visitors to a single marker. Over the next five innings New York kept the pressure on the Cleveland hurler but was unable to score another run. Meanwhile Jones was having his own problems. Through the first three innings the Indians threatened several times but a couple of timely Yankees double plays kept the home team off the board. Then in the fourth Jones's luck ran out. Five singles produced three Indians runs. An inning later Cleveland pushed across another run and, with Uhle back in control, it looked as if the Yankees' fate was sealed. That all changed in the seventh. After the first three Yankees hitters had reached base, Bob Meusel smacked a long sacrifice fly to right. Lazzeri followed with a run-scoring single and an out later pinch hitter Ben Paschal shot a single up the middle, scoring two more runs. The tallies were all the Yankees needed for the win. Having relieved Jones in the fifth, Bob Shawkey allowed just two hits through the last four innings to get the victory. The win assured Huggins and his men that even if they dropped the remaining five games, they would leave Cleveland still in first place.

The next four games did not go well for the Yankees. The day after finally beating Uhle, Ruth and company dropped a doubleheader. While Yankees pitchers did what was expected of them, Yankees hitters did not. Through 18 innings the vaunted attack could chip out only four hits, two in each game, and scored just one run. In single games the following two days, Yankees sluggers did only slightly better. In the first game they lost 5–1, and the next day Uhle redeemed himself on a four-hitter, winning 3–1. During the four games the Yankees' high point was a shouting match between Huggins and Cleveland manager Speaker that, fortunately for the diminutive Huggins, ended just short of a full scale altercation. On the field New York had scored only two runs on an anemic 13 hits. Even worse, their lead had been whittled down to 2½ games, the smallest it had been since May 16th. Though they were able to salvage the final game, the Yankees left Cleveland shaken. With eight games remaining in the season, including two doubleheaders, there was little room for error. Instead of speculating about whom they were going to be playing in the World Series, the Yankees left Cleveland trying to figure a way to start winning ball games again.

Chicago was the next stop on the Yankees journey. So far during the season the White Sox had not been much of an obstacle, losing 13 of the 18 games the two teams had played against each other. However, the story of the final four games was different. With the exception of a 14–0 blowout, New York's losing continued. In the opener the lead seesawed back and forth through the first six innings. In the seventh the White Sox unloaded, scoring four times and cruising on to a win. Chicago carried a 4–2 lead into the final frame of the second game but, for the first time in a week, the Yankees showed signs of rallying. With one out, a run in and runners on second and third, New York had a chance to pull out a much-needed come-from-behind victory. A strikeout and ground-out later, the threat was over and the Yankees had lost yet another game. After walloping the Sox the following day, the Yankees ended the series once again on a disappointing note. This time they carried a one-run lead into the bottom of the ninth. With two outs and the bases empty Chicago put together two singles and a double that scored two runs, adding to the Yankees anguish. Meanwhile the Indians crept a bit closer, taking two of three from Boston and narrowing the lead to a mere two games.

The Yankees stumbled into St. Louis for the last four games of the season. When they arrived, Huggins's crew needed a combination of wins and Indians losses totally three to bring the American League pennant back to New York. A rainout the first day in St. Louis meant that the two teams would have to play back-to-back doubleheaders. However, despite the rain the day turned out well for the Yankees. In Cleveland the Athletics beat the Indians 3–1 adding a half-game to the New York lead and reducing their "magic number" to two.

The Yankees got their bang back in the first two games against the Browns, scoring ten times in each. Babe Ruth, the biggest Yankee banger, blasted his 45th, 46th and 47th home runs of the season. In both games the New York romps started early and left little doubt about the eventual outcome. In the opener Ruth and company put up two runs in the third and fourth innings, then added five more in the fifth. Meanwhile Herb Pennock deftly maneuvered through the Browns lineup, allowing only a pair of runs. The win was Pennock's 23rd. The second game was much the same. In the sixth inning an early three-run lead turned into a seven-run rout. The beneficiary of the assault was Waite Hoyt, who held the Browns to four runs in a workmanlike performance. Appropriately Babe Ruth capped the final win with a mammoth ninth-inning clout that ended up out on Sullivan Street behind the bleachers in right field.

The double win finally brought the American League pennant back to New York. Even before the season began there was pressure on the team to regain its place atop the league. As the season wore on, expectations grew. Yankees fans wanted another championship. When the team jumped out to a giant early league lead, New Yorkers became confident that the previous year's failures were behind them. Then in September, as the team's lead steadily shrank, some again began doubting. That ended once the pennant was secured. For the next week there would be much less fan pressure. The team could relax and prepare for the season's final challenge. Of course, every Yankee knew that the American League pennant was not enough. A successful season included another championship. Yankees players and fans alike would only be satisfied after their team had won the World Series.

In early September the Cardinals left St. Louis in first place, a game up on the Reds and two ahead of the Pirates. Even though the club's final two dozen games would be played on the road, a growing number of baseball experts picked the team as the favorite to win the National League pennant. Brooklyn manager Wilbert Robinson and his Boston Braves counterpart, Dave Bancroft, both concluded that the Pirates were in disarray, needed pitching and had a bundle of doubleheaders ahead of them. The Reds had been inconsistent during the previous few weeks and they too lacked an adequate mound staff. The Cardinals, on the other hand, seemed to have it all. They were hitting the ball as well as any team in the league. Their pitching had stabilized and appeared solid, and Hornsby had his team hustling more than the other two contenders. Bancroft predicted that "the club that hustles most must win." Both managers agreed that while the road ahead would be tough, Hornsby had done a superb job so far and seemed to know exactly what his team needed to keep winning.[7]

Accompanied by a small corps of avid fans, the Cardinals began their last swing through the league with a doubleheader in Chicago. The result of two games rained out earlier in the season, the twin bill turned out to be a great start for the team's final journey. On a day when both the Reds and the Pirates were idle, the Cardinals were able to add another full game to their lead by sweeping the Cubs. The double win demonstrated what Robinson, Bancroft and others were saying about the league's leader. In the first game Alexander once again dominated his former mates (and manager), limiting them to three hits. At the plate, leadoff hitter Taylor Douthit scored one run and drove in the other in the 2–0 win. Flint Rhem was almost as effective in the nightcap, surrendering a single marker. Meanwhile the Redbirds attack, led by Hornsby and Southworth, came alive, scoring nine times. As satisfying as the wins were, the Cardinals had little time to enjoy them. As soon as they had dispatched the Cubs, the team hurried off to catch an overnight train to Cincinnati, where they were scheduled to play an important three-game weekend match up with the Reds.

The long ride from Chicago took its toll. In front of a packed house that included the governor of Ohio and several hundred St. Louis faithful, the Cardinals foundered. In the first inning a crucial error on a rundown between home and third allowed two Cincinnati runners to score. They would be the only two runs the Reds needed. At the plate Cardinals hitters, with the exception of O'Farrell, who tripled twice and scored once, were unable to put anything together. The two times that St. Louis did mount potential rallies, Reds pitcher Carl Mays stifled them on strikeouts and soft groundouts. By the end of the afternoon the Cardinals' league lead had been sliced in half.

The following game went even worse for the Cardinals. The Reds jumped on Willie Sherdel immediately, again getting all the runs they needed in the first inning. The problems started when leadoff hitter Billy Zitzmann punched a soft popup to Hornsby at second. Never comfortable with fly balls, Hornsby misjudged the ball, backpeddled, tripped over his spikes and dropped the ball. Falling backwards hard onto the ground, the Cardinals manager knocked himself out, enabling Zitzmann to end up on second base. Hornsby was quickly revived but the error began a four-run Cincinnati onslaught. Meanwhile Cardinals hitters were even less effective than they had been the day before, chipping out only five solitary singles. The loss pushed Cincinnati three percentage points ahead of St. Louis and led some reporters once again to speculate that the pressure of holding onto the league's top spot might be too much for Hornsby's young crew.

The final game in Cincinnati was played on a sunny late summer Sunday afternoon. Through the night specially chartered trains had brought more than 5,000 Cardinals rooters to the Queen City. Arriving as early as 5:30 A.M. after an all-night train ride, the St. Louis faithful joined an even larger force of Reds fans from "almost every city in Ohio, Kentucky, and Indiana and many in West Virginia" who had come to support the home team.[8] Encouraged by their own bands and carrying an assortment of flags and banners, the two contingents prior to the game paraded through the streets surrounding the ball park, trying to outdo each other. By game time more than 33,000, the largest Cincinnati crowd since the 1919 World Series, packed into Redland Field to watch the two teams battle for the league's top spot. So large was the throng that some ticket holders stood fifty deep on the field in front of the left and right field fences.

Amidst the festivities the Cardinals crew regained its punch. After a scoreless first inning, left fielder Chick Hafey opened the second with a double and O'Farrell followed with a walk. Both scored on a double by Thevenow. Two innings later Les Bell drove a ball into the crowd standing in left field. Normally the drive would have been ruled a double but because there had been no pre-game stipulations Bell was able to circle the bases for another Cardinals marker. St. Louis scored again in the fifth and two more times in the sixth as Hornsby and company opened up a six-run lead. On the mound Grover Cleveland Alexander, working with only two days' rest, "breezed along in masterly fashion."[9] Though he tired in the late innings, giving up single runs in the sixth, seventh and eighth innings, he once again rewarded Hornsby for the confidence that he had shown in his veteran hurler. By the end of the afternoon the Cardinals had regained the top spot in the league standings and were anxious to move on to Pittsburgh.

As they had over the previous few weeks, center fielder Taylor Douthit and his left field counterpart, Chick Hafey, quietly bolstered the Cardinals attack in the final game against the Reds. Both were on base twice, Douthit with a single and a double, Hafey with a double and a walk, and both scored twice. The Cardinals outfield had been a question mark at the beginning of the season. Hornsby recognized his crew of young fly-catchers had great potential but would need some seasoning. The mid–June acquisition of Billy Southworth brought a veteran who solidified the outfield. Already a bona fide star, Southworth lived up to all of his manager's expectations. In addition to his offensive production he became the leader among his young counterparts. Meanwhile Douthit, Hafey, and Ray Blades provided the depth that the team needed to contend for the pennant.

Ray Blades was arguably the most gifted athlete on the team. Growing up in St. Louis he played football, ran track and starred in the local public school baseball leagues. After high school he signed on with a semi-pro team in Iowa, but before his second season began he was part of an artillery unit fighting the Germans in France. Upon his return from the war, Blades joined a team in southern Illinois. His big break came midway through the season when his team beat Branch Rickey's Cardinals in an exhibition game. Rickey, who had watched Blades play in high school, immediately signed him and shipped him off to Memphis and later to Houston. There Blades became an outstanding second baseman and hard-hitting leadoff man.

Early in the 1924 season, after hitting .330 the previous year in Houston, Blades was called up to the Cardinals. Branch Rickey, who already had the best second baseman in baseball, had a plan for Blades. Rather than keep him at second as a backup for Hornsby, the Cardinal manager decided to put him in the outfield even though Blades had never played there before. Initially Rickey's experiment looked like a disaster. Balls that hit in front of him were a problem, and long fly balls hit anywhere but directly at him became adventures. He got a late jump on batted balls and often had trouble holding onto balls once he got to them. However, Blades worked hard to learn how to play the outfield and, despite his early problems, by the end of the season he had become adequate in his new position. Fortunately, at the plate he made up for his defensive flaws. A speedy leadoff man, he hit .311. The following season he continued to improve in the field, raised his average to .342, and scored 112 times in 131 games. By the beginning of the 1926 season Blades had developed into a reliable outfielder who Hornsby expected would soon emerge as one of the team's brightest stars.

Through the first five months of the season Blades lived up to Hornsby's expectations. Playing in left field, he was dependable and his speed enabled him to catch balls that might otherwise have fallen for hits. At the plate he continued to be an ideal leadoff man, hitting over .300 and scoring runs regularly. Then, on August 17 in a game against Brooklyn, Blades sprinted back after a deep fly ball. On the chase his spikes became tangled in a chicken

wire screen that had been built to protect players from crashing into the park's cement walls. The fall ended Blades' season. He had torn several ligaments in his left knee that would require post-season surgery.[10]

The injury did nothing to stifle Blades' determination. To Hornsby, Blades' most compelling characteristic was his fiery spirit. There was no Cardinal Hornsby respected more than Blades. He was a non-drinker and non-smoker who shunned the night life that tempted some of his teammates. He obeyed whatever order his manager gave and was unrelenting on the field. Blades' will to win rivaled even that of his manager's. In Hornsby's opinion Blades was an excellent role model for his teammates and an indispensable part of the team whether in the field or in the dugout. Despite the injury, the Cardinals manager wanted him suited up and on the bench even though he would not play again during the 1926 season.[11]

Chick Hafey struggled with health problems throughout much of the 1926 season. Prior to the start of the 1927 season he had successful sinus surgery and afterward became one of the best hitters in the National League.

With Blades out, Chick Hafey became the Cardinals' left fielder. In his first full year with the team, Hafey at the beginning of the season had been expected to challenge for a starting spot in center field. Some considered him to be one of the best pure hitters on the team. He was also blessed with a powerful throwing arm and, in fact, had originally been signed as a pitcher. Unfortunately, during the early months of the season various illnesses limited his playing time. The source of his physical problems was a chronic sinus condition. Until late June he was constantly plagued by sinus infections that came in the form of debilitating head colds and severe headaches. Eventually the infections began affecting his optic nerve and his vision. However, as the weather heated up Hafey's sinus problems were

Taylor Douthit came to the Cardinals with very little previous experience in professional baseball but established himself as an excellent leadoff hitter and a fine center fielder.

mitigated. By the time of Blades' injury, Hafey was as healthy as he had been all season and capable of filling in for the team's left fielder. Before the start of the 1927 season Hafey would adjust to his problems. After an operation on his sinuses, he began wearing glasses when he played. During the next decade the adjustment enabled Hafey to become one of the best hitters in baseball, good enough to earn him induction into the Hall of Fame in 1971.[12]

Every championship team has a player or two who perform beyond all reasonable expectations. For the Cardinals Taylor Douthit was one of those players. Douthit was the beneficiary of Hafey's early-season sinus problems. A kid from southern California who had not played organized baseball until he was a student at the University of Southern California, Douthit during his previous three seasons with the Cardinals had been used exclusively as a backup player. He possessed a good arm and excellent speed but had little power and had never hit for much of an average. Prior to 1926 his lifetime batting average of .267 consisted of 73 hits in 273 at bats. However, as the leadoff man for Hornsby's team, Douthit blossomed. He ended the season batting .308, scored almost 100 runs and stole 23 bases. Always good defensively, he also plugged the team's hole in center field.[13] Along with Hafey, Blades, and Southworth, Douthit gave the Cardinals an outstanding outfield both defensively and at the plate.

When the Cardinals arrived in Pittsburgh, the Pirates were 3½ games off the pace and fading fast. Despite claims to the contrary, the world champions were still playing under the shadow of the Carey episode. Additionally, faced with a slew of doubleheaders the pitching staff was overworked and ineffective. Clearly the team was struggling. A three-game St. Louis sweep could just about eliminate them from the pennant race.

The Cardinals took the first step in that direction with a lopsided 8–1 win in a drizzly morning makeup game. Flint Rhem was at his best, holding the buccaneers to four hits while his teammates rang up 12 of their own. Ahead by two runs in the fifth, the Cardinals left no doubt about the game's ultimate outcome with a five-run barrage. Rhem dominated the rest of the morning. The skies cleared for the afternoon game, warming the 35,000 fans who replaced the 10,000 that watched the earlier contest. Again the Cardinals jumped out to an early two-run lead, but this time the home team caught the visitors in the fifth. Two innings later the Pirates loaded the bases on a pair of bunt singles. Cardinals pitcher Alan Sothoron had a long history of misplaying bunts. While he had no problem fielding them, his throws were often erratic. Consequently, Cardinals infielders or the catcher were expected to deal with opponents' bunts when Sothoron was on the mound. As a result, a well-placed bunt became a defensive challenge. In the seventh inning, following two such Pirates bunts, Kiki Cuyler drilled a bases-loaded shot to center, scoring a pair of his teammates. The two runs held up, enabling the Pirates to salvage a split for the day.

The final game of the season between the Pirates and the Cardinals was a repeat of the previous day's first game. Willie Sherdel shut out the Pirates while Cardinals hitters, led by Douthit and Hafey, pushed eight runs across the plate. Coupled with Cincinnati's loss to the Cubs, the Cardinals' league lead grew to two games. The day's only glitch was Rogers Hornsby's back. During the previous week Hornsby had again been bothered by back spasms similar to those that had sidelined him earlier in the season. In Cincinnati a collision with the Reds catcher further aggravated the pain. A trip to a chiropractor prior to leaving Pittsburgh at least temporarily eased the pain but did not eliminate it. Fortunately, the Cardinals manager had two days to rest before his team played again. Nevertheless, even the thought of losing their star player in the midst of a tight pennant race worried Cardinals supporters.

After Pittsburgh the Cardinals were scheduled to play exhibition games in Buffalo and Syracuse. Hornsby fervently opposed team president Sam Breadon's deal to play the two games while his team was fighting for a pennant. In retaliation, the Cardinals manager, catcher O'Farrell and the team's starting pitchers instead spent their two days off watching the Yankees battle the Red Sox. Hornsby's side trip intensified his growing feud with Breadon but at the same time gave him a chance to study the Yankees hitters. Acknowledged to be as keen an observer of baseball skills, particularly hitting skills, as anyone in the game, Hornsby planned to begin concocting a pitching strategy in case his team met the Yankees in October. All season St. Louis pitchers had attributed a significant part of their success to Hornsby's observations and instructions about how to pitch various hitters.[14] If the Cardinals and Yankees ended up playing each other in the World Series, Hornsby's understanding of Yankees hitters would be invaluable.

By the time the Cardinals arrived in Boston, their league lead had grown to three games. Cincinnati had followed the Cardinals into Pittsburgh and dropped a doubleheader to the Pirates. Now with a three-game cushion and facing the league's worst four teams in 15 out of their last 16 games, the Cardinals appeared to be almost a sure thing to win their first National League pennant. Even professional odds makers had made them even money to win. Four days later, when the Cardinals left Boston, those predictions had changed.

Struggling to stay out of the National League basement, the Braves had significant incentive to play well against the Cardinals. When St. Louis rolled into town, the Braves were in eighth place, half a game behind the Phillies, who were next on the Cardinals schedule. Even a Braves split with the league's leader would certainly help the city of Boston avoid the ignominy of having its two major league teams, the Braves and the Red Sox, both finish the season in last place.

The four-game series turned out to be one of the best that the Braves played all season. In the opener both teams scored three times during the initial six innings. In the seventh the Braves exploded, bombarding Grover Cleveland Alexander with six runs. An inning later the home team added two more and coasted to a comfortable victory. The two teams split a doubleheader the following day. Jesse Haines, who had shut out the Braves twice already, continued his mastery, limiting Boston to just four hits. Haines's teammates did no better in terms of hits but in the third were able to link together doubles by Southworth and Hornsby and a Boston error to score the game's only two runs. The late game was another struggle. The Cardinals opened with two runs in the first. In the bottom of the inning the Braves matched the output. The Cards put up another run in the sixth. In their turn at bat the Braves again matched the scoring. Two innings later the Braves pushed across the winning run when third baseman Andy High lashed a one-out triple to center, then scored on a sacrifice fly.

The final game in Boston was a classic that included sensational, run-saving plays by both teams. The Cardinals jumped out to a two-run lead in the first but the Braves battled back, tying the score at four in the eighth. In the ninth both teams threatened but were stymied by spectacular plays. Through four more innings the teams battled. Then, in the bottom of 14th, Boston catcher Zack Taylor led off with a single and was sacrificed to second. The next hitter, Johnny Cooney, slapped a shot to right in front of Billy Southworth. The Cardinals outfielder quickly scooped up the ball and threw home. Taylor, who was never known for his speed, trudged around third and slid home just beneath O'Farrell's tag. Making the loss even more painful, Cincinnati was on a five-win streak that knocked the Cardinals into a tie with the Reds.

After the four losses in Boston, skeptics again warned that the young Cardinals were not mentally strong enough to deal with a tight pennant race. Hornsby vehemently disagreed. He assured fans that the problem in Boston was simply a bump on the team's road to the pennant. "Don't worry about us crackin'. You didn't see anyone crack in the field yesterday and you won't." He maintained unequivocally that: "We're a better ball club ... we'll win out yet there's no doubt of that."[15] Taking another shot at Breadon, he admitted that his team may have been tired the previous day but that was because Breadon had committed them to play yet another exhibition game, this time in New Haven, between the Saturday doubleheader and Monday's extra-inning struggle. In the exhibition game, Chick Hafey had been injured and was unable to play in the Monday game. His replacement on Monday, Wattie Holm, went hitless in six trips to the plate, including a couple of times with runners on base. Hornsby also considered the Reds' remaining schedule more difficult than his team's and promised that someone would soon knock Cincinnati off. What his team needed to do was forget about Boston and focus on taking five out of six in Philadelphia. If they did that, the pennant would be theirs.

Hornsby's words were prophetic. The Cardinals came into Philadelphia as focused as they had been all season. Winning five of the six games to be played in the following four days, even against the lowly Phillies, would be a challenge and would certainly demonstrate the young Cardinals' mental resolve. It was a challenge that Hornsby's crew was ready for. In the first five of the six games, the Cardinals dominated Philadelphia in every way possible. They outscored the home team 61 to 11 and out-hit the Phillies 89 to 48. In the field the Cardinals committed only three errors during the six games, while the Phillies committed 13. The high point came during a doubleheader on the second day of play when the Cardinals scored 33 runs, including a 23–3 blowout, while holding the Phillies to just five. Only in the last game in the series were the Phillies competitive, and even then it wasn't until their last at-bat that they were able to claim a lead. Meanwhile, just as Hornsby had predicted, Cincinnati couldn't keep pace. Though the Reds stretched their winning streak to eight games, they were bumped off twice by the Giants and as a result fell 1½ games back of St. Louis with just six games to play.

The two pennant contenders started off the final week of the season badly. The Cardinals lost a game to the Giants, then another in Brooklyn. The Reds did even worse, dropping three games in Boston. On September 22nd the Reds sat idle while the Cardinals finally turned on the power. Riding three triples from Les Bell and home runs by Bottomley and Thevenow, St. Louis drilled Brooklyn 15–7, inching them to within two games of the pennant. Two days later the Reds dropped yet another game, this time in Philadelphia. Unaware of the course of play 100 miles south, the Cards staked their hopes on the arm of their ace, Flint Rhem. However, it was not to be Rhem's day. After giving up three runs in the first inning he was quickly lifted for Sherdel. In the second St. Louis launched a comeback. Spurred by a Southworth two-run homer, the Cards struck for five runs and took the lead. It was all Sherdel needed. Over the next eight innings he held the Giants scoreless. The win, coupled with Cincinnati's loss, sealed the pennant for Hornsby and his crew.

In St. Louis, 1,500 miles away, the city was ecstatic. The victory set off spontaneous celebrations throughout the city. Car horns honked, confetti was tossed from buildings and delirious fans literally danced in the streets. When the season began few could have imagined that their team would win a pennant. Only Rogers Hornsby had steadfastly contended that with hard work and a few breaks his team had the potential to win the National League championship. Even at mid-season only a handful of fans agreed with Hornsby's prediction. But that changed the longer the Cardinals stayed in the race. Since early August normal activity in the city slowed while the team was playing. Animated scoreboards were set up so that locals could follow games on a pitch-by-pitch basis. Those who had access to radios listened intently to Cardinals games. Everywhere banners and flags supporting the team had been up for more than a month. Now everyone recognized that Hornsby had been right. St. Louis had its first championship ever. Amid the frenzy after the final victory, the city anxiously prepared for the next exciting adventure: a clash with the New York Yankees in the World Series.

9

The 1926 World Series

The 1926 World Series was memorable for many reasons. The Yankees and the Cardinals were evenly matched teams both on the mound and at the plate. The Series became a seven-game struggle that was decided by a single run. Each team had arguably the best player in its league and both teams were sprinkled with future Hall of Famers. The seven games were well played contests characterized by superb pitching performances, game-saving plays, game-winning hits and a few unexpected heroes. One of the teams was a collection of home-grown boys playing for a team from the western periphery of major league baseball. The other team was led by a group of first- and second-generation Americans from baseball's epicenter. During the Series an off-the-field episode became an integral chapter in the remarkable saga of Babe Ruth. Appropriately, the Series ended with an almost mythical confrontation between a rookie powerhouse at the threshold of greatness and a grizzled old star ravaged by alcoholism who was desperately trying to hold onto the last threads of his baseball career. The confrontation instantly became baseball legend.

The new American League champions spent the week before the World Series relaxing and preparing. Manager Huggins was particularly anxious to give his pitchers some time to rest their arms. Urban Shocker and Waite Hoyt had been inconsistent during the final month of the season. A week off would give them time to get their strength back. A few other players would also benefit from the rest. For several weeks Mark Koenig had been nursing a sore ankle. Babe Ruth's legs were again bothering him. Joe Dugan's knee ached, and the ankle that Bob Meusel had broken in June was still a bit gimpy. Huggins was certain that with a week of leisurely workouts and time off his team would be as healthy and strong as they had been all season.

Rogers Hornsby had a different plan for his crew. After finishing the season with a game in Cincinnati, he intended to take his team back to New York rather than return home to St. Louis. The Cardinals manager wanted his players to spend the week learning the various shadows, angles and dimensions of Yankee Stadium. Opened three years earlier, the stadium was unlike any other major league field. Built directly across the Harlem River from the Giants' Polo Grounds home, the stadium was a majestic structure. Boasting an official seating capacity of 57,545, periodically as many as 70,000 had been crammed into the stadium. The field's first-level grandstands encircled the entire field. Two upper decks stretched from high behind the plate out to the left and right field fences. Aside from the facility's sheer mass, its most distinguishing quality was the 15-foot copper facade that hung from the roof above the third tier. The facade gave the facility an almost regal appearance. Entering Yankee Stadium was like entering a separate world. All other ballparks had sight lines that included views of the streets and buildings outside the park. Inside Yankee Stadium there were only a few peeks of the surrounding neighborhood.

Like all other ballparks, Yankee Stadium had its own idiosyncrasies. Field boxes in most parks began close to the playing field. Yankee Stadium, on the other hand, provided ample room to chase foul popups. Likewise, there was lots of room behind home plate that could make a passed ball or wild pitch an adventure. The field's dimensions were also unique. The left field pole was just 281 feet from home plate. The fence then immediately jutted out to 395 feet in straightaway left. The right field fence was 290 feet along the line but remained at only 295 feet into dead right field. The result was that left-handed power hitters like Ruth and Gehrig had a distinct advantage. In center field the fence was 490 feet from the plate, creating a cavernous outfield. In front of the entire outfield fence was a grassy slope that warned outfielders of the approaching fence. The slope in right field especially was something outfielders needed to learn how to play. The deep grandstands behind home plate created another characteristic all fielders had to get used to. Often fly balls appeared to hang in the air for a few seconds before taking a trajectory which made it difficult for fielders to get a good jump. The height of the grandstands also produced ever-changing mid- and late-afternoon shadows that challenged both fielders and hitters alike. Hornsby realized that his players needed to learn about the stadium before they could play comfortably in the Yankees' home.

Despite owner Sam Breadon's objections, Hornsby as planned packed his team up after their final game in Cincinnati, brought them back to New York and checked them into the Alamac Hotel at 71st and Broadway. Breadon had hoped to feed Cardinals fans' frenzy with a gala St. Louis celebration,

Relations between manager Rogers Hornsby (in uniform) and Cardinals owner Sam Breaden (left) deteriorated steadily during the last half of the season. Even during the World Series tension between the two men was obvious. Beside Hornsby is his wife Mary. The other two women cannot be identified with certainty but one is Breadon's wife.

but Hornsby refused. Instead, he agreed to allow some of his players to return home but firmly announced that his starting players were going to New York. Rather than celebrate without Hornsby and some of the Cardinals stars, Breadon grudgingly deferred to his manager. Instead the festivities were rescheduled for October 4, the day after the second game in the Series, when the whole team would return home.

During the Cardinals' week of preparation, their manager experienced a personal tragedy. After the team's first workout in Yankee Stadium, Hornsby received a phone call from his aunt in Austin, Texas. She reported that his mother, Mary Dallas Hornsby, was near death. A call later the same day reported that Mrs. Hornsby had died. Hornsby was very close to his mother. His father had died suddenly when Rogers was a boy, and afterward his mother had played the central role in her son's life. In the off-season he and his family lived in Hornsby Bend to be near his mother. For almost a year Mrs. Hornsby's health had been steadily deteriorating. Even before the season began, her son suspected the seriousness of her condition. As the season proceeded he came to recognize that the end might be near. Nevertheless he was shocked by the news.

The death briefly put Hornsby's status for the first two games of the Series in doubt. However, after a few hours contemplating a hasty return to Texas, he decided to stay with his team and made arrangements to postpone the funeral until after the Series. He told reporters, "it was her greatest ambition to have me play in the World Series. My aunt told me that the last thing my mother had said was that I play in the World Series come what may."[1]

While the two teams prepared, fans in both cities also prepared. Baseball fever gripped much of the Midwest, and in St. Louis talk about the Cardinals was non-stop. Among the hottest topics was how to get tickets to the games. Since early August the Cardinals organization had been working on a plan to distribute tickets equitably. Initially Sam Breadon announced that once requests from regular box holders were filled, the rest of the available tickets would be distributed through a lottery. After reading about the lottery idea, the St. Louis postmaster quashed the plan. The post office would not facilitate a lottery. Ultimately a little over 23,500 reserved seat tickets were sent out on a first-come, first-serve basis to those who mailed in requests, though no one was permitted more than two tickets. Breadon also held back 3,100 general admission tickets and 4,100 bleacher tickets which were to go on sale an hour before game time. He had hoped to make another 7,000 tickets available by constructing temporary bleachers in left and center fields but concluded that "the temporary seats might cost the St. Louis club a championship" so he abandoned the scheme.[2] By the beginning of the Series reserved tickets had almost become an alternative commodity in St. Louis enabling scalpers to make handsome returns on their investment.

Yankees fans were also anxious for the Series to start but were a bit more subdued than their counterparts in St. Louis. New Yorkers in general were reassured that after a year's absence the Series was back where it ought to be — in one of the three city ballparks. Yankees fans were especially eager to resume what their team had started three years earlier with its first world championship. After beating the Giants in the 1923 Series, the Yankees were on the verge of replacing their rival as the city's pre-eminent team, a status that John J. McGraw's team had held since 1901. From 1921 through 1923 the Yankees and Giants had met in the World Series. The Giants won the first two times but the Yankees took the most recent one. Then came two lean years for the Yankees. Meanwhile, by adding another pennant to their collection in 1924 the Giants had re-established their standing within the city even though they lost to the Senators in the World Series. With the 1926 world championship, the Yankees could again claim to be the best baseball team in the world's best baseball city.

Baseball pundits also spent the week preparing. In a plethora of predictions and analysis, most came to the conclusion that the two league champions were evenly matched and that the Series was a tossup. Odds makers agreed. Some had the Yankees as 4 to 5 favorites while others were offering even money that the Cardinals would win, but almost no one gave long odds on either team. Baseball professionals were equally divided. In an insightful analysis, Giants manager John McGraw, writing for the *New York Times,* contended that at the plate there was little difference between the two teams. The Yankees hit more home runs but he doubted that home runs would determine the Series outcome. Rather, the team that started hitting first would win, according to McGraw. He believed that St. Louis hitters were more consistent and therefore he gave a slight edge to the Cardinals. Brooklyn manager Wilbert Robinson concurred with his cross-town rival's assessment but added that in his opinion the Cardinals pitching staff was much better than most thought.[3] Miller Huggins also agreed that the Cardinals were potent at the plate but disagreed with McGraw's conclusion. Unlike St. Louis, Huggins's club did not rely on bunts, sacrifices, or hit-and-run plays. Instead the Yankees scored in bunches and played for the big inning. Huggins argued that in a short series big innings were more important than one-at-a-time tallies. In a column of his own (ghosted by one of his agent Christy Walsh's hired writers), Babe Ruth echoed his manager's prediction, claiming, "We can hit! And this series I've got a hunch is going to be won by slugging."[4]

In the field the two teams were again evenly matched. Most preferred the St. Louis infield but considered the Yankees outfield stronger. Of particular concern to Yankees fans were the team's three inexperienced infielders—Gehrig, Lazzeri, and Koenig. Huggins agreed, lamenting that "our youngsters (Gehrig, Lazzeri, and Koenig) going into their first series cannot have the same confidence as the fellows who have been through the mill."[5] Of course St. Louis had two relatively untested infielders, Tommy Thevenow and Les Bell, of its own. In the outfield the combination of Ruth, Combs and Meusel was acknowledged to be the superior trio, but behind the plate, a Yankees weak spot all season, there was none better than the Cardinals' Bob O'Farrell.

A comparison of the two mound crews was the source of more debate. Yankees starting pitchers Pennock, Shocker and Hoyt were generally considered a bit more effective than the starters for St. Louis. However, several Cardinals pitchers, most notably Willie Sherdel and Art Reinhart, were the type that had given Yankees hitters problems all season. Cardinals pitchers had also ended the season well while the Yankees staff, with the exception of Pennock, had struggled. Grover Cleveland Alexander was another intangible. Acknowledged to be one of the greatest pitchers of all time, he was well past his prime. There were doubts about how he would do against Yankees hitters, especially the two power-hitting lefthanders, Ruth and Gehrig. Though he still had exceptional control and a deadly curve ball, Alex's fastball had obviously lost velocity. Whether he still had enough juice to get it past the two Yankees sluggers was an issue. Some also questioned whether physically "Old Pete" would be able to withstand the rigors of the Series (and stay sober). If Alexander could handle Ruth and Gehrig consistently and if he was able to pitch effectively in several games, the Cardinals staff might have an advantage. If not, the Yankees mound crew was the better of the two.

Another topic of discussion was the role that the teams' two stars, Babe Ruth and Rogers Hornsby, would play. Ruth was usually at his best when games meant the most. He was the kind of player who could carry a team through a week or two, as he had done a couple of times during the season. Ruth at his best would definitely give the Yankees an advantage. The story for Hornsby was different. Of course his bat would be critical to his club's success, but even more important would be his managerial skills. He had masterfully steered his team of youngsters through a perilous season. Several times during the final six weeks he had apparently pulled his crew together just as they were succumbing to the stress of a tight pennant race. Could he now direct his inexperienced squad through the intense pressures of the World Series? McGraw for one had complete confidence that Hornsby could, but others weren't as sure.

When all was said and done, the consensus opinion was that ultimately the Series would be won by the more confident team. The edge therefore was with the New York. Many of the Yankees had already played in at least one World Series. For Babe Ruth the 1926 Series would be his seventh, a record number. Ty Cobb, never a Yankees fan, agreed, proposing that "Almost every member of the Yankees has seen service in a world series.... The Cards lack experience. The Yanks ought to win."[6] Though he did not share Cobb's conclusion, McGraw implied much the same, writing "Some veterans get stage freight more quickly than novices.... The human element will win this series."[7] For Hornsby, hustle and hard play were far more important than experience. Likewise, the pressure of a World Series did not compare to what his team had just been through. "Now the strain is over. We have won a pennant for St. Louis and the games with the Yankees will just be ball games. There will be no great strain or worry."[8]

The 1926 World Series opened on a cool, overcast Saturday afternoon in New York City. Despite early morning showers, fans began lining up outside Yankee Stadium even before dawn. By 9:30, when the admission gates opened, the gathering had grown to more than 10,000, most of whom hoped to buy general admission tickets. In all just over 63,000, many wearing raincoats and hats, filled the stadium by game time. Unlike all previous World Series opening games, there was little pre-game celebration. There was no parade of players and dignitaries onto the field, no bands played, and no speeches were made. A few passing showers also limited pre-game batting and fielding practice. Nevertheless, by game time an excited buzz ran through the crowd. Half an hour before the start, several notable personalities arrived. The crowd cheered Jack Dempsey, promoter Floyd Fitzsimmons and their wives as they found their seats. Just a week earlier Dempsey had lost the heavyweight boxing title in his first fight with Gene Tunney, but he remained a New York favorite. The entrance of John McGraw, Wilbert Robinson and Giants star Frankie Frisch brought another rumble of applause. Most prominent among the attendees were New York's colorful mayor, Jimmy Walker, senatorial candidate Robert Wagner and baseball commissioner Kenesaw Landis, who joined Jacob Ruppert in his owner's box along the first base foul line. Walker was scheduled to make the ceremonial first pitch but at the last minute deferred to Wagner. At 1:30 sharp, under ever-threatening skies and amid flashing photograph bulbs, Wagner fulfilled his afternoon assignment and heaved out a freshly unwrapped baseball to get the 23rd World Series under way.

Thousand of excited Cardinals fans were also in the stands when the Series started. For several days special trains offering reduced round-trip rates had made the 24-hour journey from St. Louis to New York. The last arrived just three hours before game time. One group of city leaders, including Browns owner Phil Ball, arranged for their own special sleeping cars. All visitors who were asked claimed to be "fixed" for tickets but undoubtedly some were not. On the other hand, one Cardinals fan boasted that he had 90 tickets and implied that he intended to pay for his trip with his scalping proceeds.[9]

The game started well for the Cardinals. Leadoff hitter Taylor Douthit bounced Yankees pitcher Herb Pennock's fifth offering off the right field fence for a double. Billy Southworth followed with a two-strike ground ball to Lazzeri that pushed Douthit over to third. Only three batters into the series, Hornsby got a chance to put his team up early. Appreciatively greeted by a crowd that sympathized with the loss of his mother and the emotional burden he was shouldering, Hornsby failed to deliver. Instead he dribbled a ball back to Pennock, who easily fielded it, held Douthit at third, then threw Hornsby out. Cleanup hitter Jim Bottomley erased his manager's failure by looping a ball into the hole between third and shortstop and driving in the game's first run.

Back in St. Louis tens of thousands of locals cheered Bottomley's run-scoring hit. All over the city, radios had been hooked up to loudspeakers so that listeners could follow every pitch. Offices, factories, restaurants and retail stores offered their own "radio baseball" in an effort to drum up business during the game. One enterprising 12-year-old newsboy rigged up a crystal set receiver to an antenna that he had placed high atop a nearby warehouse. Listening to the game through earphones, the boy used a megaphone to shout out the play-by-play to his engrossed audience. Even through a couple of light rain showers, fans stood transfixed, following the fate of their Cardinals.

In the bottom half of the inning Billy Sherdel ran into his own problems. Until the previous day, Hornsby had refused to commit to a starting pitcher. He ultimately decided to go with lefty Sherdel's assortment of off-speed pitches rather than the right arm of Alexander. Immediately the decision appeared to be a bad one. Sherdel walked the first Yankee he faced, center fielder Earle Combs. After getting Mark Koenig on a short fly to right, he walked Babe Ruth and cleanup hitter Bob Meusel to load the bases. Anticipating the worst as Gehrig stepped into the batter's box, Hornsby signaled for Jesse Haines and Herman Bell quickly to get ready in the Cardinals bullpen. Initially the call seemed unnecessary. The Yankees first baseman punched a Sherdel fastball to shortstop Thevenow that appeared to be a tailor-made double play. Unfortunately for Sherdel, Hornsby, who was playing Gehrig to pull, had positioned himself in the hole between first and second. As a result he was late getting to Thevenow's throw and unable to make the relay to first in time to catch Gehrig. The delay allowed Combs to scamper home with the tying run. Lazzeri ended what could have been a disastrous start for the Cardinals by rolling a routine ground ball to Thevenow.

In the second inning Pennock began a string of seven near-perfect innings. Until the eighth he allowed only one baserunner, a two-out walk to Les Bell in the fourth. The Cardinals got another runner in the eighth when O'Farrell led off with a walk. Sacrificed to second, the Cardinals catcher could advance no farther. Finally, with an out in the ninth, Bottomley ended Pennock's hitless string, but the Yankee hurler kept his gem intact, easily setting down the next two batters.

Having weathered the first inning, Sherdel also settled down. In the second Dugan led off with a single but was stranded at second. Koenig, who opened the next inning with a base hit, was forced when Babe Ruth tried to lay down a sacrifice bunt. Not known for his bunting skills, Ruth tapped the ball just in front of the plate. O'Farrell jumped on it and pegged to second to get Koenig. The next hitter, Bob Meusel, sacrificed Ruth over to second but on his slide Ruth ripped out the crotch of his pants. Embarrassed, the Babe called time and dashed into the Yankees dugout for some quick mending. A few minutes later, with the repairs made, he sheepishly returned to second, where he stayed when Gehrig lifted a lazy fly to right to end the inning.

In the sixth the Yankees mounted another small rally. Ruth led off the inning. Recognizing that the Cardinals were playing him as a pull hitter, he uncharacteristically choked up on his bat, took a half-swing and lined a pitch into left field. Gehrig followed with another single and Lazzeri chipped in a hit of his own, driving in Ruth with what proved to be the winning run. Sherdel worked himself out of the inning without giving up another run, but Ruth's tally was all that the Yankees would need. Though the Cardinals lefty finished with a six-hitter and had given up only two runs, his Yankees counterpart, Herb Pennock, had done even better.

Disappointed by the first-game loss, manager Hornsby was still very confident about his team's chances of winning the Series. "The first game doesn't mean anything.... We don't have to come back in this series because we haven't gone anywhere to come back from."[10] Like everyone else who had seen the game, he attributed the loss to a superb effort by Pennock rather than a failed effort by his club. His team had played excellent defense, especially Tommy Thevenow who had made a couple of fine plays at shortstop. Aside from a bout of wildness in the first inning Sherdel had pitched an excellent game, and his team showed that they would not crack under the pressure of the Series. Hornsby was certain that the Cardinals would win the second game.

Crowds began lining up for the second game even earlier than they had for the opener. A few anxious fans had spent the night in parked cars near the stadium. Others camped out in front of the ticket booths. By dawn, lines had already begun to queue around the stadium. At 9:30, four hours before game time, those lucky enough to have tickets were allowed in. Those without waited for general admission tickets to go on sale or looked for alternative ways to get in. Scalpers sold their tickets for up to five times face value. Gate crashers tried various methods to get past the turnstiles. Some claimed to be relatives of players or Yankees officials. A few posed as reporters. Others waved around invalid rain checks. Several women simply cried when refused admittance. One ticket taker claimed he could have made up to $2,000 if he had taken the bribes he was offered.

Once inside, a festive mood reigned. Unlike the previous day a bright, warm autumn sun shone down on the field. Some who arrived early spent the morning sunning themselves in the outfield bleachers. Others played cards or dozed. Late in the morning a band began playing along the first base foul line and played until the game started. Once the players came out onto the field, fans, when given a chance, gathered around their heroes, hoping for an autograph or a handshake. Taking advantage of the perfect weather, a small army of photographers scurried around taking pictures of the players as they went through their pre-game warm-up activities. Shortly before the first pitch various celebrities entered the stadium. Once again colorful Mayor Jimmy Walker, fastidiously attired, filled a seat in owner Colonel Ruppert's box. By game time 65,000 fans, the largest crowd ever to watch a World Series game, eagerly awaited the afternoon's contest.

Among the reasons manager Hornsby was so confident that his team would prevail in Game 2 was because he would have Grover Cleveland Alexander on the mound. Through the last weeks of the season Alex had been Hornsby's most reliable hurler. With ten days of rest Hornsby expected him to be at the top of his game, and Alexander at the top of his game was as good as anyone. Opposing him would be Urban Shocker. The long rest and the mild temperature were what Yankees manager Huggins thought his pitcher needed. Like his Cardinals counterpart, Huggins also had great confidence in his second game starter.

Both pitchers ran into a little bit of trouble early. Shocker easily got past the first two Cardinals hitters before Hornsby laced a double to right. In the second the Cardinals collected two more hits but were again unable to score. Alexander's problems had bigger consequences. He opened the game uncharacteristically, walking the first batter he faced. The next hitter, Mark Koenig, lined a shot off Alexander's right hip. Quickly adjusting to the deflection, shortstop Tommy Thevenow made a sensational pickup and toss to Hornsby at second, who then fired on to first to complete a double play. The inning ended when the first confrontation between Alexander and Ruth resulted in a strike out.

In the second inning Alexander's problems grew. Quickly getting two strikes on leadoff hitter Bob Meusel, the Cardinals pitcher's next three offerings danced just off the plate. With the count full Meusel lined a single to center. Gehrig sacrificed him to second and Lazzeri followed with a single to left. On the play Meusel was waved home. Hafey's throw was on line and appeared to be ahead of the runner but for some reason Alexander, who had planted himself midway down the third base line rather than backing up O'Farrell, cut off the throw, allowing Meusel to score without a play. After the game Alex acknowledged that he had been out of position and should not have cut off the throw. Next up was Joe Dugan, who dropped a single into right field sending Lazzeri to third. Bearing down, Alexander struck out Severeid and had two strikes on Shocker when O'Farrell whipped a quick throw from behind the plate that caught Lazzeri off third. In the rundown that followed, Alexander muffed a throw allowing Lazzeri to hustle home with the second run. One strike later Alexander was out of the inning but two Yankees runs had scored.

During the Yankees time at bat O'Farrell became visibly upset with several of plate umpire Hank O'Day's calls. O'Farrell complained that umpire Bill Dinneen the previous day had not given Sherdel all of the plate to work with, and he did not want that to happen to Alexander. However, challenging O'Day was risky business. Selected by National League President John Heydler as one of two National League umpires to work the series, O'Day was considered unbending behind the plate. Christy Mathewson once lamented that arguing with O'Day was like "using a match to see how much fuel was in a gasoline tank."[11] Though his work was well respected, his taciturn, authoritarian demeanor created many enemies. Even fellow umpires complained about his acerbic personality.

O'Day began his long career in professional baseball as a pitcher but by 1895 had made the transition from the mound to calling balls and strikes. By 1926 many considered him to be one of the two or three best umpires in the game. He had almost 30 years experience behind the plate and had umpired in nine World Series. Once when asked what makes a good umpire he responded, "Never allow your eyes to see whether a uniform is white or blue, but call them as you see them." The quip became a mantra for umpires ever since. Though involved in a number of notable game decisions, his most memorable moment came during the 1908 season when he called Fred Merkle out for not touching second base in a pivotal game late in the season. Several times through the years his stubborn manner had backfired. On one occasion he was suspended because he refused to pay a fine for his on-field behavior. O'Day also has the distinction of being the only person to have ever umpired, played and managed in the National League. In 1912 he had led the Cincinnati Reds and in 1914 the Chicago Cubs, but both times returned to umpiring.[12]

One of the few umpires of O'Day's stature was Bill Klem, who was the other National League umpire assigned to the series. It was his 13th Series. Though Klem had seven fewer years experience behind the plate than O'Day, he was considered by many to be the best umpire in the game and is often referred to as the father of modern umpiring. An innovator, Klem developed a technique behind the plate that enabled an umpire to more accurately see the strike zone. He is often credited with introducing many of the hand signals that, in an age when a public address system was a megaphone, kept spectators informed. Klem became known as "The Arbitrator" and like O'Day was an autocrat on the field. He claimed that he never missed a call and never got one wrong. Frankie Frisch concurred: "If you got out of line, he'd run you out of there but he eventually got to a point where you never thought about questioning his judgment because you knew he was always right."[13] Unlike O'Day, Klem was an extrovert and a showman. Physically the two men were also a contrast. Klem stood only 5' 5" tall and weighed just 155 pounds. O'Day was 6' and 180 pounds. Two proud men who employed contrasting styles, Klem and O'Day did not particularly like each other. Klem once described O'Day as a "misanthropic Irishman."[14]

The other two umpires in the Series were George Hildebrand and "Big Bill" Dinneen. Both had played in the major leagues. Dinneen was a star pitcher and Hildebrand briefly played the outfield for Brooklyn. Pitching for three different teams, Dinneen four times won 20 games. His most notable mound accomplishment came in the first World Series, when he won three games and led his team, the Boston Pilgrims, over the Pittsburgh Pirates. Dinneen's trademarks on the mound were his fastball and his stamina. In 1904 he started and completed an incredible 37 games, winning 23 of them. When a sore arm ended his playing career in 1909 he immediately asked league president Ban Johnson for a chance to umpire. Johnson agreed and by the end of the season Dinneen had traded in his uniform for an umpire's blue suit. His first game behind the plate was at the major league level. In the years that followed he earned a reputation as a fair and congenial umpire. The 1926 Series was his sixth.[15]

Hildebrand's claim to baseball fame, even though he was an outfielder, was as the "inventor" of the spitball. One day while he was warming up alongside one of the team's pitchers, Frank Corridon, Hildebrand noticed that his teammate moistened his fingers before each pitch. Mimicking the pitcher, Hildebrand spit on the ball and whipped it to Corridon's catcher. All three were amazed by the ball's strange dipping motion. After a few days of refinement Corridon began using the new pitch in games. Later Hildebrand showed another teammate, Elmer Stricklett, how to throw a spitter. Strickett perfected the pitch and is given credit for being the first in the major leagues to use it. After Hildebrand's playing career ended in 1908, he signed on as an umpire in the Pacific Coast League, and five years later was hired by the American League to call balls and strikes. Never considered among the best behind the plate, he was affable and had good sense of humor which made him popular with players and managers. The 1926 Series was his fourth (and last).[16]

Down two runs after only two innings, the Cardinals fought back. Douthit beat out a slow roller to third to open the third inning. Southworth followed with a sharp drive to left. Hornsby then lay down a sacrifice bunt, pushing both runners up a base. The strategy paid off a batter later. "Sunny"

Jim Bottomley drilled a two-run single to right field that fell just in front of Ruth. Shocker was able to get the next two batters, Bell and Hafey, without allowing any more damage but the Cardinals had evened the score.

Given a second chance, Alexander pitched magnificently. Combs led off the third with a single, but that was the last Yankees hit and the last Yankees base runner of the day. Alexander mowed down the next 21 batters he faced. Along the way he struck out ten, including three in the fourth. Shocker wasn't quite as effective. Matching Alexander out for out through the sixth, he ran into trouble in the seventh. O'Farrell opened with a double to the gap in left center. Thevenow then lined a single to left, pushing O'Farrell up a base. After Alexander popped to second, Douthit flied out to shallow left. With Shocker one out short of escaping the inning, Southworth hit the first pitch he saw to deep right field. Ruth immediately got a bead on the ball and drifted back to the 295-foot sign. Planted at the base of the wall, he stretched up for the catch but the ball fell into the bleachers just beyond his glove. The three-run blast was all that the Cardinals needed to tie the series. Two innings later Thevenow padded the lead with an inside-the-park home run, his third inside-the-park homer of the year.

Two hours after the last out, both teams boarded trains bound for St. Louis. The 1,150-mile ride turned into a race between the Cleveland, Cincinnati, Chicago and St. Louis Railways, better known as the "Big Four," which carried the Yankees, and the Pennsylvania Railroad Company, which carried the Cardinals. The trains departed shortly after 5 p.m. All along the way rail traffic was diverted to allow the two "specials" unimpeded passage and maximum speed. Unfortunately a wreck in Altoona, PA, slowed the Pennsylvania but to make up for it the engineer sped through the last half of the trip full throttle. Despite the effort, the Big Four won the race by ten minutes. It chugged into St. Louis 23 hours and 30 minutes after leaving New York, record time according to the company.

What awaited the Cardinals in St. Louis was a celebration unlike any the city had ever seen. For several weeks plans for the celebration had been growing. When Hornsby and his crew left home on September 1 they were locked in a heated three-team pennant race. Five weeks later they were returning home as league champions, just three games short of a world title. During the time the team was away local fans had to be content following them from afar. Now the city as well as supporters throughout the entire lower Midwest was ready to unleash its pent-up glee and celebrate. The only damper on the gala was Rogers Hornsby, the most popular hero of them all. The Cardinals manager had reluctantly agreed to a parade but wanted to keep the festivities limited so that his players would have plenty of time to rest and prepare for the next day's game. Hornsby's request was ignored.

The celebration began even before the players disembarked from their train. Explosives were set off as the Cardinals train approached the city. Unfortunately, because the Yankees train arrived first it was the one that was mistakenly given the loud welcoming. Ten minutes later, when the St. Louis team train did arrive, it was engulfed by thousands of ecstatic fans. Inside the station, amid a crush of admirers, the mayor gave a brief speech, then presented each player with a variety of gifts including engraved gold watches. The best prize, a new Lincoln sedan, was saved for Hornsby. With the formalities out of the way, players were loaded two by two into limousines and paraded 34 blocks through the center of St. Louis. As the caravan crawled forward, a multitude of supporters, many decked out in Cardinals red, yelled, rang bells, blew horns, clanged noise makers and showered ticker-tape and confetti onto the limousines. Some fans jumped onto the cars' running boards and rode along with their favorite players. Hornsby's car, the last car in the procession, was especially popular. A dozen or so frenzied fans climbed onto the hood, the roof and the running boards and rode with their hero. Even after the parade ended and the players departed, the revelry continued. Long into the night cars circled the downtown, blowing their horns. Mobs pranced throughout the city center, shouting and singing. Traffic blocked streets for hours. One reporter wrote, "The entire city was a bedlam of excitement last night"[17] Another added, "The whole city blew up like a mine in Northern France."[18] Baseball Commissioner Landis agreed, claiming that the celebration surpassed all others in any major league city.

For some the celebration continued into the next morning. Rather than return home they camped out at the ballpark despite a few showers. By midnight, officials counted more than 1,000 fans bivouacked along the streets surrounding the field. They brought steamer chairs, cots, folding chairs and cardboard to sleep on. Others slept in their cars. To keep warm through the chilly night they burned trash and debris in cans or just bundled up in blankets they had brought along. Even before dawn a double line encircling the park had formed. The gates were opened at 8:30 a.m., five hours before game time, and within an hour all the $1.10 bleacher seats were filled and the $3.30 pavilion seats were almost sold out as well. Late in the morning a band set up in the right field grandstands and entertained the early patrons as those fortunate enough to have reserved seats arrived. By the time the first pitch was thrown, 37,700 paying spectators, a St. Louis record, packed into the park.

The third game of the 1926 World Series became a showcase for Cardinals pitcher Jesse Haines. Amid a roaring partisan crowd, he and his Yankees counterpart, Dutch Ruether, blanked their opposition through three innings. Then in the bottom of the fourth, after a 30-minute rain delay, the Cardinals broke through. Les Bell led off with a single to center and was sacrificed to second. O'Farrell walked to put runners on first and second. Thevenow hit a ball to second that looked like a sure double play. Lazzeri fielded the ball cleanly and tossed it to Koenig at second, but the Yankees shortstop threw the ball into the dirt and past Gehrig, allowing Bell to score. Haines was next to face Reuther. The Cardinals pitcher was not particularly dangerous with a bat in his hands. He didn't strike out much but neither did he get many hits, and almost never extra-base hits. This time was different. He drilled the first pitch he saw into the right field bleachers. The two-run shot, Haines's first home run in six years, gave the Cardinals a comfortable three-run lead. An inning later singles by Southworth and Hornsby and a sacrifice by Bottomley tacked on an insurance run.

Through the last five innings Haines dominated the Yankees. He gave up only two singles, walked two and did not allow a runner past second. After the game Wilbert Robinson remarked, "Jesse had everything we ever saw him throw and just a little more."[19] Hornsby agreed, calling Haines's performance even better than Alexander's two days earlier. Miller Huggins also complimented the Cardinals pitcher but attributed his success more to slumping Yankees hitters than Haines's pitching. Cardinals fans didn't care whether it was Haines's pitching or inept Yankees hitters. They were thrilled to have a game lead in the Series and briefly renewed the previous day's celebration.

Among those most interested in the Cardinals victory were gamblers across the country. Bookies followed the odds published in the papers as closely as investors followed stock reports. Gamblers, both sanctioned and unsanctioned, were doing unprecedented business taking wagers on the Series. One New York gambling commissioner predicted that because the two teams were so evenly matched, the amount bet during the series would surpass all other series totals. Likewise, betting on individual games was setting records. In New York alone more than $2,000,000 was bet on Game 2. In St. Louis, officials reported equally active wagering on Game 3. After the Cardinals went up a game, no one doubted that locals would raise the ante and bet even more. The prediction was correct. Betting on Game 4 set records in St. Louis.

Ticket scalpers and avaricious St. Louis hotel operators also raked in World Series profits. The city tried to limit ticket scalping but because the demand was so great and the market so large little could be done. Even though the Cardinals only sold tickets in pairs, some schemers were able to acquire dozens of tickets and then sell them well above face value. Dozens of counterfeit tickets were also sold to unsuspecting fans. The demand for hotel accommodations created another opportunity for greedy entrepreneurs.

Some hotels set up cots and packed as many patrons as they could into rooms. Other hotels resorted to price gouging by charging double or more for their rooms. All over the city there were also home owners who happily rented out a bed, a couch or space on their floor to visitors. Clearly the Series offered opportunities to those rapacious enough to take advantage of them.

After the loss in Game 3 Yankees fans were worried. Their team was in a slump and needed to start hitting immediately. Thus far in the Series the ferocious "Murderer's Row" did not have an extra-base hit. In three games the team had only 15 singles and four runs scored. It was as bad a three-game stretch as they had had all season. The prospect of facing Flint Rhem, arguably the best Cardinals pitcher, added to the New Yorkers' gloom. So concerned was American League President Ban Johnson, who hated to lose to National League teams, that before Game 4 he went into the Yankees locker room and lectured the team, "go in there and act like champions ... it is time to wake up and play ball."[20] However, amid the growing swirl of anxiety around him, Manager Huggins remained confident. His team would start hitting and despite lots of advice to use Pennock a day early, he was set to throw Waite Hoyt.

Flint Rhem opened Game 4 with a flurry, striking out the first two Yankees he faced. Then he made a mistake. He challenged Babe Ruth with a belt-high fast ball. Ruth blasted the ball into the right field bleachers. The home run was a sign of things to come. The Cardinals battled back in their half of the first. Douthit led off with an infield single. Southworth followed with a line single to right and Hornsby punched a ball up the middle to score Douthit. Off to a bad start himself, Hoyt settled down and got the next three hitters without allowing any more runs.

Both pitchers got some defensive help in the second. Lazzeri led off for the Yankees and drove a pitch to the wall in left field but was cut down by a perfect relay when he tried to stretch his double into a triple. In the bottom half of the inning Lazzeri redeemed himself with an outstanding play behind second. Ranging far to his right, he scooped up an O'Farrell ground ball and gunned the Cardinals catcher out at first. Hoyt took care of the rest, breezing past the next two hitters.

Facing the top of the Yankees order for the second time, Rhem, as he had in the first, easily got Combs and Koenig but again had a problem with Ruth. This time the Yankees slugger deposited Rhem's first pitch over the right center field bleachers, into Grand Avenue, and on one bounce the ball broke through the Wells Motor Car showroom window. Few had ever seen a ball hit as hard as Ruth's second home run of the day. In the bottom of the inning the Cardinals failed to match Ruth's tally.

The fourth inning proved no better for the Cardinals pitcher. After

Gehrig struck out, Lazzeri walked and Dugan lifted a fly to short left center field. Racing to get to the ball, center fielder Douthit and left fielder Hafey collided. Dazed, both fell to the ground. By the time the ball was retrieved Lazzeri had scored and Dugan was standing on second.

Down by two, the Cardinals came to the plate in need of some runs. Left fielder Chick Hafey got the team started with a one-out single. O'Farrell then hit what appeared to be a sure double play ball to Koenig, but once again the Yankees shortstop muffed the play. Thevenow followed with a double to right and "Specs" Toporcer, batting for Rhem, punched a sacrifice fly to center. Leadoff hitter Douthit, apparently recovered from his collision earlier in the inning, doubled in Thevenow, but one batter later was cut down at the plate by a perfect throw from Ruth after he had fielded a Southworth single. In all the Cardinals put three runs on the board to take the lead.

It was a lead that did not last long. Left-hander Art Reinhart replaced Rhem on the mound but proved even less effective. Facing the top of the order, he walked Combs, gave up a double to Koenig, then walked Ruth, Meusel, and Gehrig. With the bases loaded, no one out and two runs in, a disgusted manager Hornsby called for Herman Bell to finish the inning. Bell did as instructed but only after two more runs had scored. The four-run assault proved too much for the Cardinals. In the bottom of the inning they went down without a hit. Through the next four innings Hoyt confidently worked through the Cardinals order, giving up only a last-inning run.

Meanwhile the Yankees attack continued. In the sixth Ruth made World Series history by hitting his third homer of the day, a two-run drive to the deepest part of the park in dead center field. It was the first time in his career that he had hit three home runs in a game. As he rounded the bases, even the most devoted Cardinals fans stood and applauded the slugger's production. An inning later New York tacked on yet another run, their tenth, on a single, a sacrifice bunt and a double. By the time Ruth came to the plate in the eighth, the only uncertainty left in the game was whether or not the Bambino would add a fourth clout to his day's collection. After another standing ovation the slugger watched four straight pitches sail well out of the strike zone.

While Ruth's three home runs became the next day's headlines, the seeds of a more compelling part of the Ruth legend were planted during Game 4. In Essex Falls, New Jersey, 11-year-old Johnny Sylvester was reportedly gravely ill. He had either been kicked by a horse or had fallen from a horse and was suffering from a mild concussion, a spinal injury, and a neck injury or severe blood poisoning, depending upon the newspaper account you read. A couple of newspapers claimed Johnny's doctor had given him less than an hour to live. The boy's greatest wish was to have a baseball autographed by some of the Cardinals and Yankees players. His father was Horace Sylvester, a well-connected bank vice president. Hoping to cheer up his sick son, he telegraphed a friend in St. Louis to try to get some baseballs autographed by the two teams. The friend got the autographs and air mailed the balls back east. Along with the baseballs the boy's favorite player, Babe Ruth, reportedly sent a note in which he promised to hit a home run for the sick boy. The package was delivered just hours before Ruth hit his home runs. As Johnny listened to the game, baseballs in hand, his condition improved with each home run. By the end of the game he was well on his way to recovery.

The story was a press agent's dream (a dream created at least in part by Ruth's press agent, Christy Walsh). Though the episode received a little attention during the Series, it began to grow quickly a few days after the Series when Ruth visited the boy. How much of the story was true will probably never be completely known. Certainly the boy was ill, though the source and severity of his illness is unclear. Johnny liked baseball but in later years claimed to be a Giants supporter and not a Babe Ruth fan. Whether Ruth made a pre-game promise to hit a home run is also unclear. Nevertheless, regardless of the story's veracity, it became and remains a favorite episode in the Babe Ruth legend.

Rogers Hornsby was angry after Game 4. The targets of his ire were the first four pitchers, Rhem, Reinhart, Herman Bell and Bill Hallahan, who had pitched in the game. The Cardinals manager complained, "You can't expect to win a game as badly pitched as this one was…. Not once was Ruth pitched to properly and that's the story of the game." Only Vic Keen, the fifth Cardinals pitcher of the day and the only one who did not face Ruth, escaped Hornsby's wrath. Aside from the pitching the Cardinals manager was pleased with the way his team played, especially Tommy Thevenow who "played his usual brilliant game."[21]

Huggins agreed that "Ruth, more than anything else, accounts for the victory," but also credited the Babe's teammates. Aside from the three Ruth wallops, Yankees bats had hammered out 11 hits, five of them for extra bases. In the field the team turned in a couple of fine plays, and Waite Hoyt had pitched well. Huggins promised "We started (hitting) today and that won't stop … and that spells only one thing, victory."[22] Both managers agreed that Game 5 would be a pivotal contest. Hornsby had predicted before the Series began that his team would take at least two of the three games in St. Louis. A return to New York down a game would present the Cardinals with a very difficult task. Huggins concurred that a win in Game 5 would give the Yankees a big advantage.

As Game 5 approached the excitement throughout St. Louis grew to a fever pitch. The success of Babe Ruth and his teammates the previous day had shaken the confidence of many Cardinals rooters. To compensate, they went to new lengths to demonstrate their support. Again hundreds of fans camped out all night at the park, hoping to get prime bleacher seats. Feeding upon the ever-growing demand of anxious rooters, scalpers raised their prices, but the higher cost did nothing to deter purchasers. When the bleachers opened at 8:30, red became the color of the day. Handmade signs and team flags were carried into the park and noise makers of all kinds blared. Soon a band began playing songs designed to rally the partisan spirit further. Atop the Y.M.C.A. building behind the center field bleachers was hoisted a large balloon carrying a big, bright red cardinal that could be seen throughout the park. When the Cardinals came out to warm up before the game, the growing crowd cheered non-stop. Conversely, when the Yankees warmed up, boos echoed throughout the park. The only Yankee exception was Babe Ruth, who had his own rooting section in the left field bleachers (when in St. Louis Ruth played left field and Meusel played right which was the sun field). By game time a frenzied crowd of 39,552, the biggest in Cardinals history, was ready to howl on every pitch.

The fifth game of the Series was a rematch of the two opening game pitchers. Miller Huggins had wisely held back his ace, Herb Pennock, for the fifth game rather than throw him the previous day as many had advised him. Hornsby had tabbed "Wee" Willie Sherdel for the important assignment even before the Series began. The Cardinals manager had complete confidence that his starter could again subdue Yankee hitters as he had in Game 1. The only change from the first-game lineups was the Cardinals center fielder. The collision between Douthit and Hafey the previous day had been worse for Douthit than initially believed. He arrived at the ball park so sore that he could barely lift his arm or swing a bat. Instead Hornsby started Wattie Holm in center field and gave him Douthit's spot at the top of the batting order as well.

The game started well for Sherdel. With the crowd cheering non-stop he got the first three batters he faced, including Ruth, who grounded a ball to Hornsby at second. The Cardinals' first inning was more exciting but no more productive. Holm bounced Pennock's first pitch to short for a routine out. Southworth followed with another ground ball to short but this time Koenig rushed the play and fumbled the ball much to the delight of Cardinal fans. On the first pitch to Hornsby, Southworth stole second. A pitch later he went to third on a passed ball. With one out, Hornsby at the plate and Bottomley, who was the only Cardinal who hit Pennock well in the first game, on deck, the Yankees pitcher was in a hole. Amid thousands of screaming fans Pennock coolly dispatched Hornsby on a dribbler back to the mound and got Bottomley on a ground out to Lazzeri, temporarily silencing the partisans.

Sherdel, assisted by a double play in the second, cruised through the next four innings. Pennock had no problems in the second and third but in the fourth he could not get past Bottomley. "Sunny Jim" jolted the Yankees pitcher for a one-out double and scored when the next hitter, Les Bell, singled to right. A running catch by Ruth in left may have prevented another Cardinals tally.

The Cardinals lead held up until the sixth. Pennock led off the inning by lifting a fly to Hafey in left. Slowly backpedaling, the Cardinals outfielder slipped and fell, allowing the ball to drop behind him for a double. A couple of pitches later O'Farrell caught Pennock off second base but Thevenow dropped the throw and Pennock scampered back safely. Combs then walked and Koenig singled Pennock in for New York's first run. With no one out and runners on first and second, Ruth came to the plate. Amid hoots and hollers from his supporters, Sherdel lived up to the challenge, striking Ruth out on an assortment of off-speed pitches. Meusel flied to right. Gehrig walked and Lazzeri, with two outs and the bases full, smacked one high and deep to right. Initially the ball appeared destined for the bleachers but the wind pushed it back into play and Southworth was able to pull it in just in front of the fence to end the inning.

The Cardinals regained the lead in the seventh. Les Bell opened with a double to left. His hit pushed the noisy fans into a furor. Throughout the game the St. Louis faithful had steadily bellowed their support for the home team, their opposition to the visitors and their disapproval of numerous calls made by plate umpire Bill Dinneen. Bell's double raised the crowd volume by many decibels. When an out later O'Farrell singled in Bell with the go-ahead run the roar reached a thunderous crescendo.

Through the seventh and eighth innings Sherdel got every hitter he faced. In the ninth Gehrig popped up to short but Thevenow lost the ball in the sun and it fell for a double. Lazzeri followed with a bunt single that moved Gehrig to third. Ben Paschal was then called upon to pinch hit for Dugan. On a 2–2 pitch Paschal dropped a Texas League single into center which scored Gehrig and tied the game. After Severeid forced Lazzeri at third, Pennock came to the plate with one out, runners on first and second and a chance to win his own game. The Yankees pitcher slashed a ground ball up the middle but Thevenow made a game-saving play. Ranging far to his left, he picked up the ball and quickly tossed it to Hornsby who was covering second. Combs ended the inning by rolling a pitch to Hornsby.

The Cardinals failed to match the Yankees tally in the bottom of the ninth and the game went into extra innings. In the top of the tenth Koenig led off with a sharp single to left. Ruth walked and Meusel bunted both runners up a base. Gehrig was then walked to load the bases. With one out, rookie second baseman Tony Lazzeri became the Yankees hero of the day by driving a sacrifice fly deep to left field. In the bottom of the inning Pennock dominated the three Cardinals he faced and put his team one game away from a world championship as they headed back home to New York.

St. Louis was stunned by the loss. As the "rainbow of world series hopes faded," some fans sat in disbelief, some dejectedly ambled out of the park, and a few left teary-eyed. Rogers Hornsby was angry. "We'd have won today if the team had been up to scratch but you can't win with a team playing the way mine did today." He berated his players' efforts as indifferent, sloppy, and lacking the courage to win. He singled out Chick Hafey's poor play, ranting that his left fielder was responsible for two of the Yankees runs. Only Sherdel escaped his manager's wrath. "Sherdel pitched a great game. He was better than Pennock. He should have won." Meanwhile "Wee Willie" slumped almost inconsolably on a stool in front of his locker. Despite the tirade, Hornsby left reporters with a positive note. "We'll get them. Pittsburgh came through last year with two wins to grab the series and I don't see why we can't do the same." Over in the Yankees clubhouse Miller Huggins was, understandably, much more upbeat. "The fighting spirit won for us.... It was fight, fight, fight with my men from the time the first ball was thrown.... We have them on the run now."[23]

Within an hour of the last out of Game 5 both teams were on trains bound for New York City. The Cardinals left on the Pennsylvania Railroad's fastest special, *The American*. The Yankees, who took the New York Central's *Southwestern Limited*, almost chugged off without Babe Ruth. The slugger mistakenly showed up at the Union Station as his train pulled out. Grabbing a friend, he made a frantic drive across town to the North St. Louis station just as the last of his teammates were boarding. Of course, had he missed his train there were numerous other specials lined up to carry officials from both teams and both league offices, umpires, and fans back east. Sixteen special trains with 421 cars, including sleepers and dining cars, were assigned to carry almost 4,500 travelers to New York City for the weekend.

As they had on the trip to St. Louis five days earlier, the two railroad companies raced each other east. This time the Pennsylvania traveled obstacle-free and pulled into the Pennsylvania Station in record time: 22 hours and 40 minutes. The New York Central, which had about an additional 100 miles of track to traverse, arrived in Grand Central Station two hours later. A small gathering of fans cheered the Yankees as they arrived. As always the prime attraction was Babe Ruth, who signed a few autographs and briefly chatted with supporters. The Cardinals slipped into New York almost undetected and were quickly taxied off to their hotel.

Back in St. Louis, Cardinals fans unable to travel to New York made plans to listen to the games on radio. Baseball broadcasting was a relatively new phenomenon. The first game broadcast was on August 5, 1921, at the very dawn of the radio age in the United States. Harold Arlin at station KDKA in Pittsburgh described a Pirates game to a tiny audience. Later that year WJZ in Newark sent a scratchy account of the World Series out over the air to a handful of listeners. During the years that followed, broadcast production methods and announcing techniques improved but only a few stations were able to transmit games. By 1926 there were approximately 500 stations in the country but with a few exceptions both their range and daily programming were very limited. Many stations were on the air for less than four hours a day and had a range of about 20 miles. To carry the Series to a larger audience, WEAF in New York City organized a "gigantic hook up of 21 stations."[24] The sponsoring station, WEAF, agreed to transmit a running game account via telephone to the member stations, and the stations would then broadcast the account to listeners. Referred to as a "pick up" network, stations that joined did so exclusively to put on air each Series game. Once the game was over, each station returned to its own broadcasting activities. In St. Louis, KSD became part of the "network."

In 1926 it was estimated that one in six American households had a radio. That number, however, is a bit deceptive. Radios were comparatively expensive. The average cost of a radio was about $125. In order to facilitate more than a couple of listeners at a time, a speaker that could be placed on top of the radio set had to be purchased. The speaker typically cost another $75 to $100. At a time when a Model T cost $300 and the average American worker made approximately $1,350 annually, a $200 radio set was beyond the means of most. For rural Americans who made less and had less access to programming, a radio set was a very expensive luxury. In reality, radios in 1926 were owned by upper and upper middle class urbanites, by businesses looking for ways to attract customers, and by civic organizations. As a result few St. Louisans listened to the Cardinals in the privacy of their own homes. Instead some gathered at a neighbor's home, but most listened with others in public facilities. Listening to their hometown team play in the World Series therefore became a community activity.

To accommodate the eager fans, radios sets were put up throughout St. Louis. Sportsman's Park, the Cardinals home, transmitted the last two games to crowds so big that additional speakers were put outside the park to accommodate the overflow. At almost every intersection in the downtown district, radios and speakers were set up. At a couple of the sites crowds were so big that they stopped traffic. The biggest crowd, estimated at more than 2,000, gathered in front of the Federal building. Various schools opened their doors to neighborhood families anxious to follow the games. Many local hospitals also set up radios and speakers. The Jewish Hospital put radios in every room and reported patients were "taking a keen interest in the KSD reports."[25] The St. Louis Veterans Hospital installed a radio set in its auditorium and invited all veterans regardless of their health to stop in and listen to the games. Even the Chicago and Alton Railroad which traveled between St. Louis and Chicago installed special radio receivers in its cars for the final two games of the Series.

The voice that radio listeners heard describing the series was the best known voice in America: Graham McNamee. Trained in St. Paul, McNamee came to New York City to find work as a concert singer. In May, 1923, on a whim he walked into radio station WEAF, which was one of the biggest stations in New York, for a singing audition. Instead he was hired as the station's announcer. Later that year he was assigned to accompany and provide commentary for *New York Tribune* writer W.O. McGeehan, who had been hired by WEAF to describe that year's World Series. Midway through the first game McGeehan felt so uncomfortable behind a microphone that he left. McNamee quickly filled in even though he knew very little about baseball. From that start McNamee would become the nation's preeminent sportscaster. Through his vivid descriptions he provided listeners with a front row seat at whatever event he was announcing. He also used his powerful voice to add drama and excitement to events. Critics like sportswriter Ring Lardner periodically complained that McNamee was more interested in spectacle than in accurate reporting. Lardner once wrote, "there was a doubleheader yesterday — the one that was played and the one McNamee announced."[26] He was also criticized for reporting erroneous information, a criticism he readily admitted. Nevertheless, McNamee was revered by his listeners.

In addition to McNamee, a corps of brilliant sportswriters including Damon Runyon, Grantland Rice, Heywood Broun, Fred Lieb and young Shirley Povich provided detailed game accounts for readers. This was an era when sportswriters did more than simply report. Instead they created compelling narratives by wrapping the factual information about a game into a lively tale. Their style was characterized by the use of distinctive similes and metaphors, animated verbs and colorful adjectives. The stories focused on the players, who were usually portrayed heroically when they excelled and almost tragically when they failed. With a few exceptions, even opposing players were presented in a positive manner. To further enhance reader appeal, players were often given unique nicknames that reflected a personal quality or characteristic. Each game entailed a cast of primary characters engaged in an honorable athletic struggle. Sometimes stories also included subtle commentary that helped guide the reader to a desired conclusion.

Autumn arrived in New York City at about the same time as the Cardinals and the Yankees. The day of the sixth game was chilly and cloudy. Clearly the weather affected the mood of activities prior to the game. The patrons that ambled into Yankee Stadium looked more like a football crowd than baseball fans. Most came in heavy coats and hats rather than short-sleeve shirts. Unlike the previous games, there was no clamor to get tickets and only a few fans were waiting when the gates opened. Street vendors still had customers but lines for their ware were short. Ticket scalpers were perhaps the most adversely affected. Some reported selling tickets for as little as 20 percent of face value. Many of the police assigned to direct patrons and control traffic milled around with little to do. Inside the stadium the carousing that had accompanied the previous games, particularly the three in St. Louis, was also absent. By the time the first pitch was thrown there were only 48,500 spectators sitting in Yankee Stadium, far fewer than the 55,000 to 60,000 that were expected.

No one doubted that Rogers Hornsby was going to pitch Grover Cleveland Alexander in Game 6. There were few if any pitchers in baseball that Hornsby would have preferred for such an important assignment. Miller Huggins' choice, on the other hand, was not as clear. Most expected Urban Shocker to start for New York, and in fact just two days earlier Huggins had said it would be Shocker. However, since then the Yankees manager had begun to have second thoughts. While Shocker was well rested and anxious to pitch again he had not fared well in Game 2. On the other hand, in his two relief appearances veteran Bob Shawkey had dominated Cardinals hitters. In 4⅔ innings he had not given up a run or a hit and had struck out three. Huggins made his choice just hours before game time. It would be Shawkey in Game 6.

The Cardinals wasted no time in showing Huggins the error of his ways. Leadoff hitter Wattie Holm, again filling in for the injured Douthit, opened the game with a single. Southworth followed, hitting into a force play, and Hornsby walked. Bottomley knocked in the first Cardinals run with a sharp double into right field. The next batter, Les Bell, finished the scoring with a two-run single to center. Already staked to a three-run lead, Alexander easily cut through the first three Yankees hitters.

Past his first-inning nerves, Shawkey came out in the second and set down the next six men he faced. Through the third Alexander was almost as good, giving up only a leadoff double to Meusel in the second. In the fourth Meusel again led off. This time he lined an Alexander pitch over Bell's head at third and down the left field line. By the time left fielder Hafey, who got a bad jump on the ball, retrieved it Meusel was on his way to third with a triple. Gehrig followed with a ground ball to first that brought Meusel home with the Yankees' first run. With the help of a great play by Thevenow behind second, the Cardinals got out of the inning with no more damage done.

St. Louis matched the Yankees run in the top of the fifth. Thevenow opened the inning with a single between the shortstop and third baseman. Alexander laid down a sacrifice bunt that got Thevenow to second. Holm followed with his second hit of the game, a single to center that scored the baserunner.

Both teams failed to score in the sixth but in the seventh Shawkey fell apart. Again Thevenow led off with a single and Alexander attempted to bunt him over to second. However, this time Lazzeri, who was covering first, dropped catcher Severeid's throw. Holm then muffed a bunt that forced Theverow at third and Southworth lifted a high fly ball to left. Meusel drifted under the ball but at the last moment lost it in the mid-afternoon sun. Officially ruled a double, Southworth's fly drove in Alexander with the Cardinals' fifth run of the day. That was the end of the afternoon for Shawkey. In his place an obviously disgruntled Urban Shocker was called upon to relieve. Unhappy that he had not started the game, Shocker was even angrier that he was being used as a relief pitcher rather than being saved as a possible starter if the Series went to a seventh game as it appeared it would. Hornsby greeted him with a two-run single. The next man up, Bottomley, forced the Cardinals manager at second but then scored when Bell blasted a Shocker pitch into the left field bleachers. The five-run assault gave Alexander an eight-run cushion, far more than he would need. Pitching very deliberately through the last three innings, the Cardinals hurler gave up a pair of runs but was never in serious trouble. The veteran's biggest problem was the weather. "It was so cold that you couldn't work up a sweat. I was afraid in one of those long innings of being kept too long on the bench where it was colder than (on the field). That was my only worry. I knew I had enough to stop them but I was afraid that the cold weather might affect me."[27]

The Cardinals clubhouse was jubilant after the game. "They can't beat us now!" Specs Toporcer shouted to reporters. Teammates echoed the call, guaranteeing a win in the final game. Happy with his team's play, Hornsby focused just as much on the next day's game. "I was absolutely confident that Alex would beat them today and I am just as confident Jesse Haines will beat them again tomorrow.... We hit the ball today when we had to and we will hit again tomorrow when hits mean even more than they did today."[28] His Yankees counterpart took the loss philosophically. "We didn't hit," said Huggins. "We will tomorrow. We have too good a club to be stopped twice in a row when the championship hinges on one game. We will win tomorrow."[29]

Most odds makers gave a slight edge to the Cardinals even though they were playing away from home. John McGraw and Wilbert Robinson, who had both steadfastly predicted all along that the Cardinals would win, were more even certain about their predictions. McGraw analytically dissected the two teams and concluded that Cardinals pitching would be the difference. Haines had pitched perhaps the best game of the Series while Hoyt, though he had won, had not been particularly impressive. The Yankees' fastball hitters would again have a tough time with Jesse Haines's knuckleball. Robinson agreed.

The last day of the 1926 baseball season was cold, grey, and wet in New York City. Rain had fallen during the night and a steady drizzle continued throughout the morning. Though the weather again deterred some early arrivals, more braved the conditions than had the previous day. A few camped out all night to get the best unreserved grandstand or bleacher seats. Lines began forming at daybreak. By 9:00, when the gates opened, several thousand decked out in overcoats, raincoats, and slickers stood waiting. Fans continued to trickle into the stadium during the next few hours. Those inside huddled together under the roof or in the covered runway leading to the stands, trying to stay warm and dry. Late in the morning a band rallied ticket holders by playing fight songs. At about noon, when it was announced officially that the game would be played, the crowd began to grow more quickly. For 90 minutes taxis and the subway steadily delivered fans. Half an hour before game time the light fog that had shrouded the field all morning finally lifted. A few minutes before the first pitch, Mayor Jimmy Walker joined Commissioner Landis and the two league presidents in Colonel Ruppert's box along the first base line. Finally, with lots of seats still empty, 38,100 eager fans settled in to watch the last game between the two league champions. It was a game that they would never forget.

It became clear even before the game started that unlike the previous day this crowd would be more vocal and more partisan. As early arrivals sauntered in they gravitated to either Cardinals or Yankees rooting sections which competed against each other, cheering whenever one of their players came onto the field. Babe Ruth got the biggest ovation. Even Cardinals fans applauded the home run king. Yankees supporters reciprocated when they first saw Rogers Hornsby. The rest of the players, especially the two starting pitchers, Waite Hoyt and Jesse Haines, became fair game for catcalls and hurrahs. All through the brief warm-ups the noise built. By game time there was a distinct rumble traveling throughout the stands.

Wattie Holm, who was once again substituting for Douthit, opened the

For Waite Hoyt 1926 was a very frustrating season.

game by grounding out to Gehrig at first. Billy Southworth followed with an easy fly to Meusel in left. The first Cardinals cheer was the product of a Hornsby hit up the middle. Yankees fans retaliated when Bottomley popped to Gehrig in foul territory to end the Cardinals half of the inning. Through the first four hitters in the St. Louis lineup, Hoyt appeared to be sharp.

Like Hoyt, Haines easily retired the first two hitters, Combs and Koenig. Ruth was a different story. Hornsby had instructed his pitcher not to give the Babe anything to hit. Nibble on the corners but don't throw anything that he could drive. Haines obeyed and, with the crowd roaring, he walked Ruth on five pitches. Meusel further revved up Yankees fans by driving a single to left field. With runners on first and second and the crowd howling, Gehrig shot a low line drive toward right field but Hornsby jumped in front of it, knocked it down, then tossed Gehrig out at first.

Mixing in a couple of curveballs with his blazing fastball, Hoyt easily set down the three Cardinals batters he faced in the second. Haines again was not quite as good. After striking out Lazzeri he gave up a single to Dugan. Two pitches later Jumping Joe took off for second base. O'Farrell's throw to the bag was low but Thevenow masterfully dug it out in time to tag the sliding Dugan. With the bases again empty catcher Severeid singled down the left field line. Fortunately for Haines his pitching counterpart was next to the plate. Hoyt chopped a ball back to Haines for the final out. Through the first two innings Haines appeared to be uncomfortable on the mound. Several times he stopped to pick mud out of his spikes and to smooth out the mound. He was also having some trouble controlling his fastball though his knuckler seemed to be working well.

Under the day's only rays of sunshine Hoyt was again dominating in the third. Thevenow got to him for a leadoff single and was sacrificed to second but Holm popped to the catcher and Southworth again lifted a lazy fly to left. Facing the top of the Yankees lineup for the second time, Haines again had no problems with the first two hitters. Combs grounded to first and Koenig flew to left. Amidst thunderous cheers Babe Ruth dug into the batter's box, daring Haines to give him something he could hit. On the third pitch Ruth got what he wanted. Haines threw a pitch that was a bit too far out over the plate and Ruth delivered a missile into the right field bleachers. Completing his slow trot around the bases, Ruth smiled and doffed his cap to his delirious fans. Shaken, Haines focused on the next hitter, Bob Meusel. On the second offering, Meusel drove the pitch deep to left field but Chick Hafey got a good jump on the ball and was able to pull it in for the last out of the inning.

Down a run in the fourth, the Cardinals got a lot of help from Yankees fielders. Hornsby led off by chipping a ground ball back to the mound. Bottomley followed with the Cardinals' third hit of the day, a single to left. Bell hit Hoyt's first pitch sharply to short for what looked like an inning-ending double play. However, Koenig mishandled the ball and both runners were safe. Hafey then loaded the bases with a seeing-eye single that fell just behind Koenig and in front of Meusel. The next Cardinals hitter was Bob O'Farrell, who in the fourth game had singled twice against Hoyt. This time he lifted a ball to left center field. Combs and Meusel both moved to the ball but Meusel called for the catch because he had a much stronger arm and might be able to get Bottomley at home if he tried to tie the score. Meusel positioned himself, reached up for the ball, had it in his glove and dropped it. A collective gasp went through the stands. The entire stadium was momentarily stunned. The muff enabled Bottomley to score and both Bell and Hafey to move up a base. Tommy Thevenow, who was the Cardinals' leading hitter throughout the Series, compounded the error by driving a single to right that scored two runners. Still in a bases-loaded jam, Hoyt overpowered Haines, striking him out, and then got Holm on a routine ground ball to Koenig.

As he walked off the mound trailing thanks to three unearned runs, Hoyt may have had flashbacks to the seventh game of the 1921 World Series against the Giants. He pitched a brilliant four-hitter but lost 1–0 when an error by Yankees shortstop Roger Peckinpaugh allowed the game's only run to score.

Now up by two runs, Haines continued to struggle. He started the inning by walking Gehrig and then escaped two long fly balls by Lazzeri. The first went foul into the right field mezzanine and the second was caught by a sprinting Holm in the deepest part of center field. Anywhere else in the stadium Lazzeri's shot would have probably tied the score. Dugan was next to the plate and tapped one toward third. Haines pounced on the ball, threw Dugan out at first but allowed Gehrig to move up to second. On Haines's first pitch, Severeid smashed a line drive that appeared headed for left field. As the ball sped over his head, Thevenow made a desperate leap and somehow speared the ball. The inning-ending catch saved a run and the Cardinals' lead.

Hoyt was back on track in the fifth. He cut through the heart of the St. Louis lineup with ease. He then led off the Yankees half of the inning by grounding out to shortstop. Combs followed with a clean single to center. Koenig flew out to left and Ruth, the potential tying run, came to the plate. The raucous Yankee fans were anxious to see the Babe duplicate his third-inning shot but this time, amid a chorus of boos, Haines stayed with the game plan and walked the slugger. Meusel came to the plate with a chance to redeem himself. An extra-base hit would tie the score; a home run would put the Yankees ahead. Instead he grounded the ball back to Haines.

The only problem for Hoyt in the sixth inning was an error by Dugan, but that was quickly erased when Severeid threw out the runner trying to steal. Though he certainly did not know it as he left the mound, Hoyt's day had come to an end. He had pitched as well as he had all season, throttling the potent Cardinals attack as few had.

Gehrig led off the Yankees sixth with a smash up the middle. The ball seemed destined for center field but Thevenow again came to Haines's rescue. Ranging far to his left and stretching as far as he could, the Cardinals short-stop gloved the ball, pivoted and threw Gehrig out at first. It was yet another in a growing collection of sensational plays by Thevenow. Haines had an easier time with Lazzeri, striking him out on four pitches. Dugan followed with his second hit of the game. Severeid was the Yankees' next hitter. After Haines missed the strike zone with his first three pitches, the last of which O'Farrell was barely able to catch, Hornsby went to the mound to talk to his pitcher. Two strikes later Hornsby watched Severeid drill a double to left that pulled New York to within a run of the Cardinals. With the tying run on second, Huggins pinch-hit for Hoyt. Ben Paschal was sent to the plate. The only time he had previously faced Haines, Paschal had walked. This time he grounded the ball back to Haines to end the Yankees threat.

Yankees ace Herb Pennock was called on to pick up for Hoyt. Already with two wins in the Series, Pennock had given up only three earned runs in his 19 innings on the mound against the Cardinals. Though he had pitched last only three days earlier there was no doubt that he could hold St. Louis for nine more outs. In the seventh his only mistake was a pitch that Haines hit for a single. The other three batters he faced, Thevenow, Holm and South-worth, were all easy outs.

The Yankees half of the seventh inning is one that will forever be remembered by baseball fans. It started when Combs singled just over the glove of a leaping Tommy Thevenow. Playing for a run, Koenig laid down a sacrifice bunt that got Combs into scoring position. There was little question about how Haines was going to pitch Ruth. Amid a storm of boos, the Cardinals hurler walked the Babe on four pitches. With runners on first and second, Haines and O'Farrell met between the mound and the plate to figure out how to pitch to the next batter. Bob Meusel was coming to plate with another chance to atone for his earlier misplay. Once again he failed. Instead, he hit a ground a ball to third where Bell, hoping to start a double play, moved to his left, fielded the ball and threw it to second for an out. Hornsby's relay, however, was not in time to get Meusel at first.

Gehrig was the next to come to the plate and he walked on four pitches. From the way Haines threw each pitch to Gehrig, it became clear that something was wrong with him. All four pitches had floated up to the plate and each one was farther from the strike zone than the previous one.

As Gehrig trotted down to first, Hornsby called his infield in for a conference on the mound. Haines's problem was the index finger on his pitching hand. Five days earlier, late in his first game against the Yankees, a between-pitches throw back from his catcher had hit the tip of the index finger on his pitching hand and smashed the nail. It was a freak accident. Haines toughed it out through the rest of the game but the next day the finger was bruised and the nail was loose and bloody. Hornsby knew about the finger and between innings of the seventh game checked on it. Each time Haines had said it was alright. By the seventh, the combination of the injury and the effects of throwing his knuckleball had transformed Haines's nail into a bloody mess. This time when asked, Haines acknowledged that he could not continue. The next question was: who should replace him? The logical choice was Sherdel. Wee Willie had pitched two excellent games against the Yankees even though he had lost them both. He was also well rested and was ready. Flint Rhem, the Cardinals' fireballing 20-game winner, was also rested and ready as was most of the rest of the pitching staff. The only pitcher that seemed unavailable was Grover Cleveland Alexander, who had pitched nine innings the previous day. Hornsby knew all the circumstances and knew exactly whom he wanted even before coming to the mound. When he saw Haines' bloody finger he made the call.

By the time that Haines left the game, the afternoon had become even more gloomy and colder than it was when the game started. The sun that had peeked through the clouds a few innings earlier was long gone, and instead a misty fog had begun to descend upon the field. Late afternoon shadows further darkened the stadium. Through the gloom and the mist and the shadows 38,100 hushed fans peered out toward the left field bullpen to get a first peek at whom Hornsby was bringing in. When the bullpen door opened the grey silhouette of an unidentifiable Cardinals player emerged. Not an imposing figure but taller than Sherdel and more stooped than Rhem. He was wearing a bright red Cardinals sweater and his cap was tipped a bit to one side. As he slowly tramped through the mist and onto the outfield grass, a quiet whisper began to circulate throughout the stadium. "It's Alexander," "Grover Cleveland Alexander," "Alex the Great," "Old Alex."

Alexander sauntered in toward the infield while Tony Lazzeri waited at the plate, knocking mud off his spikes. The new Cardinals pitcher strolled past center fielder Wattie Holm and patted his glove. Then he passed Tommy Thevenow and patted gloves again. Hornsby trotted out across the infield to meet his new pitcher. "Well, the bases are full," he told Alexander. "There just don't seem to be no place to put Lazzeri. I guess I'll have to get him out," was the droll reply.[30] On the mound Alexander told his manager and catcher O'Farrell how he planned to pitch Lazzeri. Hornsby, who would have told any other pitcher how to handle a hitter, simply stood and listened. The plan was to get ahead of the Yankees slugger, a fastball or two up and in, then break curveballs off the outside part of the plate. Alexander took only three warm up pitches and then called for a hitter.

The rugged old veteran stared in at his powerful young adversary and let go of the first pitch: a fastball high and tight for ball one. Then came a called strike across the inside part of the plate. Working quickly as he always did, Alex dished up another fastball, this time well inside. Lazzeri swung hard and pounded the ball deep down the left field line. Hornsby at second watched the ball fade, fearing the worst. Lazzeri's teammates who saw the drive arching down the line jumped to the top step of the dugout, sure that the young slugger had driven one out of the park. All 38,100 fans leaped to their feet as the ball soared toward the bleachers. And then as the ball approached the fence it appeared to bend just a shade to the left. Bell and O'Farrell, who were standing on the line, knew from the moment it was hit that the drive was foul. Third base umpire Hank O'Day and plate umpire George Hildebrand knew it was foul too, but almost everyone else in the stadium thought that Lazzeri's blast was a grand slam. And then it landed well over the fence but several feet foul, a long strike two.

Undaunted, Alexander's next pitch, just as he had promised, was a sharp curve off the outside part of the plate that dove almost in the dirt. Lazzeri swung hard but missed: strike three. Yankee Stadium exploded with noise. The grizzled old-timer whose baseball career appeared over just three months earlier had at least temporarily saved a world championship for the Cardinals.

Alexander knew that the story hadn't ended with Lazzeri. He knew that there were two innings left in the game and calculated that if he got every hitter he faced, the last batter to come to the plate would be Babe Ruth. While his teammates batted in the eighth he sat at the end of the dugout with his sweater on, trying to stay warm. He watched Hornsby lead off with a single and Bottomley bunt him over to second. But that's as far as the Cardinals manager went. Bell popped to center, Hafey was hit by a pitch and O'Farrell grounded to short.

In the bottom of the inning Old Alex was as good as ever. Mixing curves and fastballs, he got Dugan to ground out to Thevenow. Pat Collins, who had replaced Severeid in the seventh, popped one to Bottomley and Pennock hit a lazy fly to Hornsby.

The Cardinals went down in order in the ninth. Three outs away from possible defeat, the top of the Yankees order came to the plate. Combs hit a two-strike pitch to Bell at third for the first out. Koenig did the same. And now Babe Ruth stepped in to face Alexander one last time. The greatest slugger of all time battling one of the greatest pitchers of all time with two outs in the last inning of the seventh game of the World Series. There was electricity in the air. Hornsby came in to talk with his pitcher. Yankees fans cheered their home run hero. Alexander, who never took a windup, threw in the first pitch, a strike, then a ball, and then a foul for strike two. The next three pitches teased the slugger but all three missed the plate. Ruth walked to first and Bob Meusel came to the plate. The only Yankees hitter who had given Alexander trouble was Bob Meusel. The previous day the Yankees left fielder had doubled and tripled and scored one of the two New York runs. In the first game against Alexander, Meusel had one of the Yankees' four hits and had scored a run. Now he was at the plate with a chance to tie or win the game.

The first pitch to Meusel was a called strike but as Alexander released the pitch Ruth inexplicably broke for second. O'Farrell caught the pitch, raised up and fired a strike to Hornsby covering the bag. The Cardinals manager caught the ball cleanly and tagged the sliding Ruth out. The game, the Series and the season were over. The Cardinals were the new baseball world champions.

After the game Ruth explained that he tried the steal on his own. He figured that with Alexander pitching as well as he was, the Yankees would be lucky to get a hit off of him and if they did Ruth wanted to be in scoring position. Additionally, Alexander didn't have a very good move to first and wasn't paying much attention to the baserunner. Under similar circumstances the previous day, the Babe had stolen a base and thought he could do it again. He was wrong.

Hornsby's tag set off a gala two-day celebration 1,000 miles to the west. Within minutes of the final out St. Louisans flooded the city's business district as well as neighborhoods throughout the city and surrounding suburbs. They came in cars, in buses, and in streetcars, and they walked. They brought horns and noise makers; they carried Cardinals pennants and signs; they painted their faces red, black and white; and they wore Cardinal-red shirts, jackets, and dresses. "It was as if dynamite had been planted in a hundred spots and all touched off at the same instant."[31] For hours spontaneous parades closed streets and halted traffic. The city was truly delirious. Jubilant fans pranced and paraded, sang and howled, and honked their horns until the early morning, and then the next afternoon they did it all over again when the players arrived home. This time there was no parade because city officials were concerned that the crush of the crowd might injure someone. Instead the team was taken to Sportsman's Park, where 40,000 ecstatic fans roared inside and more roared outside. Brief speeches were made, a few gifts given to the team, and the players were hailed as conquering heroes.

Several players were given special recognition. At the top of the list was Grover Cleveland Alexander, who was redubbed "Alexander the Greatest" by happy fans. Praise for Alexander's play came from far and wide. Sam Breadon lauded his pitcher the greatest of all time. The Governor of Missouri formally commended his feat and invited him to dinner. John McGraw called Alex's Series pitching performance the greatest since Christy Mathewson's three consecutive shutouts in 1905. It was an assessment echoed by knowledgeable baseball people everywhere. Across the country, baseball fans extolled the old warrior's accomplishment. To Alex it was far more acclaim than he deserved, but despite his humility and his efforts to share the glory with his teammates, most considered him the Series hero.

Tommy Thevenow's play also garnered grand acclaim. The unheralded shortstop led the team in hitting with a .417 average. His play in the field was simply sensational. Time and time again he magically transformed base hits into outs that several times saved games. Just about everyone agreed that, even though Alexander was the Series hero, without Thevenow's contributions there would not have been a seventh game and the Cardinals would not have beaten the Yankees. Hornsby argued that "it was Tommy Thevenow who won the game for us.... Alexander saved it."[32] Alexander concurred.

The third of the fan favorites was the only Cardinal who had not traveled back to St. Louis. As soon as the series ended Rogers Hornsby and his family boarded a train to Texas for his mother's funeral. While the Cardinals manager had not had a great World Series (he batted only .250) he was the brains behind the Cardinals success all season. He had guided his young crew through a nerve-wracking pennant race and then past the Yankees to a world championship. From the beginning of the season, whenever people doubted his team's chances he had steadfastly defended his players and explained why the doubters were wrong. He had masterfully maneuvered his pitching staff and initiated the mid-season acquisitions of Southworth and Alexander which proved crucial to the Cardinals success. Every time his team was confronted with a challenge, he figured a way past it. Though his World Series performance was only mediocre, to St. Louis fans he deserved as much adulation as any of his teammates.

What Hornsby and his fans did not know was that he had played his last inning in a Cardinals uniform until the twilight of his playing career seven years later. The differences between Hornsby and owner Sam Breadon had grown to such proportions that the two men could barely tolerate each other despite the team's success. The final battle came during contract negotiations. Hornsby was contracted through 1927 but wanted a $20,000 raise. Breadon vehemently refused. Instead the Cardinals owner contacted Giants owner Charles Stoneham, who had previously made several offers for Hornsby. When Stoneham suggested trading his disgruntled star, Frankie Frisch, for Hornsby, Breadon eagerly agreed. Hired in part to serve as John McGraw's assistant manager (McGraw was having health problems) Hornsby, as he had in St. Louis with Breadon, ended the season feuding with Stoneham. By the beginning of the 1928 season, Hornsby was in Boston as the player-manager of the Braves.

Financially the Series was the most successful that had ever been played. More money was spent for tickets, over $1.2 million, by more fans, 328,000, than ever before. Cardinals players took home $6,254 compared to the previous high in 1923 when the Yankees earned $6,140. In 1926 the losers were paid $4,168, about $100 more than in 1923. Gamblers did well also.[33] Though estimates varied, it was generally agreed that more than $20 million had been wagered, again an all-time record for a World Series. In St. Louis the value of the Cardinals skyrocketed as a result of the team's success. Sam Breadon claimed to have bought the team for $39,000. After the Series he conservatively estimated his team's value at more than $1 million.

For the Yankees, the 1926 World Series was the first of three consecutive trips to the post-season. The following year most of the team would return and establish itself as one of the all-time great teams. Ruth, Gehrig, and the rest of "Murderer's Row" waltzed to the 1927 pennant, winning by 19 games, and then swept the Pirates in the World Series. The team got a bit of revenge in 1928 when they swept the Cardinals in that year's World Series. However, the Cardinals team was a different one than it had been 1926. More than half of the roster that had been part of the Cardinals' world championship team was gone. Hornsby, Bell, Southworth and O'Farrell among others had moved on. By 1930, the next Cardinals World Series appearance, five more from the 1926 team, including Sherdel and Alexander, were gone as the famous "Gas House Gang" was being assembled.

Sadly, during the days and months and years that followed the Cardinals victory, the shine on Grover Cleveland Alexander's performance became unfairly tarnished. Some game-day reports claimed that Old Alex was drunk when he pitched to Lazzeri. As the stories went, after winning Game 6 he had celebrated most of the night. When he arrived at the stadium the next day he was suffering from a hangover. To ease the pain and fight the cold of the dugout, he nursed a bottle of whiskey all afternoon. By the time Hornsby called him into the game he could barely walk. Somehow, through his drunken stupor, Alex had been able to strike out Lazzeri and throttle the Yankees for two more innings.

The story made good copy. It was no secret that Old Alex drank more than he should. The media embraced the story and quickly it became "fact," which it remained for decades. However, the truth is that Alexander was completely sober when he faced down Lazzeri. With one exception, everyone who interacted with him that afternoon agreed that he had not been drinking and knew exactly what he was going to do. Third baseman Les Bell, when asked years later, emphatically defended the pitcher. "They say that Alec was drunk, or hung over, when he came in.... All a lot of bunk!" Though less profusely, Jim Bottomley and Tommy Thevenow, both of whom were with Alexander when he arrived on the mound, agreed with Bell. Hornsby was another who denied the claim. He had told Alex the night before that he planned to use him in relief if necessary and that Alex should postpone any celebrations. There was no doubt in Hornsby's mind that Alexander had abided by the request. Several teammates in the Cardinals dugout that afternoon also denied that Old Pete had been sipping whiskey during the game. Aimee Alexander, his wife, was another who disputed the charge. Only catcher Bob O'Farrell years later gave credence to the story. Nevertheless, the tale became part of the Grover Cleveland Alexander legend and baseball lore as well.

Part of the reason the story lived as long as it did is because Alexander himself did not refute it. Instead he acquiesced and moved on with his life. Several days after the Series, a reporter asked him about the rumor and how it felt to be the World Series hero. Alex laconically replied, "I'm a hero. I been a hero before but not a hero like this. But say — take my advice: don't you be a hero."[34]

Chapter Notes

Chapter 1

1. *New York Times*, April 9, 1925.
2. Leigh Montville, *Big Bam: The Life and Times of Babe Ruth* (New York: Doubleday, 2006), 198–203; Robert Creamer, *Babe: The Legend Comes to Life* (New York: Simon & Schuster, 1974) 281–290; Marshal Smelser, *The Life That Ruth Built: A Biography* (New York: Quadrangle Press, 1975).
3. Gehrig's presence in the Yankees starting lineup on June 2, 1925, has one of a few explanations. In one Pipp showed up at Yankee Stadium with a headache and when looking for aspirin was told by manager Huggins to take the day off. I have found little to verify this account. Another account has it that Pipp was neither beaned nor did he have a headache. Instead, like several of his teammates he had not been playing well. Jonathan Eig in *Luckiest Man: The Life and Times of Lou Gehrig*, 64–66, makes a strong case that Pipp was simply benched. He contends that Huggins was anxious to play Gehrig more as well as send a message to other Yankees starters. I have chosen the beaning story because of an interview that Pipp gave in 1953. *New York Times*, August 31, 1953.
4. As with Babe Ruth, there are many good biographies of Lou Gehrig. The two I found most useful were: Jonathan Eig, *Luckiest Man: The Life and Times of Lou Gehrig* (New York: Simon & Schuster, 2005); Ray Robinson, *Iron Horse: Lou Gehrig in His Time* (New York: W. W. Norton, 1991).
5. *New York Times*, June 3, 1925.
6. *The Sporting News*, June 3, 1925.
7. Lee Lowenfish, *Branch Rickey; Baseball's Ferocious Gentleman* (Lincoln: University of Nebraska Press, 2007), 148.
8. Lowenfish, 149–50.
9. Breadon File, Baseball Hall of Fame Library.
10. John Heidenry, *The Gashouse Gang* (New York: Public Affairs Press, 2007), 21–22; Lowenstein, 119–124.
11. *The Sporting News*, November 5, 1925; December 10, 1925.

Chapter 2

1. Jack Sher, "Rogers Hornsby: The Mighty Rajah," *Sport*, July 1949, 62–63; Jonathan D'Amore, *Rogers Hornsby: A Biography* (Westport, CT: Greenwood Press, 2004), 42.
2. *New York Times*, January 13, 1928; D'Amore, 80, 89–90.
3. *The Sporting News*, October 21, 1953; D'Amore, 51.
4. *Harrisburg Patriot News*, December 31, 1966.
5. *St. Louis Post Dispatch*, March 21, 1926.
6. *Ibid.*
7. *The Sporting News*, October 21, 1953.
8. *St. Louis Post Dispatch*, January 3, 1963; Fred Lieb, *Baseball as I Have Known It* (New York: Coward, McCann & Geoghegan, 1977) 57; D'Amore, p 142. Hornsby once revealed to Fred Lieb that he had been a member of the Ku Klux Klan.
9. *The Sporting News*, March 25, 1925.
10. *St. Louis Post Dispatch*, May 1, 1930.
11. Harold Seymour, *Baseball: The People's Game* (New York: Oxford University Press, 1990), 188–98; Jules Tygiel, *Past Time: Baseball As History* (New York: Oxford University Press, 2000), 5–9.
12. Seymour, 203–12.
13. *The Sporting News*, March 25, 1925;

Tommy Thevenow file, Baseball Hall of Fame Library.

14. *St. Louis Post Dispatch,* October 21, 1926; May 1, 1930; August 7, 1957.

15. *St. Louis Post Dispatch,* May 1, 1930. The reporter was Gordon McKay.

16. *The Sporting News,* January 21, 1926.

17. D'Amore, 55; Peter Golenbock, *The Spirit of St. Louis: A History of the St. Louis Cardinals and Browns* (New York: Spike, 2000), 100.

18. *The Sporting News,* April 15, 1926.

19. Leo Trachtenberg, *Yankees Magazine,* August 4, 1983; *The Sporting News,* December 31, 1925.

20. *New York Sun,* April 15, 1926.

21. Roger Daniels, *Coming to America: A History of Immigration and Ethnicity in American Life* (New York: HarperCollins, 1990) 189.

22. Serial Set no. 5865, Senate document 747/1, sessions 61–63, session date 1910, 1911, vol. 1, 23–29.

23. Immigration Act of 1924. The law permitted only 3845 Italians to enter the country each year.

24. John Higham, *Strangers in the Land* (East Brunswick, NJ: Rutgers University Press, 1955), 80–87.

25. Leonard Dinnerstein and David M. Reimers, *Ethnic Americans: A History of Immigration* (New York: Harper & Row, 1988), 74; Charles C. Alexander, *The Ku Klux Klan in the Southwest* (Lexington: University of Kentucky Press, 1966), 22.

26. Higham, 90–92; Dinnerstein and Reimers, 69–70; Daniels, 198–200.

27. Isabel Leighton, ed., *The Aspirin Age, 1919–1941* (New York: Simon & Schuster, 1976), 169–189.

28. *The Sporting News,* December 31, 1925; Tony Lazzeri file, Baseball Hall of Fame Library.

29. Mark Koenig file, Baseball Hall of Fame Library; Leo Trachtenberg, *Yankees Magazine,* June 4, 1987.

30. *St. Paul Dispatch,* February 20, 1925.

31. Leigh Montville, *The Big Bam: The Life and Times of Babe Ruth* (New York: Doubleday, 2006), 218–21.

32. *New York Times,* April 11, 1926.

Chapter 3

1. *The Sporting News,* April 15, 22, 1926; *New York Times,* April 11, 1926.

2. Jesse Haines file, Baseball Hall of Fame Library.

3. *St. Louis Post Dispatch,* April 19, 1926.

4. *St. Louis Post Dispatch,* April 22, 1926.

5. A. Scott Berg, *Lindbergh* (New York: Putnam Press, 1998), 59–74; Kenneth Davis, *The Hero: Charles Lindbergh and the American Dream* (New York: Doubleday, 1959), 79–88.

6. Berg, 86–90; Dominick A. Pisano and Robert van Der Linden, *Charles Lindbergh and the Spirit of St. Louis* (New York: Harry N. Abrams, 2002) 25–29; Davis, 126–140.

7. *The Sporting News,* April 8, 1926; *New York Times,* April 11, 1926.

8. *New York Times,* April 14, 1926.

9. www.Retrosheet.org.

10. *New York Times,* April 18, 1926. The reporter was James B. Harrison.

11. *New York Times,* April 22, 1926.

12. Creamer, 292–301; Montville, 206–07.

13. Miller Huggins file, Baseball Hall of Fame Library.

14. *Philadelphia Public Ledger* July 25, 1915.

Chapter 4

1. *New York Times,* May 5, 1926.

2. *New York Herald Tribune,* May 2, 1926; *Washington Post,* May 2, 1926.

3. Charles Alexander, *Ty Cobb* (New York: Oxford University Press, 1984), 83.

4. *New York Times,* May 9, 10, 1926; *The Sporting News,* May 20; *Detroit Free Press,* May 9; Jonathan Eig, *Luckiest Man: The Life and Death of Lou Gehrig* (New York: Simon & Schuster, 2005), 61–62; Ray Robinson, *Iron Horse: Lou Gehrig in His Time* (New York: W. W. Norton, 1990), 102–03. Eig and Robinson provide fine descriptions of the episode but both have the year of the fight wrong. Eig puts it in 1924 and Robinson a year later in 1925.

5. *Cleveland Plain Dealer,* May 12, 1926; *New York Herald Tribune,* May 17, 1926.

6. *New York Times,* May 19, 1926.

7. Edith L. Blumhofer, *Aimee Semple McPherson: Everybody's Sister* (Grand Rapids, MI: William B. Erdman's, 1993), 281–90; Daniel Mark Epstein, *Sister Aimee: The Life of Aimee Semple McPherson* (Orlando: Harcourt, Brace, 1993), 283–310; Isabel Leighton, ed., *The Aspirin Age, 1919–1941* (New York: Simon & Schuster, 1976), 56–72; *Los Angeles Times,* 1926–January 1927; *New York Times,* 1926.

8. *New York Times,* May 12, 1926

9. Leo Trachtenberg, *Yankees Magazine,* November 28, 1977, 26–28.

10. Earle Combs file, Baseball Hall of Fame Library; *New York World,* February 24, 1924, June 14, 1925; *The Sporting News,* January 19, 1933; David M. Vance, *From Pebworth to Cooperstown,* The Eastern Kentucky University 1970 Alumnus Magazine, Spring 1970

11. *Boston Globe,* May 9, 1926.

12. *New York Times,* May 26, 1926.

13. *New York Times,* May 30, 1926.

14. Charles Alexander, *John McGraw* (Lincoln: University of Nebraska, 1995), 272–74.

15. Vic Keen file, Baseball Hall of Fame Library.

16. *St. Louis Post Dispatch*, August 27, 1926.

17. *Ibid.*

18. Bob O'Farrell file, Baseball Hall of Fame Library.

19. *Philadelphia Inquirer*, May 20, 21, 1926.

20. *St. Louis Post Dispatch*, May 23, 1926; *Philadelphia Inquirer*, May 23, 1926; D'Amore, 59. With some irony, the same day it was "Grover Cleveland Alexander Day" in Chicago and he was given a car.

21. *Cincinnati Enquirer*, May 25, 1926.

Chapter 5

1. *The Sporting News*, April 1, 1926.

2. Seymour, *Baseball: The Golden Age* (New York: Oxford University Press, 1971), 59–66; Craig Harlene, *Sunday: A History of the First Day* (New York: Doubleday, 2007), 351–359; Lee Lowenstein, *Branch Rickey* (Lincoln: University of Nebraska, 2007), 15–6, 64–5.

3. *New York Times*, June 11, 1926.

4. *St. Louis Post Dispatch*, June 15, 1926.

5. *Sporting News*, October 30, 1930.

6. Jon C. Skipper, *Wicked Curve: The Life and Times of Grover Cleveland Alexander* (Jefferson, NC: McFarland, 2006), 76–7; Peter Golenbock, *The Spirit of St. Louis: A History of the St. Louis Cardinals and Browns* (New York: Avon, 2000), 101.

7. Golenbock, 103.

8. *Ibid.*

9. *The Sporting News*, February 13, 1930, February 11, 1948; *The Sporting Life*, September 1923, Herb Pennock file, Baseball Hall of Fame Library.

10. *New York Times*, June 10, 1926.

11. *New York Times*, June 12, 1926.

12. *Ibid.*

13. *Ibid.*

Chapter 6

1. *New York Times*, July 14, 1926.

2. Cait Murphy, *Crazy '08* (New York: Harper Collins, 2008) 208–09; *www.baseball-refernce.com/bullpen/Spitball*; Thomas Boswell, "Salvation Through Salivation," *How Life Imitates the World Series* (New York: Penguin Books, 1982) 197–206.

3. Harold Seymour, *Baseball: The Golden Age* (New York: Oxford Press, 1971), 9–11, 311–16, 319–2; Benjamin Rader, *Baseball: A History of America's Game* (Chicago: University of Illinois Press, 2002), 90–1, 111–12, 118–19.

4. *The Sporting News*, February 4, 1926.

5. *St. Louis Post Dispatch*, April 29, 1926.

6. *The Sporting News*, April 8, 1926.

7. Daniel E. Ginsburg, *The Fix Is In: A History of Gambling and Game Fixing Scandals* (Jefferson, NC: McFarland, 2003), 164–82.

8. Charles Alexander, *John McGraw* (Lincoln: University of Nebraska Press, 1988), 262–65; Ginsburg, 187–89, 193.

9. Timothy M. Gay, *Tris Speaker* (Lincoln: University of Nebraska Press, 2005), 226–32; Charles Alexander, *Ty Cobb* (New York and London: Oxford University Press, 1984), 185–94; Ginsburg, 199–208.

10. David Schwartz, *Roll The Bones: A History of Gambling* (New York: Gotham Press, 2006), 337–40; 370–72.

11. *New York Times*, July 12, 1926.

12. *New York Times*, July 17, 1926.

13. *New York Post*, July 26, 1926.

14. George Toporcer file, Baseball Hall of Fame Library; *Sports Collectors Digest*, June 1, 1989.

15. *The Sporting News*, July 29, 1926.

16. *St. Louis Post Dispatch*, July 17, 1926.

17. Jeffrey A. Miron, "Alcohol Consumption During Prohibition," *American Economic Review*, vol. 81, no. 2, May 1991, 245–47.

18. Edward Behr, *Prohibition: Thirteen Years That Changed America* (New York: Arcade, 1996), 147–49.

19. Miron, 246; The National Prohibition Law, *Subcommittee on the Judiciary United States Senate*, 69th Congress, April 1926, 13, 15.

20. The National Prohibition Law, 40–58; Edward Behr, *Prohibition: Thirteen Years That Changed America* (New York: Arcade Publishing, 1996), 147–49; Miron, 246; The National Prohibition Law, 13, 15, 40–58.

21. *http://prohibiton.osu.edu/content/laguardi.cfm.*

22. *St. Louis Post Dispatch*, July 25, 1926.

Chapter 7

1. *The Sporting News*, July 29, 1926.

2. George Donellson Moss, *America in the Twentieth Century* (Upper Saddle River, NJ: Prentice Hall, 1997), 127–29; William Leuchtenburg, *The Perils of Prosperity, 1914–32* (Chicago: University of Chicago Press, 1993), 172–75.

3. Hornsby and Bill Surface, *My War with Baseball* (New York: Coward and McCann, 1962), 43–45; Jonathan D'Amore, *Rogers Hornsby: A Biography* (Westport, CT: Greenwood Press, 2004), 64–65.

4. Bottomley file, Baseball Hall of Fame Library; *Washington Star*, March 9, 1924.

5. Peter Golenbock, *The Spirit of St. Louis: A History of the St. Louis Cardinals and Browns* (New York: Harper Entertainment Books, 2000), 92–95.

6. *St. Louis Post Dispatch*, August 28, 1929.

7. http://bioproj.sabr.org/bioproj.cfm?a=v&y=I&bid=8938&pid=2513.

8. *St. Louis Post Dispatch*, August 16, 1926.

9. *New York Post*, July 27, 1926.

10. *New York Tribune*, November 27, 1916.

11. Leo Trachtenberg, *Yankees Magazine*, May 5, 1988, 70–71.

12. Urban Shocker file, Baseball Hall of Fame Library, *New York Herald Tribune*, December 16, 1924.

13. *The Sporting News*, August 12, 1926.

14. *The Sporting News*, August 19, 1926.

15. *New York Times*, August 25, 1926.

16. *New York Times*, August 27, 1926; *New York Herald Tribune*, August 27, 1926.

17. Robert Stanley, *The Celluloid Empire: A History of the Motion Picture Industry* (New York: Hastings House, 1978), 10–13.

18. Lewis Jacobs, *The Rise of American Film: A Critical History* (New York: Teachers College Press, 1967), 292.

19. Douglas Germany, *Shared Pleasures: A History of Movie Making in the United States* (Madison: University of Wisconsin Press, 1992), 20, 34–39; William K. Everson, *American Silent Film* (New York: Oxford University Press, 1978), 174–76; 196–97.

Chapter 8

1. *New York Times*, September 7, 1926.

2. Leo Trachtenberg, "He Could Pick It, That Jumpin' Joe," *Yankees Magazine*, September 18, 1986.

3. *New York Evening World*, December 29, 1926.

4. William A. Cook, *Waite Hoyt: A Biography of the Yankees' Schoolboy Wonder* (Jefferson, NC: McFarland, 2004), 86–87.

5. Trachtenberg, "Jumpin' Joe," 10.

6. Joe Dugan file, Baseball Hall of Fame Library.

7. *St. Louis Post Dispatch*, September 4, 1926.

8. *Cincinnati Enquirer*, September 6, 1926.

9. *Ibid*.

10. *St. Louis Post Dispatch*, February 19, 20, 1953.

11. Ray Blades file, Baseball Hall of Fame Library.

12. Charles "Chick" Hafey file, Baseball Hall of Fame Library.

13. Taylor Douthit file, Baseball Hall of Fame Library.

14. *St. Louis Post Dispatch*, September 10, 1926; *Sporting News*, September 16, 1926.

15. *St. Louis Post Dispatch*, September 14, 1926.

Chapter 9

1. *New York Times*, September 30, 1926.

2. *Sr. Louis Post Dispatch*, September 27, 1926.

3. The *Sporting News*, September 30, 1926.

4. *New York Times*, September 25, 1926.

5. *New York Times*, September 29, 1926.

6. *St. Louis Post Dispatch*, Sept 30, 1926.

7. *New York Times*, October 1, 1926.

8. *St. Louis Post Dispatch*, October 1, 1926.

9. *Ibid*.

10. *St. Louis Post Dispatch*, October 3, 1926.

11. Tom Simon, ed., *Deadball Stars of the National League* (Cleveland: Society for American Baseball Research, 2004), 20.

12. Henry "Hank" O'Day file, Baseball Hall of Fame Library.

13. *The Sporting News*, January 13, 1973.

14. William "Bill" Klem file, Baseball Hall of Fame Library.

15. William Henry Dinneen file, Baseball Hall of Fame Library.

16. George Hildebrand file, Baseball Hall of Fame Library.

17. *Brooklyn Eagle*, October 5, 1926.

18. *Evening World* (New York), October 5, 1926.

19. *New York Times*, October 6, 1926.

20. *New York Times*, October 7, 1926.

21. *St. Louis Post Dispatch*, October 7, 1926.

22. *New York Times*, October 7, 1926.

23. *New York Times*, October 8, 1926.

24. *St. Louis Post Dispatch*, October 5, 1926.

25. *St. Louis Post Dispatch*, October 3, 1926.

26. Thomas Moore, "Sports Announcer by Accident," *Sports Illustrated*, October 12, 1964; Graham McNamee file, Baseball Hall of Fame Library.

27. *New York Times*, October 10, 1926.

28. *St. Louis Post Dispatch*, October 10, 1926.

29. *New York Times*, October 10, 1926.

30. *St. Louis Post Dispatch*, October 11 1926; Peter Golenbock, *The Spirit of St. Louis* (New York City: Avon Books, 2000), 114–15.

31. *St. Louis Post Dispatch*, October 11, 1926.

32. *New York Times*, October 11, 1926; *St. Louis Post Dispatch*, October 11, 1926.

33. *New York Times*, October 11, 1926.

34. *St. Louis Post Dispatch*, October 16, 1926.

Selected Bibliography

Books

Alexander, Charles. *John McGraw.* New York: Viking Press, 1988.

_____. *Rogers Hornsby.* New York: H. Holt, 1995.

_____. *Ty Cobb.* New York: Oxford University Press, 1984.

Allen, Lee. *The National League Story: The Official History.* New York: Hill and Wang, 1961.

Broeg, Bob. *Redbirds! A Century of Cardinals Baseball.* South Bend, IN: Diamond, 1981.

Cook, William A. *Waite Hoyt: A Biography of the Yankees' Schoolboy Wonder.* Jefferson, NC: McFarland, 2004.

Creamer, Robert W. *Babe: The Legend Comes to Life.* New York: Simon & Schuster, 1974.

Curran, William. *Big Sticks: The Batting Revolution of the Twenties.* New York: William Morrow, 1990.

D'Amore, Jonathan. *Rogers Hornsby: A Biography.* Westport, CT: Greenwood Press, 2004.

Deford, Frank. *The Old Ball Game: How John McGraw, Christy Mathewson, and the New York Giants Created Modern Baseball.* New York: Atlantic Monthly Press, 2005.

Devaney, John. *The Greatest Cardinals of Them All.* New York: Putnam, 1968.

Deveney, Sean. *The Original Curse.* New York: McGraw-Hill, 2010.

Eig, Jonathan. *Luckiest Man: The Life and Death of Lou Gehrig,* New York: Simon & Schuster, 2005.

Felber, Bill. *A Game of Brawl: The Orioles, the Beaneaters, and the Battle for the 1897 Pennant.* Lincoln: University of Nebraska Press, 2007.

Frommer, Harvey. *Five O'Clock Lightning.* Hoboken, NJ: John Wiley & Sons, 2008.

Gallagher, Mark, and Neil. *Baseball's Greatest Dynasties: The New York Yankees.* New York: Gallery Books, 2002.

Gay, Timothy M. *Tris Speaker: The Rough-and-Tumble Life of a Baseball Legend:* Lincoln: University of Nebraska Press, 2005.

Ginsburg, Daniel E. *The Fix Is In: A History of Baseball Gambling and Game Fixing Scandals* Jefferson, NC: McFarland, 1995.

Golenbock, Peter. *The Spirit of St. Louis: A History of the St. Louis Cardinals and Browns.* New York: HarperCollins, 2000.

Gutman, Dan. *Baseball's Greatest Games.* New York: Viking, 1994.

Heidenry, John. *The Gashouse Gang.* New York: Public Affairs, 2007.

Hornsby, Rogers. *My War with Baseball.* New York: Coward-McCann, 1962.

Kavanagh, Jack. *Ol' Pete: The Grover Cleve-*

land Alexander Story. South Bend: Diamond, 1996.

Kohout, Martin Donell. *Hal Chase: The Defiant Life and Turbulent Times of Baseball's Biggest Crook.* Jefferson, NC: McFarland, 2001.

Levitt, Daniel R. *Ed Barrow: The Bulldog Who Built the Yankees' First Dynasty.* Lincoln: University of Nebraska Press, 2008.

Lieb, Frederick G. *Baseball As I Have Known It.* New York: Coward, McCann & Geoghegan, Inc., 1977.

_____. *The St. Louis Cardinals: The Story of a Great Baseball Club.* 1944. Carbondale: Southern Illinois University Press, 2001.

Lowenfish, Lee. *Branch Rickey: Baseball's Ferocious Gentleman.* Lincoln: University of Nebraska Press, 2007.

Macht, Norman. *Connie Mack and the Early Years of Baseball.* Lincoln: University of Nebraska Press, 2007.

Montville, Leigh. *Big Bam: The Life and Times of Babe Ruth.* New York: Doubleday, 2006.

Murdock, Eugene C. *Ban Johnson: Czar of Baseball.* Westport, CT: Greenwood Press, 1982.

Murphy, Cait. *Crazy '08: How a Cast of Cranks, Rogues, Boneheads, and Magnates Created the Greatest Year in Baseball History.* New York: Smithsonian Books, 2007.

Peterson, Richard, ed. *The St. Louis Reader.* Columbia: University of Missouri Press, 2006.

Pietrusza, David. *Judge and Jury: The Life and Times of Judge Kenesaw Mountain Landis.* South Bend: Diamond, 1998.

Rader, Benjamin G. *Baseball: A History of America's Game.* Urbana: University of Illinois Press, 2002.

Robinson, Ray. *Iron Horse: Lou Gehrig in His Time.* New York: W. W. Norton, 1990.

Seymour, Harold. *Baseball: The Early Years.* New York: Oxford University Press, 1960.

_____. *Baseball: The Golden Age.* New York: Oxford University Press, 1971.

_____. *Baseball: The People's Game,* New York: Oxford University Press, 1990.

Shannon, Bill, and George Kalinsky. *The Ballparks* New York: Hawthorn Books, 1975.

Skipper, John C. *Wicked Curve: The Life and Troubled Times of Grover Cleveland Alexander,* Jefferson NC: McFarland, 2006.

Sowell, Mike. *The Pitch That Killed.* New York: Collier Books, 1989.

Stout, Glenn, and Richard Johnson. *Yankees Century: 100 Years of New York Yankees Baseball.* Boston: Houghton Mifflin, 2002.

Thomas, Henry W. *Walter Johnson: Baseball's Big Train.* Lincoln: University of Nebraska Press, 1998.

Tygiel, Jules. *Past Time: Baseball as History.* New York: Oxford University Press, 2000.

Votano, Paul. *Tony Lazzeri: A Baseball Biography.* Jefferson, NC: McFarland, 2005.

Newspapers and Journals

Boston Globe
Brooklyn Eagle
Chicago Tribune
Cincinnati Enquirer
Cleveland Plain Dealer
Detroit Free Press
New York Daily News
New York Times
New York Tribune
New York World
Philadelphia Inquirer
Pittsburgh Post
Sporting Life
St. Louis Globe
St. Louis Post Dispatch
The Sporting News
Washington Post
Yankees Magazine
Websites
Baseball-almanac.com
Baseball-encyclopedia.com
Baseballhistorians.com
Baseballlibrary.com
Bioproj.sabr.org
Retrosheet.org
Stlouiscardsblog.com

Index